The Evidence Behind HR

The Evidence Behind HR: An Open Evaluation of Contemporary HR Practices is a critical take on the assumptions and strategies used within modern HR practice. This book takes a detailed look at some of the latest academic and practitioner work used to justify mainstream HR practices. Chapters evaluate specific HR practices, including diversity training, organisational change management, and emotional intelligence-based selection. This work's engaging and informative tone presents quality and transparency as a priority for research to inform future directions for modern HR practice.

Using an open scholarship perspective, *The Evidence Behind HR* questions the quality of evidence used to inform modern HR practices, such as diversity training, stress management interventions, and in-house evaluations. This book simplifies, summarises, and synthesises the latest research developments into accessible and actionable recommendations. Perfect for practitioners, students, and academics alike, this work provides practical support to help readers explore how to evaluate evidence, improve practices, and change thinking.

This book supports criticality surrounding taken-for-granted HR assumptions, and encourages reflective practitioners, academics, and students to be more interested and critically engaged with "evidence", and to change ways of thinking surrounding day-to-day practices.

Thomas R. Evans is an Associate Professor in Occupational Psychology at the University of Greenwich, UK.

The Evidence Behind HR

An Open Evaluation of Contemporary HR Practices

THOMAS R. EVANS

Routledge
Taylor & Francis Group

LONDON AND NEW YORK

Cover image: © Danielle Navarro. https://art.djnavarro.net

First published 2023
by Routledge
4 Park Square, Milton Park, Abingdon, Oxon OX14 4RN

and by Routledge
605 Third Avenue, New York, NY 10158

Routledge is an imprint of the Taylor & Francis Group, an informa business

British Library Cataloguing-in-Publication Data
A catalogue record for this book is available from the British Library

Library of Congress Cataloging-in-Publication Data
Names: Evans, Thomas R. (Thomas Rhys), 1992– author.
Title: The evidence behind HR : an open evaluation of contemporary HR practices / Thomas R. Evans.
Description: Abingdon, Oxon; New York, NY: Routledge, 2022. | Includes bibliographical references and index. |
Identifiers: LCCN 2022004621 (print) | LCCN 2022004622 (ebook) | ISBN 9780367476717 (hardback) | ISBN 9780367476724 (paperback) | ISBN 9781003035794 (ebook)
Subjects: LCSH: Personnel management.
Classification: LCC HF5549 .E853 2022 (print) | LCC HF5549 (ebook) | DDC 658.3–dc23/eng/20220302
LC record available at https://lccn.loc.gov/2022004621
LC ebook record available at https://lccn.loc.gov/2022004622

ISBN: 978-0-367-47671-7 (hbk)
ISBN: 978-0-367-47672-4 (pbk)
ISBN: 978-1-003-03579-4 (ebk)

DOI: 10.4324/9781003035794

Typeset in Avenir and Dante
by Newgen Publishing UK

All supplementary information and materials to this book can be found at https://osf.io/ytkad/

Contents

The Current State of Evidence Behind HR

1

In one of my former workplaces, the human resources (HR) team completed everything though an online portal. If I have a new member of staff, wish to report changes to contracts, or raise issues, there is a specific online form for each. After working out exactly which form I need, I dutifully fill these out, sweating over the specific details which are undoubtedly inconsequential to anyone (*hmm yes, Steve is a Virgo which might make him clash with Imran and yes this possibly should make the risk assessment form*). I then stare mindlessly at my inbox, waiting to delete the automated response that acknowledges my trouble-making and promises to return with a rapid response. There's a rumour that there aren't even any people on the other side – it's simply a randomiser dictating speed of response, name of HR personnel, and one of three automatic responses: 1) Thanks, this action has been completed, 2) Please fill out this other form/the same form again, and 3) no response. In principle, I'm sure there are many reasons why this online form system is beneficial, and to be honest my experience of it wasn't too negative (I got response 1 on my last three spins so I was on a lucky streak). For the record, I started the rumour and my vote is on a late seventeenth century automaton running the show.

The latest research argues that employees' perceptions of HR, potentially more so than the HR policies themselves, are important predictors of employee and organisational performance (Van Beurden et al., 2021) so clearly HR – and perceptions of HR – matter. Whilst I joke about HR automatons, HR already gets a bad enough press. The general TV tropes of HR are generally pretty negative. Often characters are seen as either too scared to talk to HR, whose existence is based upon enforcing rules in an emotionally devoid drone as the "human" face of the company, or they are hopelessly friendly yet ineffective and hold a token position in maintaining an air of authenticity/professionalism

DOI: 10.4324/9781003035794-1

for the organisation. This inherent conflict between being the friendly face of the company, whilst also the enforcer, is a real issue for many working in this sphere. For example, HR have a responsibility to promote staff wellbeing, whilst also structuring the work environment to do "more with less" (Kowalski & Loretto, 2017). There are many such contradictions to negotiate. Ultimately, HR are designed to help and protect the organisations' most valuable asset – the people: they are structured to make sure the workplace is safe and you are appropriately supported and trained to thrive. HR are, however, also paid by the organisation to protect the organisation's interests: they are structured to support senior management visions and to fulfil and enforce legal requirements. Clearly, these goals can be contradictory.

So, who works in HR and why write a book about it? There are a reported 5.6 million individuals working in HR in the US (US Bureau of Labor Statistics), and HR work represents roughly 1% of the UK workforce (Prospects, 2021). This large community is the backbone of small and large businesses alike, ensuring the core organisational structure and processes are in place to complete essential functions. Unfortunately, HR are increasingly being expected to fulfil central functions with minimal resources, expand their responsibilities, and to enforce what often feels like increasingly bureaucratic form-filling and policies. HR can represent a diverse range of individuals and challenges and they deserve our attention in improving and supporting practices (van der Togt & Rasmussen, 2017).

The value of the work completed by HR is unquestionably fundamental. Unquestionably fundamental but not to be left unquestioned, however. This book was born to question some of the functions that have entered modern HR practice and to look more closely at the evidence informing them. Do we even need any of these new practices? Emotional intelligence-based selection, diversity training, change management planning; what is the evidence behind these practices? Is it time to revaluate things?

If there's one thing that annoys me at work, it's to carry on doing something inefficiently because it's the expected process or norm, rather than acting on what is the best strategy in the given situation. "It's just a formal hoop you have to jump through…" "It's just a tick-box exercise…" "It's just how it's done around here…". Sound familiar? When do we really ever stop to question the value and evidence behind the practices we perpetuate? When do we ever feel sufficiently empowered and respected for challenging what we do? When was the last time you heard someone state "this is probably no longer a good idea, let's stop"? When do we say, now is the time to review some of these decisions and processes and try to improve things? When do we say, let's have a look at what evidence is out there to improve how we do things? HR should be evidence-based (Briner & Barends, 2016; van der Togt & Rasmussen, 2017).

We should be using practices underpinned by quality evidence to maximise desirable outcomes and mitigate negative ones. This book is an opportunity to pause and reflect on what we're all doing and how we might be able to drive more positive change by re-evaluating the evidence. We're going to challenge the assumptions, whilst avoiding the tendency for us to add things rather than take away to fix problems (Adams et al., 2021). Sometimes the answer is to just stop. Let's see.

As an academic and practitioner, I often work closely with HR teams on commercial research and enterprise projects. Because of my academic credentials, I am expected to apply the latest academic understanding to solve organisational issues, creating rigorous evidence-based recommendations sufficiently impactful to make my consultation financially justified. Let's go through a common (and somewhat more simplified) example of a consultancy situation. I might get approached by a CEO/manager who gives me a problem to fix or a project to facilitate. Here's what a brief work log might look like:

Day 1: So, I have been contacted again by company X and they have offered me some more work. It's to support them select a senior manager. It sounds really exciting, is well-paid and it sounds like they already have someone in mind. They just need me to go through the process so it's legally defensible. Sounds like a relatively easy job! Sign on the line!

Day 2: I've had a quick read through their generic HR procedure for recruitment and selection and it all seems pretty clear. The company like to use this particular personality psychometric questionnaire at all levels: that seems fine as some aspects of personality are strong predictors of future performance, and also I don't need to rock the boat by questioning everything. They briefed me and it sounds like they have already written a set of criteria based upon what they want through a brainstorm together – strategic leadership, media relations experience, project management skills, stakeholder management, resource and budget management... All the usual leader clichés, so no particularly complex niche needs to be negotiated here.

Day 3: I need to put together a plan. I have put together a checklist which maps the skills they noted before to as few activities measuring them as possible. I feel under quite a bit of pressure to minimise the amount of time and costs invested. I have decided upon four different components – the personality test they like, a structured interview (all the literature I can find suggests that unstructured interviews are too subjective, so this is evidence-based practice!), a portfolio of prior work, and a project simulation task. I'm really excited about this last one – they have to meet the team they will be managing and design a micro project lasting for a day that could be implemented within their first six months. Can't call that anything but a realistic job preview!

Day 4: They said no. Too much. Might be too much of a burden for participants and take too much team time, so they dropped the simulation as they were running out of time. OK, so three things to manage; if anything that makes it easier for me. We can score them all out of 100 and best candidate wins! I wanted to be involved in the interview and portfolio review so I can get a clear overview over the project and I have been trained to implement these types of interventions. I am confident that it will go well. The interviews go relatively smoothly based upon my plan of questions. The panel clearly tried to hide their commitment to their preferred candidate but I felt I had control of the situation. The portfolio reviews we are doing independently and they want me to send mine over ASAP (I know they haven't done theirs yet but I'm done and I have to get this project off my desk to progress with other work!).

Day 5: OK so let's have a look at how they have all been scored. We had four candidates and they have been pretty generous with their scoring for a certain someone. I have a look through and they have been relatively consistent in applying the criteria we agreed though. I add up the scores and it looks like they are quite close but with their preferred candidate just ahead. Oh, wait a minute, damn it, I should have checked... They seem to have missed out three of the eight criteria on their portfolio checklist. I'll email them now to finish it fully.

Day 6: They responded by saying that they found the criteria too restrictive so didn't do the ones they thought were problematic and adjusted their scores. It would be fair enough if it didn't exclude their preferred candidate from being assessed on their weakest areas! Either way, if the criteria aren't relevant to the post then it's sufficiently justified to drop them. OK so I have submitted my final report and recommendations. I don't think there's much between the highest two scorers and, without knowing, I might have given it to someone else. That could have been a little trickier, but it's fair – they had the highest score and were the favourite from the beginning. Submit report. Submit timesheet. *Voila*. Pina coladas for all.

Day 7: OK, so it's good practice to feedback into the community to share my experience, and I have written a LinkedIn post about the project. The new senior manager seems to have settled in well and the CEO is happy, so I think that's a good job done! Might as well crack out the old self-congratulatory trumpet and give it a good blast on social media. #jobwelldone

Take a moment to reflect – to what extent have any rules been broken in this situation? Whether or not you agree on all the decisions made, we can all agree that this sort of approach is not rare in organisational practice. The scenario looks even more normal if you consider that for some individuals this is part of their job and so no contract negotiation is required. Imagine this same situation but for an internal HR employee who feels all the pressures to conform and not challenge authority – it seems pretty standard. It even feels normal for an external individual because it's part of the consultancy cycle – part of the process that nearly all external contractors, and indeed internal employees, typically adopt when completing work. The consultancy cycle has six key processes: negotiating the contract, gathering information and analysing the issues/situation, formulating an evidence-based plan, implementing the solution, evaluating outcomes, and finally sharing the outcomes with the relevant parties and reflecting upon the experience. As you can see, this stage-like process quite clearly maps onto the diary above.

So, it's clear that the practices described are pretty typical for organisational life. And that's not always a bad thing – we need to adopt a consistent approach to tackling key responsibilities, and using what others do as a template can often give us structure and clearer expectations. But what if, by adopting the norms, we simply recreate the same poor practices? Normal or typical doesn't necessarily mean good or bad. So, what are we doing? Let's reconsider the previous example, but instead of being distracted by the positive tone, we can view the same practices from a negative perspective. Note that none of our actions or decisions have been changed, but the attitude/approach is different:

Day 1: I have been contacted again by company X and they have offered me some more work. It's to support them select a senior manager. They have already made the decision, so I don't really need to do much. It's well-paid and sounds like I just need to go through the motions so it's legally defensible. Seems like an easy job! Sign on the line!

Day 2: I have skim-read the policies. The company has decided on one assessment (personality tool) which they implement at all levels. They aren't going to change their mind because they have financially committed to it long-term, so it's not worth even pointing out how problematic that might be. They have told me how they want things to happen and what criteria to adopt so this easy job has just got easier.

Day 3: I need to put together a plan. I have mapped skills they noted to as few activities as possible – it needs to be legally defensible, it doesn't have to be the most stringent or high-quality recruitment process – they have already made the decision after all and I'm not going to bite the hand that feeds me! I decided on four components: personality test, structured interview (even a basic Google tells us that unstructured interviews are bad practice, so let's just do the opposite, which makes it more legally defensible too), portfolio of previous work, and a project simulation task. Can't say I haven't tried at presenting a robust method.

Day 4: They said "no" to the simulation – might put off their preferred candidate and take up too much staff time. I don't have enough time to come up with something similarly rigorous to replace it. OK, so three things to manage, if anything that makes it easier for me. I'm going to score them all out of 100 (sounds much more credible than 10). I wanted to be involved in the interview and portfolio review, time is money after all, and again, this helps me make sure it's legally more justifiable to any outside evaluation. I have been trained to implement these types of interventions and am confident that it will go well. The interviews were based upon my plan of questions, and they were fine. They didn't stop the panel clearly evidencing their preference for a certain candidate but meh there's nothing I can do about that. The portfolio reviews we are doing independently, and they want me to send mine over ASAP (I know they haven't done theirs yet but, hey, I have to get this project off my desk to progress with other work!). Quick review. Send.

Day 5: OK, let's have a look at the surprise scoring. We had four candidates and they have been pretty generous with their scoring for their preferred candidate. A surprise win; not! I give it all a cursory skim-read and whilst they have been consistent in applying the criteria we agreed, they seem to have missed off a few. I'll send it back just to make sure everything is covered. Dot the Is and cross the Ts and all that.

Day 6: Ha! They responded by saying they found the criteria too restrictive so didn't do the ones they thought were problematic. Dodgy. This sounds totally dodgy. But who am I to argue when they seem confident in their justification? By excluding these elements, they have made the preferred candidate come out on top. Right. I'm done with this already – it's fine to get on with it. They have found their perfect match and I have found my next pay-check. Submit report. Submit timesheet. *Voila*. Pina coladas for all.

Day 7: OK, I'm done but I need to boost my profile so I should write a social media post about my amazing work. The CEO got exactly what they wanted and I made that happen so I think that's a good job done! Might as well crack out the old self-congratulatory trumpet and give it a good blast. #jobwelldone

Let's take a moment to pause and reconsider this again – are you similarly happy with the decisions that were made or are you a little more concerned this time around?

Suboptimal practices are common in day-to-day business, and they don't have to be catastrophic in terms of outcomes. It's OK to make mistakes or to not get things exactly optimal. We're human and things don't always go to plan, even with the best of intentions. It's also OK because it's impossible to avoid bad decisions, even in high-impact industries like healthcare and high-speed contexts like the stock exchange.

One field that has been granted immunity from making errors, subjective decisions, or otherwise inconclusive or inconsistent answers, at least in the public eye, is that of science. Science is traditionally considered objective due to the use of the scientific method and formal publication system – ask big questions, use existing understanding to focus the idea, and then form a plan of how to answer the question and consider what might happen (a hypothesis). The researchers will then test the hypothesis using whatever method is most suitable (e.g. observation, experiment, etc.), analyse the data, and draw objective conclusions based upon the data. They then write this all up to the best of their ability and submit it to journals in the form of a formal (and often long) document. The journal editor then reads the work and makes a judgement as to whether it should undergo review by experts in the field or should be rejected. For the latter, the researcher might be able to make some changes based upon feedback (if there is any) and submit it do a different journal. If the editor sends it for review, researchers in the same field to the paper (peer-reviewers) are invited to give detailed scrutiny of the document and provide comments. These are used to help the editor to make a decision as to the extent of changes needed before it can be published. Sometimes this loop can continue for a number of iterations. Finally, the decision will be made to either accept or reject the document. The purpose of this process is to weed out bad practices and enhance the quality of the document – a rubber-stamp of quality to increase quality and legitimacy. The result: quality science!

Science is too often considered to be white (frequently bearded) men in lab coats – the "experts", making objective decisions from test-tubes that ominously bubble. The reality is not that simple, nor innocent. In most cases, scientists working in the field of psychology and human resource management are predominantly laptop-bound, and unfortunately, they are human too. They are making subjective and suboptimal decisions in an attempt to secure the same things we all want in life – meaning and/or a sense of achievement, comfortable finances, recognition, and an endless supply of biscuits. This obviously has consequences for the "objective" science. For example, we know that agreement between peer-reviewers about manuscripts, and indeed research funding applications, is extremely weak (Kravitz et al., 2010; Pier et al., 2018), and that peer review often adds minimal quality enhancements to manuscripts (Carneiro et al., 2020; Klein et al., 2019).

Let me share with you a little about what's going on right now. Science as a whole – but particularly the fields of medicine and social science – are facing a

Figure 1.1 Scientist. Wait, no. Who let this happen?! No beard? *Get him out of here!*

crisis.[1] We're not just talking a minor life crisis where we buy expensive flashy lab equipment – oh no. We're in a state of shock following what has been called the replication crisis. Unless you work in science you probably haven't heard of it – a recent survey found relatively few of the German population had heard of it (Mede et al., 2021) and probably for good reason – we don't want to lose your trust in science!

The replication crisis (also referred to as the replicability crisis and reproducibility crisis) began only a few years ago. In 2011, three crucial developments were made. The first was an article published in the *Journal of Personality and Social Psychology*, a highly respected scientific journal, by an academic called Daryl Bem. It was 18 pages of gold. In this work, Bem (we "scientists" refer to people by surnames – I'm not sure why) presented nine experiments which converged in presenting evidence for human Extrasensory Perception (ESP). Knowing something before it happens. We can predict the future. Buy me a lottery ticket, Derren Brown has got nothing on me!

---

1 In reality it's a bit of a bad time for us, we're experiencing a few crises – of theory, of measurement, and higher education is really facing the squeeze, with many facing redundancies – I guess we're really not OK right now. I'm just going to focus on the replication crisis though, if that's OK. I can only tackle one issue at a time and we're going to touch upon some of the others as we go along.

In one of the experiments, 100 participants were invited to decide which side of the screen an image would later appear in. Both sides featured an initial image of some theatre curtains and following their choice the experimental software would then randomly select a side and an interesting picture would be unveiled. The fun thing about this research is that for only half of the 36 guesses each participant made, they were observing very standard images: a picture of a bride and groom, for example. The others, well they were "erotic" – originally described as "couples engaged in nonviolent but explicit consensual sexual acts". Can't say psychology isn't sexy! The results for this particular experiment? 49.8% of guesses for non-erotic images were correct. No evidence for ESP there! Unfortunately, Daryl got a little too excited when 53.1% of all guesses with erotic imagery were correctly predicted. This is hardly much greater than 50% – the chance of picking correctly at random – but it was concluded to be "statistically significant" and evidence for precognition. Want to know my favourite statistic for this paper? The word "erotic" is used 82 times.... Daryl! Filthy!

I hope that it comes as no surprise that some other academics didn't necessarily take the claims on face value and ran some independent replications. Replications are attempts to re-evaluate conclusions by collecting new data which can use similar or different methods. Unfortunately for Bem, these replications were far from supportive of the clams made, and as a whole they provided no convincing evidence of such a controversial effect (e.g. Galak et al., 2012; Ritchie et al., 2012). Furthermore, more critical examinations of some of the decisions Bem made with data collection and analysis suggested that perhaps the reviewers of Bem's work could have probably predicted that this was nonsense and misleading (LeBel & Peters, 2011; Wagenmakers et al., 2011).

One particularly exciting replication attempt is called the Transparent PSI Project (Kekecs et al., 2019). Attempting to replicate the study described above, they use all the very best practices known to psychological research to provide the most rigorous evaluation of the original research. They state their methods and analysis strategy in detail and before data collection (called preregistration, see Chapter 7). They make sure researchers don't know any information about what might happen for each participant (known as masking), so they can't influence participants. They even upload data being collected from participants live to ensure there is no data tampering or manipulation. For those working in science, I recommend reading the research plan. It's ambitious and provides a preview of some scientific practices that I anticipate are likely to soon become mainstream. I was originally part of this project, but unfortunately my institutions at the time of data collection wouldn't grant me ethical approval to collect data for the study. Apparently, showing university students erotic images is an unacceptable ethical risk. Even with a warning that they might see such images and when they chose which based upon their sexual preference. Even if a fellow student ran the data collection and couldn't see the participants' screen. Even if they weren't in the room with the participant at the time. I really tried.

Whilst the results of this project have not yet been released, the general conclusion of replication attempts have been that evidence is most compatible with no such effect existing. Sorry. The bad decisions with studying ESP didn't end there, however. For example, a rigorous attempt to replicate the original findings was rejected by a number of popular journals on the basis of being *only* a replication, including the original works' home: the *Journal of Personality and Social Psychology*, and the *British Journal of Psychology* (who invited Bem to review the work, where he unsurprisingly encouraged rejection, for hopefully obvious reasons). The critical replication was eventually published (Ritchie et al., 2012) but the cracks in science were showing and were seen to be on the verge of more strongly supporting claims that science as a whole was broken and that scientific evidence shouldn't be trusted (Ioannidis, 2005).

Despite its relatively obvious absurdity, and its likely use to encourage those interested in conspiracy theories and anti-science, the impact of Bem's controversial work has likely been net positive in my view. The Bem paper provided the scientific community an irrefutable example of the many flaws in science. It was a "reputable" journal. It underwent peer review and was vetted by at least one editor and two peer-reviewers. Statistical decisions were flawed. The evidence was nowhere near as convincing as you might want it to be to make claims that humans can predict events before they happen (Schwarzkopf, 2014). Nevertheless, these claims were being championed by "science". Whilst taking science into dispute and exposing weaknesses, these series of events also contributed to reform and have driven a big shift in thinking (LeBel & Peters, 2011).

The second motivator for an increased critical self-awareness for the scientific community was made through an article by Simmons, Nelson, and Simonsohn (2011), but for this we're going to need to return to hypotheses for a minute. Hypotheses are specific predictions about what might happen in a study. For example, individuals who attend a training event on accessibility will be more likely to use accessible fonts, colours, and formats in their subsequent meeting presentation slides than those who didn't attend the training. That's our hypothesis. It's the purpose of our research. It makes it clear to all as to what we expect to occur. The null hypothesis is then often written as the opposite, that there would be no such impact – that is, there will be no difference in accessibility of fonts, colours, and formats in meeting slides between those who did and did not attend the accessibility training session.

A paper by Simmons et al. (2011) made a convincing argument for how simple it is to incorrectly reject our null hypothesis, thereby accepting our main hypothesis when it is not true. This is what is referred to as a false-positive result. We make claims for an exciting effect when no such effect truly exists. You may have come across this term when getting results back from medical tests – false positives tell you that you have an illness when you don't really have it. In medicine, false negatives are probably more problematic – when you are told you don't have the illness being tested for when you do, but, in science, false-positive results are only ever bad news. They lead to false confidence, which is hard to correct, questions the legitimacy and credibility of the scientists and scientific practices, and leads to more academic and practitioner investment into fields which are not impactful and are unlikely to drive the intended changes.

The Simmons paper provides a number of examples where decisions researchers make (called "researcher degrees of freedom") can influence the outcome of a study towards it becoming misleading. For example, let's imagine we are running some meeting accessibility training in our workplace. We could analyse our data each time we run this new training session under the innocent assumption that if our training is effective then it'll be easy to make that call, regardless of when we stop collecting data. Indeed, in a survey of behavioural scientists in 2010, 70% reported doing this (John et al., 2012). But this is problematic. If we were to analyse our data on the difference in meeting slide accessibility between each and every meeting held, we would be more likely to make a false-positive conclusion after only a few meetings. The more regularly we test the data, the more likely we would be to draw such a misleading conclusion. Only when we have a meaningful amount of data (to what constitutes meaningful, see "Power" in Chapter 4), can we draw robust conclusions. The paper challenged many norms and assumptions. For example, that an effect seen with a small sample size is likely to be seen in a larger sample. Big early results are not indicative of big robust effects. The only solution? More robust and transparent practices.

The third major development was the natural development of a system and community which is "excessively orientated to uncritical confirmation of one's own ideas and to finding appealing but theoretically superficial ad hoc results" (Levelt et al., 2012): Fraud. In that magic year (2011), Diederik Stapel, a widely liked and respected Professor in Cognitive Social Psychology and Dean of School at Tilburg University, was suspended, voluntarily returned his doctorate, and underwent formal investigation for a breach of scientific integrity through use of fictitious data in publications. The first formal retraction of his work was of a paper published in *Science* (still perceived to be one of *the* most prestigious journals) and has since expanded into a list of retractions to 58 at the time of writing (2021). A range of interim and full reviews have subsequently been published on his practices criticising both his ongoing abuses of the system and the scientific communities' inability to prevent them. His autobiography,

translated into English by Nick Brown and freely available at http://nick.
brown.free.fr/stapel, describes his addiction-like escalation from "massaging"
data through minor alterations in specific data points to complete fabrication
of experiments. In 2013, Stapel accepted a pre-trial settlement of 120 hours of
community service and agreed not to claim further finances from the university, this having been deemed reasonable because he never misappropriated his
research funding.

Stapel's case was widely discussed, but he isn't the only one. Consider one
of the most eminent and highly-recognised, cited and respected academics –
Hans Eysenck, who took tobacco-industry funding to misrepresent the cancer
risks of personality such that the role of cigarettes could be suppressed (Pelosi,
2019, see also his RIOT Science Club talk for an entertaining and engaging
overview: www.youtube.com/watch?v=IP6ccNUU4ks). Amongst a range of
concerns raised about his scientific practices, including data manipulation and
both statistical and ethical misconduct, he also took funding from, and adopted
advisory roles for, groups focussed upon eugenics, scientific racism, and white
supremacy. He was a dominant figure within the field of psychology and
beyond – a strong voice in the psychic phenomena and astrology community.
And such was his popularity that he also featured in *Mayfair* and was publishing
in *Penthouse* (if you don't know, these are, ahem, "naughty" magazines). Whilst
Eysenck received substantive critique as early as 1991, retractions of his work
are only now being issued to highlight the problematic practices identified
(Pelosi, 2019).

There are many more examples like Stapel and Eysenck. Just consider the
group of academics who are referred to as "hyper-prolific", publishing an academic journal article every few days (Price, 2018). Are we confident in the
rigour of their work, particularly if it was influential for what is recommended
as "evidence-based practice"? At my most efficient and collaborative, I publish a
few papers each year.

So, humans can't mind-read. They can make bad decisions to improve their
personal circumstances, and indeed they frequently do. The sum of these
developments is a state of understanding where denial of the issues with
current scientific practices could only be reserved for the hopelessly naïve. You
might think this to be a little harsh when there is still lots of evidence that such
problems continue to exist through most of the academic community, but these
three major events in 2011 did not occur in isolation. These works encouraged
the academic community to act quicker on some of the long-standing literature around the concerns with the status quo in scientific practices, encouraging
greater criticality and rigour (e.g. Cohen, 1962; Feynman, 1974; Lakatos, 1976;
Meehl, 1978; Sterling, 1959). Fortunately, many scholars have picked up this
baton and attempted to turn the replication crisis into a credibility revolution. It

first started by working out how bad the situation could be. Here, replications were the order of the day.

Replications can be really insightful. They are typically used to explore whether effects differ when studied in different ways, with different samples, in different countries, etc. It's what's known as the boundary conditions of an effect: what are the minimum conditions required for a result to replicate – do you have to measure your outcome in a specific way, test a specific sample, etc.? This sort of work is really useful for refining theory and for making claims about the generalisability of results for practice (Hüffmeier et al., 2016). For example, I published a replication using different (better) measures than the original to provide better quality evidence on whether emotional intelligence could be integrated into theoretical models of cognitive ability (Evans et al., 2020). Instead of this developmental approach, in light of this concern that research perhaps wasn't quite as trustworthy as hoped, replications were instead wielded to question the trustworthiness of an effect, as was the case with exploring ESP. If you could run a study in a near-identical way, you would hope that you would find similar results, and that would be a more convincing basis for trust and thus action.

The greatest damage was done by the Open Science Collaboration, who, in 2015, published the results of 100 substantive replications. Where 97 of the original studies reported "statistically significant" results, only 36 of the replications reported the same. Furthermore, when they looked at the effect size – e.g. the strength of relationship between variables, or the size of differences between groups being studied – the replication studies on average reported effects half the size of the original. A number of further large replication projects were subsequently started, including the Many Labs 2 project (Klein et al., 2018) where 14/28 studies replicated as expected, and the median effect size reduced to a quarter of the size originally reported by the original works. Replication initiatives have now covered a wide range of fields within and outside of psychology, and whilst rates of "successful" replication do tend to vary, they broadly tell us the same thing – when you use more rigorous methods, evidence often become less convincing. Science is clearly not the objective ideal we had hoped.

The reasons why some effects replicate and others don't is clearly complex. However, as we noted above, the scientists themselves play a key role – whether that be through overt fraud, poor decision-making, or simply following problematic norms. If we want to get to the bottom of this, we need to question errors at every part of the scientific method (Munafò et al., 2017). As we discussed earlier, the scientific method represents the various stages we follow to produce scientific evidence. It's a cycle that starts with generating some big ideas to study and ends with publishing and disseminating findings to inform others' hypotheses.

The research cycle starts with picking a focus and specifying the hypotheses and/or research question to be addressed. As with all decisions, these can be influenced by our own ideas, values, understanding, and beliefs, whether they be implicit or explicit, so that we end with desirable outcomes. There are many good examples where personal views have influenced the focus of a study. For example, there are many works attempting to support or encourage eugenics or racism through scientific racism – studies which attempt to present those of certain backgrounds as fundamentally superior or inferior to others. It's enough to boil blood that science is used as a veneer of credibility and objectivity to justify some of the most disgusting forms of discrimination. The biggest body of evidence in this respect examines IQ differences between different ethnic groups. Indeed, the term eugenics was coined by Sir Francis Galton, a scientist interested in intelligence development. The half-cousin of Charles Darwin, Galton coined the term "nature versus nurture" to explain biological and environmental effects upon development, in addition to a variety of other commonly adopted ideas including the statistical concept of correlations (relationships) and the practical study of psychometrics. His work continues to be influential, yet his dogged pursuit to disseminate racial differences in intelligence has had a catastrophic impact for fuelling hatred and dividing societies through scientific racism. His beliefs about the world clearly informed his decision-making on research foci and methods. This may be an extreme example, but we should be real: all research is motivated. Much of my earlier research was guided by the belief that many managers were terrible managers and could be better if they used humour, praise, and compassion more effectively (e.g. Evans & Dobrosielska, 2019; Evans & Steptoe-Warren, 2018; etc.). I made decisions based upon this belief and this informed study designs and methods. We shouldn't ever try to pretend to be objective, apolitical, or impartial; that is an idealistic mirage that can compromise our critical faculties. We should instead focus on being transparent about what we do and why. This reflexivity will help others to evaluate our work in context and support making more conscious decisions about what we do and why. My personal research focus has since changed and is now orientated towards addressing the Global Goals. I hope many others follow me in this regard and prioritise investment of their expertise into the most socially impactful and important directions.

The second stage is study design. Much like a tailor when creating a pattern to follow during manufacturing, we can use our creative freedom to make design choices. A button up here, not down there. Should the bow be bigger? Rigid material or soft and flexible? A short pencil skirt or a long flowing dress? There are many valid ways of creating clothes, but each decision can have an impact on the final outcome produced. Studies are much the same and as we create the blueprint for each opportunity to collect data, we make decisions that impact the final study outcome. Should we collect data over different time points (longitudinal) or at the same time (cross-sectional). Should we use an experimental manipulation or a hypothetical scenario? Should we measure our outcome directly or ask participants to self-report? All these decisions change the results. This of course is not a problem, except remember that we typically get taught to design in specific ways, we get told that certain things "work" and others don't (although it might be difficult to explain why that might be). We also often have real world trade-offs between easy and immediate results and well-considered and long-lasting outcomes. Imagine I am resource-poor. I want to create a skirt with as little material and process as possible. I'm going to go for a miniskirt or pencil skirt, not a maxi skirt with reams of cloth and many complicated pleats. I'm going to use a thin cotton rather than a durable denim. Much in the same way, if I have limited time or resources, I'm going to design a very simplistic study and limit the number of participants I recruit to minimise the use of precious resources. The particular issue of sample size is one that is particularly problematic in the design stage because, as we discussed above, low power to detect an effect if it exists means we increase the likelihood of drawing erroneous conclusions. The final quality of the study, or indeed the skirt, is only as good as the design decisions made. For both research and clothing, it's time for a culture change towards minimising consumption and choosing more rigorous and long-lasting designs, instead of prioritising cheap and immediate results that don't last.

The third stage in the research cycle is the implementation of the study design and data collection. Here, a number of issues surrounding quality control can influence the creation of data and thus subsequent conclusions drawn from the research. For example, a researcher can fail to accurately log contextual factors which may influence data collection, such as a recent redundancy announcement, or perhaps a mobile phone going off during a task requiring focus and concentration. These issues might be considered to have relatively minimal impact, but consider whether this happens at random. For example, let's imagine a researcher was testing the impact of different briefing strategies upon decision-making, comparing a detailed strategy to a control group who were given no instructions. If the researcher did not treat the groups equally, perhaps by engaging more with their mobile when with the control group than when with the intervention group, we might expect that some of the difference between groups may be due to the distracting actions of the researcher rather than some inherent effect of the structured briefing strategy. If these disruptions are not transparently reported, the results may therefore be misleading in not acknowledging the potential role of the researcher. For these types of reasons researchers can use masking when comparing groups – a strategy well established in clinical study design. Single-masked studies are typically those where participants don't know which experimental group they are within (so don't have any placebo effect or disengagement from the control group). Double-masked studies are those where both the participants and researcher collecting the data don't know which condition participants have been allocated to. Finally, triple-masked studies build upon double-masked designs such that those who analyse the data don't know which groups represent which interventions. Intervention and control groups are labelled group A and group B etc., and they are only revealed once analysis is complete. We'll discuss the role of the researcher in the analysis more below, and in Chapter 2.

The next stage in the process is the analysis of data. The problem is that there is a wide range of very small decisions, made as part of the process of analysis. It's a garden of forking paths, and researchers have the freedom to choose any route they wish (researcher degrees of freedom) so long as they justified it somehow. Do we include or exclude participants who produced extreme scores (outliers), and which might distort findings? What cut-off point do we adopt to suggest our model is a good fit to the data? More on this in Chapter 2, but as null results are less desirable to publish (see the final stage), there is good evidence to suggest that researchers commonly "massage" their analysis decisions to lead to the greatest likelihood of securing a "statistically significant" result. This is called p-hacking. It's often seen in exploratory research when researchers collect a wide range of outcomes to increase the likelihood that at least one will be positive. Such strategies can capitalise on false-positive results and could lead to highly misleading conclusions.

The penultimate stage in the process lies with the interpretation of results. We have collected data and ran some analyses, now we have to work out how best to "sell them" so they convince readers to trust and act upon the conclusions. This isn't problematic when results are as you expect, but what happens when results show no effect, or directly contradict your hypotheses? This isn't itself a bad thing, but it's easy to worry that peer-reviewers can use this as an easy reason to reject your manuscript – either you chose a poor theory to frame your study, or you have designed your study poorly to capture the effect. One easy route to make publication easier is to correct the narrative so that results were as expected. This is a major issue at this stage of the research process, and it's called HARKing: Hypothesising After Results are Known. If you can't change the data/analyses then you can always change your hypotheses and narrative so you "expected" them! The same can be seen in clinical trials where they change the narrative to focus upon the most "exciting" results. This is called outcome switching (Goldacre et al., 2019). A great strategy to increase the likelihood of publication, but another distortion of understanding to the evidence base.

The final stage in the process is the publication and dissemination process. Getting the findings of the research into the hands that can do the most with them. This stage completes the loop by allowing the work conducted thus far to inform decisions upon future work. We've already reviewed the academic publication process and the problems with peer review as a gatekeeper of quality, but there are a wide range of other issues to consider. One major barrier to progress is called publication bias. This is when the outcome of the study impacts the likelihood of it being published. There is a tendency for "statistically significant" findings, those telling us a particular intervention type has been "successful", for example, to be more likely to be published than those suggesting an intervention has little or no effect. So, what does this do? First up, this motivates researchers to create "positive findings" – something which could be done subconsciously or purposefully, by picking more certain routes of study, capturing a larger number of outcomes to secure a hit, and practices like p-hacking, selective reporting, and data fabrication. The result of all these factors is a distorted body of literature where the majority reports significant results and findings. It's therefore likely that most bodies of evidence over-exaggerate the likelihood and strength of an effect. We'll discuss this more in Chapter 7, but when researchers are promised publication before the results are known, they are far less likely to report "statistically significant" findings (Scheel et al., 2021). My final concern with the publication process is that when null findings get rejected for publication… where do they go? The death of many such works is the file-drawer. They get stored away like some secret shameful failure and prevent other researchers from learning about what does and doesn't work. This is called the file-drawer effect (Rosenthal, 1979). So much important research is hiding in people's file drawers, Dropbox files, or indeed boxes under their desk, because null findings are less desirable to publishers who like "novel" and "impactful" research. In my view, null findings are just as useful. For example, if we found out that workplace diversity training had no effect upon important outcomes, or even a mixture of positive and negative effects, we would hopefully stop running that training and invest the resources to target more structural barriers which prevent diversity. Null findings are just as useful as "statistically significant" results. Unfortunately, they are not treated as such by the companies who act as the main gatekeepers of academic research – journals. So where else can null findings end up – on social media, LinkedIn posts, or organisational reports. This sort of "grey" literature has few barriers to dissemination, but are not considered as equivalent in quality by many (although the quality of the work is nearly completely independent of the publication route). So null findings here can be more accessible, but less easy to systematically identify, and often receive a wider audience with those who can implement findings (practitioners) than academics. As there are few barriers, it also means that poor-quality work can be easily disseminated amongst quality null results, which means that the work with some of the least accountability and transparency can be much more easily shared with those who can action it than those who can critically challenge it (Evans et al., 2021).

The reason why this is important to be aware of is that this research process, with all the subjectivities discussed above, has built the evidence base we're currently living our lives based upon. Whether that be the techniques we use to recruit individuals, the types of training we chose to run and how we determine that it "works", or the strategies we use to negotiate day-to-day stressors and change. Not to worry you, but it's also the body of evidence upon which our public health campaigns, our drugs and our healthcare policies are based upon (read the book *Bad Science* by Goldacre (2010) if you want to know more in this field). Our current understanding is based upon scientific practices that are suboptimal at best. A full response from the scientific community tackling such substantive issues is long overdue and fortunately there are now a wide range of initiatives to encourage reform, challenging these issues across the scientific method. However, this does leave us with the question of what to do with current HR practices. There are many calls for evidence-based practice: judicious, explicit, and conscientious use of various sources of information to support better decision-making (Briner & Barends, 2016). Unfortunately, the use of the term widely outruns the rigorous application of the method. The body of evidence available to inform evidence-based practice is often poor (e.g. Evans, 2020). The point of this book is to re-evaluate the evidence base for just a few HR practices and encourage some wider critical reflections upon what we can do, as members of the HR community, to improve practice.

It may be difficult to see how we as individuals can improve the state of play, but let's just have one more read through of our consultancy situation, this time looking at is from a problematic research perspective:

Day 1 / 2: Being approached for work with an expected outcome is likely to drive bias. They already made the decision as to who to hire. I could have walked away, refused to do the work, or perhaps challenged their assumptions. Instead, I went ahead with their intentions and secured the outcome they wanted.

Day 3: I design the plan based upon speed and resources, not quality evidence collection. I have relatively little data from which I need to make a big decision. They said no to something which would improve data quality and I did nothing to challenge the decision either.

Day 4: I collect the data, poorly. I don't try to design out or adjust for the biases demonstrated by the others involved in the process. I don't enforce quality control in any way.

Day 5/6: The others involved have looked at my data and fabricated their own responses accordingly to produce the outcome they want. They p-hacked the data by dropping the criteria which would go against the end outcome they intended. The outcome could never be anything else except what had been decided at the beginning, and the decision was based upon compromised data.

Day 7: I'm going to selectively disseminate what I want others to hear about how good I am. I've told people that use of the organisations' personality tool was helpful. I've presented my design as an objective and rigorous process establishing the blueprints and reinforcing the norms for other people to work from. I've made myself look good and that's all that matters.

This example directly mirrors the issues reported from across the research cycle. Naughty! And it's worth reflecting here that there are many issues, with responsibility spread across all those involved in the research process. Part of the issue was not challenging norms and authority, but that was only part of the story. The point was that the various decisions made, and actions taken, were common. It's normal. Standard. Typical. Yet it was problematic in many different ways.

These are the sorts of issues we're going to be tackling throughout the book. It's going to make us question whether current practices really are fit for purpose and can be claimed to be based on any quality evidence. We're going to raise our heads out of the sand and take a good hard critical look at ourselves. It might be uncomfortable, but, as Simmons et al. (2011) argue, we should embrace these developments as if the credibility of our profession depended on them: "Because it does".

A brief note before we continue. It should be evident from your reading thus far that this book is not designed to be a formally written comprehensive guide to HR. In my primary role as an academic, I am normally very limited in my style of writing, often required to focus on specific numbers (and often to three decimal points – wow, precision!) to impress only a few other academics who probably don't have enough time to read much more than what is necessary to get the general gist of what I wrote, not say to scrutinise the numbers to *three* decimal points. Instead, this book is for everyone. I may walk us through some numbers, and possibly even statistical concepts, but I promise to do it in a way that is accessible and – I hope – enjoyable to read.

The next five chapters look at some of the actions that have persisted or entered modern HR practice. We'll cover in-house analysis of HR work, emotional intelligence-based selection and assessment, diversity training, workplace stress interventions, and organisational change interventions. Throughout,

I will cover my own experiences of these practices as a scientist-practitioner, alongside a critical review of the evidence behind each one.

After Chapter 6, you would be forgiven if you were to think all prior academic study of organisations have been shambolic misdirection to keep shoulder-patch sewers in business. (Please tell me you know we don't still wear those right?). I'm known for being positive yet constructively critical, so my responsibility lies not solely with burning down the unstable house, but also with identifying resources that may act as more robust foundations for the future. As such, I spend the subsequent two chapters covering two principles which I think will be fundamental to overcoming some of the issues in evidence quality highlighted throughout – preregistration and collaboration.

I hope this book leaves you feeling cautiously optimistic about the future and ready to challenge current practices. I'll attempt to negotiate the current state of disarray and balance it with the power of some new tools and approaches academics and practitioners can use to build a more robust and progressive state of understanding and practice. We'll revisit some of the ideas and principles first raised in this chapter and look at the wider context offered by the replication/credibility crisis to ask ourselves whether HR is really in crisis and whether there is any hope for progress. In reading this, I challenge you to begin to question your own practices and approaches, and to join me in working towards a more transparent and robust evidence base to build HR practices upon. Ready?

References

Adams, G. S., Converse, B. A., Hales, A. H., & Klotz, L. E. (2021). People systematically overlook subtractive changes. *Nature*, *592*(7853), 258–261.

Bem, D. J. (2011). Feeling the future: Experimental evidence for anomalous retroactive influences on cognition and affect. *Journal of Personality and Social Psychology*, *100*(3), 407–425.

Briner, R. B., & Barends, E. (2016). The role of scientific findings in evidence-based HR. *People and Strategy*, *39*(2), 16–20.

Carneiro, C. F., Queiroz, V. G., Moulin, T. C., Carvalho, C. A., Haas, C. B., Rayêe, D., ... & Amaral, O. B. (2020). Comparing quality of reporting between preprints and peer-reviewed articles in the biomedical literature. *Research Integrity and Peer Review*, *5*(1), 1–19.

Cohen, J. (1962). The statistical power of abnormal-social psychological research: A review. *Journal of Abnormal and Social Psychology*, *65*(3), 145–153.

Evans, T. R. (2020). Improving evidence quality for organisational change management through open science. *Journal of Organizational Change Management*, *33*(2), 367–378.

Evans, T. R., Branney, P., Clements, A., & Hatton, E. (2021). Improving evidence-based practice througrh preregistration of applied research: Barriers and recommendations. *Accountability in Research*, 1–21. 10.1080/08989621.2021.1969233

Evans, T. R., & Dobrosielska, A. (2019). Feedback-seeking culture moderates the relationship between positive feedback and task performance. *Current Psychology*, *40*(7), 3401–3408.

Evans, T. R., Hughes, D. J., & Steptoe-Warren, G. (2020). A conceptual replication of emotional intelligence as a second-stratum factor of intelligence. *Emotion, 20*(3), 507–512.

Evans, T. R., & Steptoe-Warren, G. (2018). Humor style clusters: Exploring managerial humor. *International Journal of Business Communication, 55*(4), 443–454.

Feynman, R. P. (1974). Cargo cult science. *Engineering and Science, 37*(7), 10–13.

Galak, J., LeBoeuf, R. A., Nelson, L. D., & Simmons, J. P. (2012). Correcting the past: Failures to replicate psi. *Journal of Personality and Social Psychology, 103*(6), 933–948.

Goldacre, B. (2010). *Bad science: Quacks, hacks, and big pharma flacks.* McClelland & Stewart.

Goldacre, B., Drysdale, H., Dale, A., Milosevic, I., Slade, E., Hartley, P., ... & Mahtani, K. R. (2019). COMPare: a prospective cohort study correcting and monitoring 58 misreported trials in real time. *Trials, 20*(1), 1–16.

Hüffmeier, J., Mazei, J., & Schultze, T. (2016). Reconceptualizing replication as a sequence of different studies: A replication typology. *Journal of Experimental Social Psychology, 66*, 81–92.

Ioannidis, J. P. (2005). Why most published research findings are false. *PLoS Medicine, 2*(8), e124.

John, L. K., Loewenstein, G., & Prelec, D. (2012). Measuring the prevalence of questionable research practices with incentives for truth telling. *Psychological Science, 23*(5), 524–532.

Kekecs, Z., Aczel, B., Palfi, B., Szaszi, B., Szecsi, P., Zrubka, M., ... Dubrov, D. (2019, August 1). *Raising the value of research studies in psychological science by increasing the credibility of research reports: The Transparent PSI Project – Preprint.* Accessible: https://doi.org/10.31234/osf.io/uwk7y

Klein, M., Broadwell, P., Farb, S. E., & Grappone, T. (2019). Comparing published scientific journal articles to their pre-print versions. *International Journal on Digital Libraries, 20*(4), 335–350.

Klein, R. A., Vianello, M., Hasselman, F., Adams, B. G., Adams Jr, R. B., Alper, S., ... & Sowden, W. (2018). Many Labs 2: Investigating variation in replicability across samples and settings. *Advances in Methods and Practices in Psychological Science, 1*(4), 443–490.

Kowalski, T. H., & Loretto, W. (2017). Well-being and HRM in the changing workplace. *International Journal of Human Resource Management, 28*(16), 2229–2255.

Kravitz, R. L., Franks, P., Feldman, M. D., Gerrity, M., Byrne, C., & Tierney, W. M. (2010). Editorial peer reviewers' recommendations at a general medical journal: are they reliable and do editors care? *PLoS One, 5*(4), e10072.

Lakatos I. (1976) Falsification and the Methodology of Scientific Research Programmes. In: Harding S.G. (eds) *Can Theories be Refuted?* Synthese Library, vol 81. Springer, Dordrecht. Accessible: https://doi.org/10.1007/978-94-010-1863-0_14

LeBel, E. P., & Peters, K. R. (2011). Fearing the future of empirical psychology: Bem's (2011) evidence of psi as a case study of deficiencies in modal research practice. *Review of General Psychology, 15*(4), 371–379.

Levelt, W. J. M., Drenth, P., & Noort, E. (2012). *Flawed science: The fraudulent research practices of social psychologist Diederik Stapel.* Accessible: https://web.archive.org/web/20130112204021/www.tilburguniversity.edu/nl/nieuws-en-agenda/finalreportLevelt.pdf

Mede, N. G., Schäfer, M. S., Ziegler, R., & Weißkopf, M. (2021). The "replication crisis" in the public eye: Germans' awareness and perceptions of the (ir) reproducibility of scientific research. *Public Understanding of Science, 30*(1), 91–102.

Meehl, P. E. (1978). Theoretical risks and tabular asterisks: Sir Karl, Sir Ronald, and the slow progress of soft psychology. *Journal of Consulting and Clinical Psychology, 46*(4), 806–834.

Munafò, M. R., Nosek, B. A., Bishop, D. V., Button, K. S., Chambers, C. D., Du Sert, N. P., ... & Ioannidis, J. P. (2017). A manifesto for reproducible science. *Nature Human Behaviour, 1*(1), 1–9.

Open Science Collaboration. (2015). Estimating the reproducibility of psychological science. *Science, 349*(6251).

Pelosi, A. J. (2019). Personality and fatal diseases: Revisiting a scientific scandal. *Journal of Health Psychology, 24*(4), 421–439.

Pier, E. L., Brauer, M., Filut, A., Kaatz, A., Raclaw, J., Nathan, M. J., ... & Carnes, M. (2018). Low agreement among reviewers evaluating the same NIH grant applications. *Proceedings of the National Academy of Sciences, 115*(12), 2952–2957.

Price (2018) Some scientists publish more than 70 papers a year. Here's how—and why—they do it. Accessible: www.sciencemag.org/news/2018/09/some-scientists-publish-more-70-papers-year-here-s-how-and-why-they-do-it

Prospects (2021) Overview of the UK's HR and recruitment industry. Accessible: www.prospects.ac.uk/jobs-and-work-experience/job-sectors/recruitment-and-hr/overview-of-the-uks-hr-and-recruitment-industry

Ritchie, S. J., Wiseman, R., & French, C. C. (2012). Failing the future: Three unsuccessful attempts to replicate Bem's 'Retroactive Facilitation of Recall' Effect. *PLoS One, 7*(3), e33423.

Rosenthal, R. (1979). The file drawer problem and tolerance for null results. *Psychological Bulletin, 86*(3), 638–641.

Scheel, A. M., Schijen, M. R., & Lakens, D. (2021). An excess of positive results: Comparing the standard Psychology literature with Registered Reports. *Advances in Methods and Practices in Psychological Science, 4*(2), 25152459211007467.

Schwarzkopf, D. S. (2014). We should have seen this coming. *Frontiers in Human Neuroscience, 8*, 332.

Simmons, J. P., Nelson, L. D., & Simonsohn, U. (2011). False-positive psychology: Undisclosed flexibility in data collection and analysis allows presenting anything as significant. *Psychological Science, 22*(11), 1359–1366.

Sterling, T. D. (1959). Publication decisions and their possible effects on inferences drawn from tests of significance—or vice versa. *Journal of the American Statistical Association, 54*(285), 30–34.

US Bureau of Labor Statistics (2000). *Occupational Outlook Handbook.* Bernan Press.

Van Beurden, J., Van De Voorde, K., & Van Veldhoven, M. (2021). The employee perspective on HR practices: A systematic literature review, integration and outlook. *International Journal of Human Resource Management, 32*(2), 359–393.

van der Togt, J. & Rasmussen, T. H. (2017). Toward evidence-based HR. *Journal of Organizational Effectiveness: People and Performance, 4*(2), 127–132.

Wagenmakers, E.-J., Wetzels, R., Borsboom, D., & van der Maas, H. L. J. (2011). Why psychologists must change the way they analyze their data: The case of psi: Comment on Bem (2011). *Journal of Personality and Social Psychology, 100*(3), 426–432.

DIY Analysis

2

I sit here writing this chapter from my sofa. It's not a particularly comfortable place to work, is open to distractions from the road outside and the kitchen next door, and I know it's probably doing terrible things to my posture. But I'm here, and I'm happy. Want to know why? *I* made the sofa. OK, so not from scratch (most of my skills are pretty limited to those contained within these pages, although I have recently replaced a bathroom tap and electric shower, so try not to look too surprised). But I *constructed* it. That counts as "making" right? I place disproportionate levels of value in the sofa, because I (partially) created it. In the academic study of bias, this is called the IKEA effect. IKEA is known for products that have to be self-assembled (like my sofa). Also meatballs.

We can transfer this same phenomenon to the workplace. You have set up a new policy/procedure, established a new working group, recruited a new colleague – by investing in this process, you are often also invested in the outcomes. You want them to succeed, and to be recognised for making a positive contribution. Because you have been involved, you may be biased in placing disproportionate value in them. Now, imagine I am running an intervention in your organisation. We have spent significant time and resources in creating and evaluating the work. We have both invested in making it "work". This isn't a problem if the results were generally clear and consistent, but what if the results were ambiguous? I am far more likely to suggest it was a success in comparison to someone who was not attached or involved in the process. Often judgements on whether something is successful are subjective – particularly as targets might be partially met, malleable, or vaguely defined. These all allow my biases to kick in, claiming a successful intervention where perhaps the evidence isn't quite so conclusive.

DOI: 10.4324/9781003035794-2

There are plenty of ways in which the distance between organisational demand for a project and shiny PowerPoints concluding success can be negotiated. To illustrate this clearly, let's talk about a specific example from some of my previous research. My undergraduate dissertation project was interested in the relationships between managerial humour use and employee outcomes. My dissertation planning started off by using Google Scholar to look up fields of interest. I wanted to build an evidence base to determine whether managerial offerings of cake/baked goods had substantive impacts upon the manager–employee relationship, but, alas, I did not have the resources or vision for a randomised control trial for that at the time. Instead, I found two papers of interest. The first was by Dr Rod Martin, a now-retired Professor who dedicated his career to understanding humour and laughter.

If I were to describe an individual as humorous or using lots of humour, you're likely to picture this person as positive, nice, friendly, or similar. Humour is considered "ideologically positive" (Billig, 2005), such that we tend to consider any use of humour positive, however, humour can be used to achieve all sorts of outcomes. I'm sure we can all remember experiences when someone has used humour to make a joke about us. Humour has been referred to as a rubber sword – you can attack someone with it but hopefully not hurt them. Such uses of humour are often based upon a kernel of truth, so represent a valid critique, yet when questioned on it the user can then defend themselves by saying a joke is only a joke and doesn't mean anything (a Cavalier Humour Belief, Hodson et al., 2010). Humour can be used to probe, violate norms, ingratiate, tease, and maintain or change the hierarchy, amongst many other functions. It's not an innocent or passive process. As such, Martin et al. (2003) developed a multidimensional model of humour (see Figure 2.1). It's based upon two continuums – valence (benign/negative) and target (self/relationships). What we tend to think of as humour, the social glue to build and reinforce relationships, is that of affiliative humour. Like sending around a joke to colleagues: "Why was there no headache medicine left in the jungle? Parrots ate 'em all. (read: paracetamol)". I got told that one by a firefighter when doing some training on humour and communication, so don't blame me.

We can also use humour to benefit ourselves but at the cost of others – a specific individual or group (competitor organisation, estate agents, women, etc.), and this aggressive humour can range from friendly teasing to bullying and abuse. Unsurprisingly, outcomes from this type of humour tend to be negative. Then there are the uses of humour which relate to the self – either using humour to rise above situations (self-enhancing, sometimes referred to as coping humour) or to enhance relationships at the cost of the self (self-defeating humour).

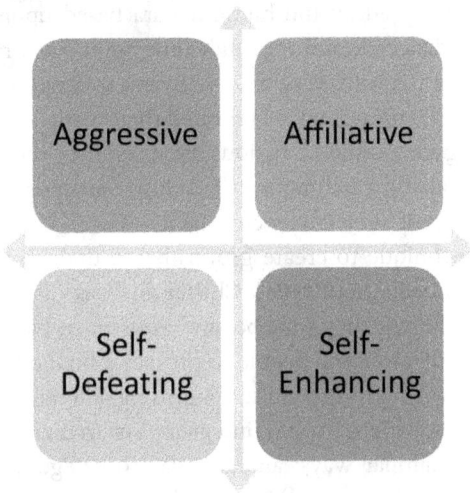

Figure 2.1 The Martin et al. (2003) framework for humour types

A little simplistic, and sometimes difficult in practice to definitively classify examples, but this framework has driven substantive bodies of evidence and appears to be quite useful to discuss different relational consequences of humour types. Unfortunately, now you know about this model, it'll be really difficult not to classify how friends and loved ones use humour. I wouldn't recommend watching a comedy film or similar this evening...

The second paper annoyed me. I would go so far as to say that it represents some of the worst of academia – cherry-picking unfounded claims to encourage action and using the allure of an academic tone to inspire confidence, but without any clear justification or robust evidence. The paper was a "model" in the broadest sense, in that it suggested various relationships between the four humour types and various organisational outcomes (Romero & Cruthirds, 2006). This must be where my current academic cynicism and curiosity began. I took it as my own personal mission to test all the relationships proposed because I wasn't convinced that the evidence matched the claims. Even I can hear how annoying I must have been questioning everything, but my supervisor, and now ongoing friend and mentor Dr Gail Steptoe-Warren, thankfully saw this inquisitiveness as indicative of potential, rather than a warning sign for ongoing annoyance. My undergraduate dissertation therefore became a critical evaluation of this proposed model.

After my undergraduate studies I completed various fixed-term research and teaching roles for a year before I jumped into my PhD (more on this in

Chapter 3). During this time I re-analysed all the humour data based upon concerns that lots of relationships in data collected at a single time point (known as a cross-sectional design) might not tell us very much (Evans & Steptoe-Warren, 2019). I had data from over 200 participants who rated their manager's use of the four humour types, alongside ratings of various dimensions of their workplace experiences. I applied a statistical technique called cluster analysis to this data, and this is where the buckets of subjectivity creeped in.

Cluster analysis is a statistical technique to create groups based upon any number of variables – in this case, four humour types. Cluster analysis always creates groups regardless of how different they may be, and in its most basic form it tries loads of different ways of grouping people to present a final out-come that maximises differences between groups whilst minimising differences within groups. My thought was that maybe we could find groups of managers who use the four humour types in similar ways; an easy way to categorise people based upon their humour use. For example, we might expect a Lord Alan Sugar-type character who uses quite a lot of aggressive humour – humour to establish dominance over others, and little of any other humour type. If there were a few different types of these groups of humour user then maybe I could create a viral Buzzfeed quiz and my life would be set up for a very early retirement.

So, cluster analysis is quite a flexible technique. You can use different methods to tell you how many groups are most likely within the data, or you can dic-tate the number of groups you would like to extract and it can calculate how best you can group these individuals. I used the latter. It sounds objective to let an equation decide, but where was the theory? What made the differenti-ation between groups meaningful? When I tried to create four groups (as might have been recommended by other studies using a similar approach) the results were pretty difficult to build a convincing narrative around. For example, there was one group who had average self-defeating humour use, a little more than average affiliative and self-enhancing humour, and used lots more than average aggressive humour. It's not easy to picture this type of person. This isn't a par-ticularly clear or convincing humour profile. I didn't like it, so I didn't run with it. Instead, I looked at only three groups, and here I found an easier narrative to present, including an aggressive "Lord Sugar" profile exactly as I had hoped. For transparency, I reported both analyses where there were three and four groups in the final paper. But, I took the easier road in providing further analysis on only the three groups. Instead of embracing the complexity and messy reality of the findings, I chose to take an easier road. I found a group who used lots of all the humour types, a Lord Sugar profile, and a group who used the posi-tive types more than average and the negative types less than average. Simple to communicate, but was this really the right decision? Both solutions, three groups or four, are equivalent in principle, but I had control and flexibility over what I could do, and I used that power to try and make a stronger argument through a simpler message.

There was a recent project within psychology where researchers declared when they had lost confidence in their own prior findings or conclusions (Rohrer et al., 2021). I don't think my research fits the criteria for this, and I stand by my initial research conclusions as they are, particularly as the cluster analyses were exploratory and I was explicit about my concerns surrounding the meaningfulness of groups discussed. As you might imagine, however, I wasn't quite happy with leaving things there. It raised an important question for me as to the extent to which science is self-correcting. Science is generally considered by academics and the public to be self-correcting, but with so many biases I'm not sure I fully endorse that statement. Mistakes, of course, happen and can get corrected – replication works have challenged various well-established psychological effects on what feels like a weekly basis, but replication works are a big commitment, and the quantity of academic publications is only increasing. Furthermore, science retractions and corrections are slow, inconsistent, and painful processes. Just ask Dr Bik, whose attempt to retract academic works based upon obvious fabrications through image manipulation are infrequently appreciated (Bik et al., 2016). See her brief talk on bad science and image manipulation for the RIOT Science Club here: www.youtube.com/watch?v= F_cd0IqGwwU. Instead, I took some time to reflect about what would represent a test of how meaningful these groupings are, and I took to Twitter. I certainly wasn't content in accepting the status quo and I made a plan to question this as objectively as is possible. Cue the montage where the superhero-underdog protagonist goes to various places across the world to recruit a motley crew (I use this term affectionately) of crime fighters with specialist talents.

This time I had bigger ambitions. I got the support of collaborators in Poland, the Netherlands, and across the UK, so we could try to replicate the groups I previously identified across different countries (Evans et al., 2020). This might be able to tell us whether the groups are consistent across samples and cultures, and if they are meaningful. Not only that, but we also stated how we would analyse the data before we collected it (more on preregistration in Chapter 7). We collected data from over 900 people who self-reported their humour and various outcomes in personal wellbeing and relationships. To cut to the shock conclusions, as all montages inevitably do, the findings were messy. The groups were inconsistent across cultures and didn't seem to map clearly to existing work on humour using cluster analysis. Not only that, but we tested to see whether these groupings were important for the prediction of outcomes. They didn't predict the outcomes well at all and were less helpful than just considering the individual humour types by themselves. Luckily, this time, we had anticipated and were accepting of inconsistencies, but again I was left without a Buzzfeed quiz to rest my hat upon.

For this project we had journal acceptance before the results were known (an initiative called Registered Reports; see Chapter 7), so there was no pressure to tell a coherent story. But what if we didn't? If I were to return to this data, I am confident that with enough tinkering and time, I would be able to make it tell us the perfect narrative, and perhaps even argue that they are meaningful and useful groupings. Please be reassured that I'm not going to do this, even to prove a point (the data is open so there's nothing stopping you though!). This situation is often called the "garden of forking paths" (Gelman & Loken, 2014). We accept that the outcomes and conclusions we draw can change depending upon the strategies we use to manage the data – whether we control for demographic variables, remove extreme values (outliers), etc. These are all decisions we make that influence the outcomes and conclusions we draw. One might suggest that if we go down a variety of these paths and still return the same outcomes then the conclusions might be considered somewhat more robust. Various versions of this type of thinking have been referred to as multiverse analysis (Steegen et al., 2016) and specification curve analysis (Simonsohn et al., 2015). Here we go down various paths to work out how these analytical decisions change the outcomes and what this might mean for how confident we should be in these conclusions. This is super useful when applied to previous research where we see that the conclusions drawn were often driven by a single arbitrary analysis decision.

So, couple this analytical freedom and flexibility with the IKEA effect discussed earlier – that we over-value our work when we are more involved in it. One can then see how some of the questionable research practices highlighted in Chapter 1 come about. For example, when reviewing feedback comments from an intervention I have delivered, having lovingly crafted the content over many years, I may interpret negative feedback as less severe and positive feedback as more prominent. One might be fooled into thinking: "Yes! they recognised and valued the fact I spent a lot of time negotiating the nuances of the topic". Was this the most salient or dominant factor in their evaluation of the intervention or have I just chosen it to highlight it because it's what I felt was my most meaningful contribution to the project?

Couple these factors with incentive structures around science, discussed in Chapter 1, and practice. An HR manager knows they will be under pressure to evidence that their intervention has been effective, so they make decisions along the way when collecting and analysing that data to make it tell the story needed to remove that pressure. Indeed, there has been a paper published in the field of psychological therapies (Cuijpers & Cristea, 2016) as to how to make ineffective interventions appear effective, many principles of which would be relevant here. For example, assessing many outcomes and only reporting those which report positive results, or providing excessive enthusiasm in communications about the intervention to increase expectations of positive outcomes. We could keep going, adding further biases and contextual factors, but I think the message is clear – there is a lot of freedom in the analysis and interpretation of data and this can (but not always!) distort findings to the point that they become misleading.

So, all of this raises the question: should HR staff be leading the analysis/ interpretation of their own initiatives?

The Argument Against

HR staff should not be leading the analysis/interpretation of their own initiatives.

First up, they are biased. We are all biased. The IKEA effect, and all the other such personal biases we hold, mean we are not always fit to portray an independent assessment of our own work. This is particularly true because the real world is messy, and initiatives often have many and mixed impacts that we can only understand in context. Any ambiguity in outcome offers opportunities for exploitation.

We have a stake in the outcome, and no-one wants to be associated with a sinking ship. The systems we work in operate on definitions of success that are not orientated towards transparency or rigour, they are based upon the type of results you report. A biased assessment only increases the likelihood of exaggerating the benefits, minimising concerns or problematic practices, and simplifying complex accounts. Such an obvious outcome seems inevitable when considering the extent of questionable practices seen by those in science who (apparently) endeavour for the selfless goal of improving scientific understanding, rather than working within an organisation explicitly driven by results. Designing evaluations with poor designs, reporting different outcomes (outcome switching), keeping uncomfortable conclusions in the file-drawer, disseminating specific conclusions without appropriate context; all likely practices which replicate the problems reported in the academic literature. So, if you want a less biased account, we shouldn't be doing the analysis or interpretation of our own initiatives.

Second, education is a potential issue. Let's take training evaluation as a good example. I have been to way too many training events where their evaluation has been a brief survey immediately after the event asking how much I enjoyed it, felt I learnt, or how great I thought the training was. We all know that this initial response to training is not an effective way to evaluate training. One of the most well-known models of training evaluation is that of Kirkpatrick (1959). His model ranges from looking at direct business results (level 4, e.g. return on investment) to immediate self-reported reactions (level 1) as the outcome. Now, let's be honest with ourselves. We all know that an initial response assessment doesn't really mean much and is likely to be heavily biased by social factors and training approach rather than reflecting training content. That's not to say it can't be useful information, but its ease of use and accessibility mean it's adopted far more regularly than is justified. This four-level model is problematic in of itself (Bates, 2004), but helps us to highlight the simplicity of most evaluations.

Similar issues are experienced in research, and it happens across all levels of seniority. For example, let's consider the concept of a p-value which underpins judgements around whether findings are "statistically significant". It's the probability of a given test observing the same effect, or greater, given that no such effect exists. It is a really difficult thing to get your head around, and whilst many of my students can repeat the definition by rote and can interpret whether a p-value is "statistically significant", understanding what it means (and thus being able to identify when things are not right) is difficult. It therefore comes to no surprise that an estimated 89% of psychology textbooks on research methods, written by experts in the field, perpetuated inconsistencies and errors in definitions and understanding (Cassidy et al., 2019). If these are the materials used to teach students on their way towards careers in research, it is hardly controversial to suggest that education is an ongoing contributing factor to suboptimal practices.

The immediate conclusion is not to suggest that we always need to look for "experts" to do the work for us. Even experts get it wrong, although hopefully less so than non-experts, and sometimes they introduce their own biases when they become the faces of certain approaches, products, or services. We should instead, if we think analysis and evaluation is that important, outsource analysis *until* evaluation and analysis skills are better embedded into HR-based curricula and training. Otherwise, we need to consider whether building HR groups from multi-disciplinary teams where responsibilities are allocated meaningfully (e.g. analysis to the data analyst) may bring sufficient consistent involvement to drive beneficial outcomes, but sufficiently independence from subject specific areas, to act more objectively. So, rather than move the work beyond HR, perhaps we should move the scope of HR to better capture the work completed?

Finally, we should acknowledge the wider context in which the work is completed. Finding "good" outcomes in our projects increases the likelihood of securing good outcomes for ourselves. The current reward structure is designed in such a way that it encourages and motivates actions driven by the aforementioned biases, rather than the rigour or quality of the work conducted. If we know we're going to be positively rewarded for positive results, then we're going to suppress negative results, over-emphasise modest findings, and reduce complex messages into positive take-homes, and in doing so we're going to mislead others. Doing analysis of our own work is no encouragement to act transparently. The current system rewards game-playing and places a damaging emphasis on the results of the work rather than the quality of process adopted.

The same can be said about the avoidance of a negative outcome. As part of the modules I lead every semester, I get evaluated and rated by my students. This gives the students voice, gives me feedback, and gives my employer a seemingly objective insight into my teaching prowess. This information, alongside other metrics like student grades in my module, are used to evaluate my perform-ance. I know many staff are scared of having their teaching questioned or nega-tively evaluated, and in doing so go well above their duties to support, reassure, and in some cases, spoon-feed their students. Is this environment conducive to challenging students with difficult questions and complex content? Is this envir-onment conducive to encouraging students to explore and learn for themselves? Or is this an explicit structural motivation to inflate grades, treat students like customers, and attempt short-term initiatives to increase satisfaction?

The issue is often the application: rather than being used to reward high performers, these evaluations are used as a way of seeming to enforce quality standards and weed out poor performers. In this specific case, the problem is also the tools used for evaluation: student assessments of teaching are systemat-ically biased against women (Mengel et al., 2019) and individuals from minority cultures (Chisadza et al., 2019), and are influenced by as little as a chocolate cookie (Hessler et al., 2018). The broader issue (beyond the power of biscuits) is that we have counterproductive structures when they are based upon good outcomes rather than good processes. So, until we have a sustainable struc-ture capable of rewarding quality work, and to embrace failures, complexity and inconsistency, it seems of value to have external parties provide evalu-ative judgements, thereby hopefully navigating any internal pressure to drive misleading results.

The Argument in Favour

HR staff should be leading the analysis/interpretation of their own initiatives.

It important to recognise that evaluation work should not be done for free. If it is of value to the organisation, then it should be fully resourced. This seems likely to be problematic for a bias-free interpretation (should such a thing be possible). Imagine I am a consultant and have been asked to analyse and inter-pret the data evaluating an intervention. Am I likely to be critical and reduce the likelihood of securing further business from this organisation by getting a reputation for being the "grumpy" one, or am I instead motivated to find some positive messages which might present myself and the organisation is a better light? It seems likely that the introduction of financial motivations will benefit the process, but is there a way to manage this without financial incentive? This too looks to be problematic. Imagine two organisations swopping data to analyse for each other? GDPR alone would make this problematic and even if they were not direct competitors, one still might expect some contextual biases towards either criticality (due to perceived competition) or positivity (if there was some motivation to help continue/manage the relationship between organisations). As such, financially, it seems most justifiable that HR teams evaluate their own work.

There is also something to be said about changing the culture surrounding feedback and failure too. In an environment where individuals feel responsible for their work, but also sufficiently supported and empowered to make mistakes, have unsuccessful projects, and be openly critical to others, there are far fewer issues with evaluating internal work. I appreciate this might not sound like everyone's workplace, but there are implications for not encouraging criticality. Outsourcing critique and relying upon others to provide critical comments on work sets a dangerous precedent in communicating to others that they cannot be trusted, should act in-line with expectations, and are not responsible for outcomes.

Another factor to acknowledge is that if you say HR are not the best individuals to provide an impartial evaluation of the data, are they likely to be the best individuals to provide impartial evaluative designs or data collection? So, if you want a robust evaluation of work, do you have to excuse yourself for all of it, placing the weight of responsibility onto others for evaluating it? Where do you end this cycle? The team might have a good understanding of the content domain, but to involve experts in content creation, communication, IT, project management, etc. means the HR team would have very limited involvement, and it would no longer become their own work to take ownership of. This is an exaggerated viewpoint, against the current trend of generalisation rather than specialisation, but it does highlight the issue in thinking there is always someone "better".

The other factor to consider is the assumption that an external individual would not bring their own biases to the table. For example, I often get approached to review commercial and academic works. I can read a project featuring buzzwords like "mindfulness" and "emotional intelligence" and the transformation into criticality begins quickly. My temperature will rise, I suddenly become hyper-aware of the tightness of my watchstraps against my wrist, and shouts emanate from the next room because I am "sighing too loudly". I'm instantly approaching this work with caution, applying my beliefs about these terms as an indicator of the quality of the work. Colleagues who review the same work might be a little more forgiving, open to considering the quality of work on other bases, and that may go in favour or against the work. We all have our own idiosyncrasies, and they manifest in different ways. Research looking at the degree of agreement between markers, peer-reviewers and grant-reviewers all show us that this subjectivity should be an expected part of the process (e.g. Kravitz et al., 2010; Pier et al., 2018).

One is never going to remove human idiosyncrasies and biases away from data analysis and interpretation. One might hope that if you give the same data set with the same research question to a diverse range of analysts that there would be a strong consensus in conclusion, but that simply is not the case. When Silberzahn et al. (2018) did this with 29 different teams, giving them the same hypothesis and data to test it, there was a high level of variability in conclusions drawn. Recent critique suggested this was likely due to there being a vague research question (Auspurg & Brüderl, 2021) but a second attempt of this nature drew similar patterns – individual differences in decision-making at various stages of the analysis process influence the conclusions drawn (Breznau et al., 2021). I have since been involved in a similar project which analysed data looking at the relationship between computer use and depression in young adults. The results have yet to be fully published, but the conclusion is again the same. The number of different conclusions is the same as the number of analyst groups. The different approaches taken by the various teams will be interpreted through multiverse analysis, and I am confident the results will only reinforce the importance of these discussions surrounding subjectivity. So, really, one might suggest that involving others with perhaps less buy-in or insight into the nuance of the project might muddy the picture further and cause ambiguity, and introduce different types of biases into the interpretations.

Another factor to consider surrounds the norms of interaction and communication. Rejection, critique, and negative feedback hurts. In academia this is really common (grants, module evaluations, journal articles, engagement opportunities, etc.), but it still can hurt. So many of my colleagues can tell you word for word their last scathing student module evaluation comments. This (typically) honest feedback comes at a cost. It's very easy to become defensive, to double-down on justifications, and to take any critique personally. Accepting the well-meaning but critical advice or feedback of others can be unpalatable and can lead to any potential gains from the feedback to be dismissed. We should rarely avoid soliciting feedback due to concerns for its reception, however, the high level of variability in quality of delivery is a meaningful barrier to effect change. There is often little support for those giving or receiving feedback, and appropriate structures and standards in place to protect both parties. This reflects a deficit in our current understanding (and subsequent practice) for delivering critical feedback, an area that I expect to receive significant attention in the near future due to the evolving nature of collaboration and communication. So, we might be able to solicit critical input, but whether this becomes an influential driver of results is often questionable and unquestioned.

Finally, the most obvious reason why we can't hire lots of people to be critical of everything. The financial costs. Bringing in external individuals who are suitably qualified, or allocating time from existing internal teams, to complicate and potentially delay completion of core activities would likely be costly and thus avoided. It's unlikely that all core activities are sufficiently important that they would require such funded work, so a cost-benefit analysis of external contributions may be of benefit. Creating a market for paid critical work also inspires further discussions, however... There are career critics in many domains of life, and I am confident I would be capable of being a restaurant critic, but are there many who would make the jump to dedicate the majority of their time to challenging, pushing, and questioning others' research and practice? Many similar negotiations are taking place through initiatives to normalise funding for peer-reviewing of journal articles (@450Movement) and critical input into research (@RedTeamMarket). Norms around appreciation of the value of feedback need to change, and until they do, sourcing additional resources for project work is likely to be a major barrier.

Let HR do it. It's easier. It's cheaper. It's normal practice. It avoids ruffling feathers. That's a compelling case. No-one is advocating for an all-or-nothing perspective, however. There are several factors for choosing one response over another and we can all recognise some circumstances look to gain much from considering external critique. To make things even more difficult, let's explore some alternative approaches to critique.

Red Teams

My first suggestion comes in the form of "red teams": a concept first born out of security, technology, and defence industries. White-hat hackers are a term for ethical hackers, sometimes employed by the organisation they are hacking, who provide information on weaknesses and vulnerabilities to support developments to strengthen internal systems. Groups of white-hat hackers have been referred to as "red teams". A similar "red team" concept has been used in military contexts: groups who attempt to think like their enemy to provide critical suggestions for improving defence. Building upon these, the idea of red teams within research is now slowly spreading too (Lakens, 2020). The idea is that red teams will provide critical feedback, question assumptions, and provide an alternative external perspective.

My friend, we'll call him "Derek", has a Daily *ahem* Newspaper policy at work. They ask: how would it look if we had the rationale behind any given decision appear on the front-page of a newspaper? The red team go even further than attempting to minimise embarrassment – they ask critical questions to support creativity in decision-making and higher-quality outcomes. Going beyond a devil's advocate approach, which can often be passively arguing for the purpose of considering an opposite viewpoint, red teams are formed from individuals whose dedicated role is to improve the project by providing critical feedback, making the evidence behind decisions explicit, and challenging that evidence. They might be considered an in-built defence against the IKEA effect.

Whilst some researchers have advocated for involving external analysis teams for data analysis, the red team idea is beginning to spread across psychological research as a happy middle ground to such approaches, and an additional source of critical input in addition to peer review. All reputable journals currently require research to be reviewed by several peers who have experience in the specific field of interest or methodological approach. This is considered as a central defence of quality. Unfortunately, peer review is highly variable in quality and has not represented a strong defence against dissemination of low-quality research. Indeed it acts as no guarantee of quality and there is often a lot of disagreement between peer-reviewers when evaluating works (Kravitz et al., 2010). At its best, peer review can substantively change the quality of the methodology and thus the conclusions drawn, although this level of contribution is infrequent due to its timings – applied at the end of the research cycle, and we'll discuss this more in Chapter 7. I suspect progress in red team adoption has been relatively limited by the amount of expertise and time required to critically evaluate every detail of a study, and thus the barriers surrounding recognition of the contributions of such work. I have led a number of critical error detection projects that have not led to publications or outputs that will meet my personal or organisational targets. This has not discouraged me from this work, as it's all in the same pursuit: for good science. I now have a section of my CV dedicated to this type of work to try and acknowledge the method behind error detection and correction (see Chapter 4 for an example). This work can be slow and, going even further than being unrecognised/under-appreciated, it is often highly negatively received and defended against.

Business interest in red teams to date has been predominantly concentrated in military contexts, but I think red teams could be used in HR, potentially helpful in minimising bias during data evaluation and interpretation. In practice, a "red team" could be an individual (preferably external to the team) allocated for each project to encourage creativity, give advice or guidance, and provide the opportunity to revisit and re-evaluate decisions. Revisiting some of the discussions above, red teams could be involved in the design of the evaluation (rather than just in the interpretation of results collected), and because they are resource-intensive, could be prioritised where the decision-making is particularly impactful, e.g. in high-stake situations.

The idea of red teams could be adopted quite flexibly. For example, the team or individual could be internal or external. There isn't much evidence on evaluation of red team implementation at this moment to know which decisions can bring about most positive changes, but we can apply some findings from other fields. For example, being purposefully challenging, imaginative, and inquisitive is likely to be better fitted to some personality types than others, but it seems unwise for one individual to consistently adopt this role – they may be seen as obstructive, uncooperative, and turn the role into a symbolic criticism rather than driving a more meaningful creative and developmental process. I hope to see some metascience research evaluating use of these teams soon.

This suggestion, like the other systems in place, e.g. peer review, are really only as good as the investment given to them. Peer-reviews conducted over a series of hours, with carefully constructed constructive feedback, are great; a token gesture of criticality conducted by a friend over a quick glance of the work is less so. For red teams to be effective in evaluating HR projects, they should be given adequate time, resources and recognition, with the power to be able to support major changes. Without this, the red team will likely lead to nothing more than a token gesture providing the illusion of having received critical feedback, thereby providing further misplaced confidence in the conclusions drawn.

Collaborative Frameworks

An alternative approach to DIY analysis might be through formalising the opportunities available to collaborate. For example, one could imagine a database where organisations put calls for evaluation design/data analysis/interpretation work with a brief description of what is required, commitment, timeframes, etc. and academics or practitioners from different organisations can volunteer in exchange for an agreed output. The equivalent of Cilla Black in a spreadsheet. The work could be described in broad terms under a pseudonym, the non-disclosure/data-sharing agreement signed, and then a formal negotiation of work could follow. The outcomes could include external acknowledgement of the work for impact case studies, agreement to facilitate future data collection within their organisation, or cash. Following project completion, feedback could be given by each party and then publicly released on the system to help inform future collaborations of the suitability or problematic practices to be expected.

I am confident the legalities of such work would need a little more consideration, but this sort of framework could be an important gateway to opportunities for individuals and organisations alike. A structured collaboration network could be a valuable opportunity for early career researchers and practitioners to build relationships with organisations, and to expand their portfolio of skills. Organisations could get a chance to diversify their bank of consultants and to secure external input into important projects. It may also support changes against use of old-boy networks, diversify talent identification, and allow individuals to adopt roles where their experience can have a direct impact on real-world business practices.

There is scope for such ideas to be exploitative – either individuals engaging in work they are insufficiently experienced or qualified to complete, or organisations capitalising on individuals prepared to complete work for free. Some of this could be mitigated through the post-project feedback, and by setting requirements and tests, e.g. qualification checks or similar, however, this is clearly not foolproof.

Some additional considerations to such a framework could be whether organisations could buy into the system, exchanging time of some employees in some areas of their organisations to support other groups in other organisations: a scheme where reciprocated commitment supports collaborative gain. Similar to law fields, we might also expect some opportunities for organisations with few resources, or those engaging in socially beneficial aims, to receive pro bono support and expertise. A good example of this in current practice, although of a more geographically limited (that is, local) nature, is how universities become highly engaged in their local communities by providing investment into their industries. This sort of collaborative agreement is therefore not a new concept.

The "open" stance and structured nature of the idea presents a real opportunity to be innovative and inclusive, however, collaborations between academia and industry are already common and represent nothing new. Whilst I have thus far situated these two groups separately, this is a false divide: most of the brilliant academics I work with also have commercial work or external engagement projects. I am employed as an academic, but I have benefited much, personally and professionally, from my applied and commercial research (Evans & Steptoe-Warren, 2019). Academics are often heavily motivated by making a difference in the world, and the opportunity to engage with industry decision-making is a pathway to do this (Lam, 2011). Furthermore, commercial engagement is desirable to many universities who now capture commercial activity and use this as a basis for progression and recruitment decisions (Cohen et al., 2020). As such, greater communication and interaction between academia and industry can often lead to exciting opportunities for mutually beneficial outcomes (D'Este & Perkmann, 2011). We'll talk more about collaboration in Chapter 8.

Conclusion

So where does this all leave us? We know that analysing and interpreting our own data is problematic, but so is involving others, or asking others to do it. So, what do we do? My recommendation is that of a negotiation across these solutions. My central consideration would be the importance of outcome and subsequent decision-making. If the outcome strongly drives decisions, the decision effects many others, and it could have large long-term considerations for the organisation, then bringing in others, either to provide critical support or to complete the work, would be a clever strategy. If the outcomes are less central, then this is likely to tip the cost-benefit balance. Similarly, where the project targets are set in advance and require relatively objective outcomes (e.g. number of days to process an action) then the involvement of others is probably more costly than it is beneficial. Contrary to that, where expected outcomes might be diverse and unexpected, not easily captured through standard metrics, or ambiguous or flexible in interpretation, external involvement could provide greater value. Having originally highlighted the problematic nature of subjective interpretations, my solution to DIY analysis is to make another subjective decision, this time based upon a number of complex and inter-related factors as to whether and how you require external involvement. Simple?

References

Auspurg, K., & Brüderl, J. (2021). Has the credibility of the social sciences been credibly destroyed? Reanalyzing the "Many Analysts, One Data Set" project. *Socius*, *7*, 23780231211024421.

Bates, R. (2004). A critical analysis of evaluation practice: the Kirkpatrick model and the principle of beneficence. *Evaluation and Program Planning*, *27*(3), 341–347.

Bik, E. M., Casadevall, A., & Fang, F. C. (2016). The prevalence of inappropriate image duplication in biomedical research publications. *MBio*, *7*(3), e00809–16.

Billig, M. (2005). *Laughter and ridicule: Towards a social critique of humour*. Great Britain: Sage.

Breznau, N., Rinke, E., Wuttke, A., Adem, M., Adriaans, J., Alvarez-Benjumea, A., … Nguyen, H. H. V. (2021). *Observing Many Researchers Using the Same Data and Hypothesis Reveals a Hidden Universe of Data Analysis*. Accessible: https://doi.org/10.31222/osf.io/cd5j9

Cassidy, S. A., Dimova, R., Giguère, B., Spence, J. R., & Stanley, D. J. (2019). Failing grade: 89% of introduction-to-psychology textbooks that define or explain statistical significance do so incorrectly. *Advances in Methods and Practices in Psychological Science*, *2*(3), 233–239.

Chisadza, C., Nicholls, N., & Yitbarek, E. (2019). Race and gender biases in student evaluations of teachers. *Economics Letters*, *179*, 66–71.

Cohen, W. M., Sauermann, H., & Stephan, P. (2020). Not in the job description: The commercial activities of academic scientists and engineers. *Management Science*, *66*(9), 4108–4117.

Cuijpers, P., & Cristea, I. A. (2016). How to prove that your therapy is effective, even when it is not: a guideline. *Epidemiology and Psychiatric Sciences*, *25*(5), 428–435.

D'Este, P., & Perkmann, M. (2011). Why do academics engage with industry? The entrepreneurial university and individual motivations. *The Journal of Technology Transfer*, *36*(3), 316–339.

Evans, T. R., Johannes, N., Winska, J., Glinksa-Newes, A., van Stekelenburg, A., Nilsonne, G., ... & Masson, I. (2020). Exploring the consistency and value of humour style profiles. *Comprehensive Results in Social Psychology*, *4*(1), 1–24.

Evans, T. R., & Steptoe-Warren, G. (2018). Humor style clusters: Exploring managerial humor. *International Journal of Business Communication*, *55*(4), 443–454.

Evans, T. R., & Steptoe-Warren, G. (Eds.). (2019). *Applying Occupational Psychology to the Fire Service: Emotion, Risk and Decision-Making*. Palgrave Macmillan.

Gelman, A., & Loken, E. (2014). The statistical crisis in science: data-dependent analysis – a "garden of forking paths" – explains why many statistically significant comparisons don't hold up. *American Scientist*, *102*(6), 460–466.

Hessler, M., Pöpping, D. M., Hollstein, H., Ohlenburg, H., Arnemann, P. H., Massoth, C., ... & Wenk, M. (2018). Availability of cookies during an academic course session affects evaluation of teaching. *Medical Education*, *52*(10), 1064–1072.

Hodson, G., Rush, J., & MacInnis, C. C. (2010). A joke is just a joke (except when it isn't): Cavalier humor beliefs facilitate the expression of group dominance motives. *Journal of Personality and Social Psychology*, *99*(4), 660–682.

Kirkpatrick, D. L. (1959). Techniques for evaluating training programs. *Journal of ASTD*, *11*, 1–13.

Kravitz, R. L., Franks, P., Feldman, M. D., Gerrity, M., Byrne, C., & Tierney, W. M. (2010). Editorial peer reviewers' recommendations at a general medical journal: are they reliable and do editors care? *PLoS One*, *5*(4), e10072.

Lakens, D. (2020). Pandemic researchers-recruit your own best critics. *Nature*, *581*(7807), 121.

Lam, A. (2011). What motivates academic scientists to engage in research commercialization: 'Gold', 'ribbon' or 'puzzle'? *Research Policy*, *40*(10), 1354–1368.

Martin, R. A., Puhlik-Doris, P., Larsen, G., Gray, J., & Weir, K. (2003). Individual differences in uses of humor and their relation to psychological well-being: Development of the Humor Styles Questionnaire. *Journal of Research in Personality*, *37*(1), 48–75.

Mengel, F., Sauermann, J., & Zölitz, U. (2019). Gender bias in teaching evaluations. *Journal of the European Economic Association*, *17*(2), 535–566.

Pier, E. L., Brauer, M., Filut, A., Kaatz, A., Raclaw, J., Nathan, M. J., ... & Carnes, M. (2018). Low agreement among reviewers evaluating the same NIH grant applications. *Proceedings of the National Academy of Sciences*, *115*(12), 2952–2957.

Rohrer, J. M., Tierney, W., Uhlmann, E. L., DeBruine, L. M., Heyman, T., Jones, B., ... & Yarkoni, T. (2021). Putting the Self in Self-correction: Findings from the Loss-of-Confidence Project. *Perspectives on Psychological Science*, *16*(6), 1255–1269. https://doi.org/10.1177/1745691620964106.

Romero, E. J., & Cruthirds, K. W. (2006). The use of humor in the workplace. *Academy of Management Perspectives*, *20*(2), 58–69.

Silberzahn, R., Uhlmann, E. L., Martin, D. P., Anselmi, P., Aust, F., Awtrey, E., ... & Carlsson, R. (2018). Many analysts, one data set: Making transparent how variations in analytic choices affect results. *Advances in Methods and Practices in Psychological Science, 1*(3), 337–356.

Simonsohn, U., Simmons, J. P., & Nelson, L. D. (2015). Specification Curve: Descriptive and Inferential Statistics on All Reasonable Specifications. Accessible: https://ssrn.com/abstract=2694998 or http://dx.doi.org/10.2139/ssrn.2694998

Steegen, S., Tuerlinckx, F., Gelman, A., & Vanpaemel, W. (2016). Increasing transparency through a multiverse analysis. *Perspectives on Psychological Science, 11*(5), 702–712.

Tartari, V., & Breschi, S. (2012). Set them free: scientists' evaluations of the benefits and costs of university–industry research collaboration. *Industrial and Corporate Change, 21*(5), 1117–1147.

Selection and Assessment of Emotional Intelligence **3**

I have been researching emotional intelligence (EI) for the last seven years. In truth, I stumbled upon the field as I was developing project ideas for my PhD, inspired by my supervisor's interest in applying EI within the Fire Service. I was struck by the number of bold claims made for its value, with a number of consultancies, test publishers, and business-support groups keen to endorse EI for a whole range of reasons. It was originally my intention to evaluate the impact of EI interventions within higher education. I had one cohort of 350 psychology undergraduate students answering a whole range of EI and outcome questionnaires before and after several weeks of EI interventions, and another cohort with an "active-control" employability intervention. Hundreds of students and teaching hours, thousands of questions answered across multiple time points, and my future academic career at stake. No pressure. But this study didn't even feature in my final PhD. I didn't even write it up. I was distracted.

Carl Sagan famously stated: "extraordinary claims require extraordinary evidence". I was initially concerned that EI might not be able to achieve all the things it claims to do. After all, the claims were both bold and diverse. This was what I originally focussed my PhD upon – exploring whether the evidence might not be strong for all these claims, and I focussed upon student outcomes as an accessible and high-impact priority. But the more I went digging, the more something more fundamental didn't feel right. My spidey-senses were tingling. To create a robust and replicable EI intervention, I needed to define EI, and this became a problem, which then became an obsession – taking over as my primary PhD focus. This wider idea of being critically aware of everything has since defined my research profile and motivated this book – asking lots of uncomfortable questions about the state of understanding and quality of research being conducted.

DOI: 10.4324/9781003035794-3

So within the field of HR, there have been a number of strong claims about the value of EI for improving various organisational outcomes like performance and job satisfaction (Zeidner et al., 2004). Recommendations to integrate EI within many organisational practices have therefore followed, with a number of commercial groups with proprietary measures of EI ready to help (for a fee!). Based upon misleading and unsubstantiated claims that "use of EI for recruitment decisions leads to 90-percentile success rates" (Watkin, 2000) and that EI accounts for over 85% of outstanding performance in top leaders (Goleman 1996), using EI for selection has been one of the most recommended applications (Cadman & Brewer, 2001).

HR has not been tentative in embracing the concept of EI. In a sample of 2,662 hiring managers in the US (CareerBuilder, 2011):

- 71% valued EI more than cognitive ability (often called IQ).
- 58% would not hire someone who has high IQ but low EI.
- 75% would be more likely to promote a worker with greater EI over one with higher IQ.

Before we get carried away and apply EI, we should satisfy a few assumptions. So, to apply EI for selection purposes, we need to know: a) what EI is, b) how EI is measured, c) whether EI can be measured robustly and without bias, d) the extent to which EI predicts desirable outcomes, and e) the extent to which EI predicts desirable outcomes beyond the practices currently adopted. Without these, we run the risk of making things worse, not better. Without these, we cannot be confident in what we are doing. Without these, we should not be using EI. So, let's have a look at the evidence – fingers crossed everyone!

Assumption 1: We Know What EI Is

Bear with me, let's try a thought experiment. This isn't of my own design but it's incredibly powerful for starting a conversation. First thing I want you to do is to write down your answer to the following question:

What is a sandwich?_____

Most tend to say it's two pieces of bread, with some other food-stuffs in the middle, often savoury. Wikipedia calls it "a food typically consisting of vegetables, sliced cheese or meat, placed on or between slices of bread, or more generally any dish wherein bread serves as a container or wrapper for another food type".

So, let's explore this. I'm going to list several foods – you need to state whether each one is a sandwich, according to your definition…

- Filled baguette, panini, or bagel. It's not two pieces of bread but one big piece cut down the middle.
- A hotdog. Is this any different to a baguette really?
- Filled croissant. One piece but it's a pastry not a bread.
- A burger. Is this so different to a filled bagel?
- Keto sandwich/burger. The bread is replaced by vegetables/salad.
- Open top sandwich. Only one slice of bread with food on top.
- A piece of toast. If an open top sandwich is a sandwich, is that any different?
- A pizza. This is a piece of bread with food on top.
- A calzone. Like a pizza but fully enclothed in dough – is this more of a sandwich than a pizza?
- A taco. It's a piece of dough with some food in the middle.
- Stuffed ravioli. They are two pieces of dough with goodness in the middle.

Far from easy. Indeed, there have been many legal disputes on the basis of the definition of sandwich. In 2006, there was a case which was decided upon through this very issue. A shopping mall had a contract with a sandwich shop which limited the mall owner to no further leases where sandwiches contributed to more than 10% of sales. The mall subsequently leased space to Qdoba, a Mexican restaurant selling burritos, tacos, and quesadillas. The sandwich shop objected and sued, stating such items were sandwiches. The case was eventually denied by adopting a common language definition of sandwich and began many interesting discussions on whether ambiguous terms in contracts should be held to usual interpretation or specific definition (e.g. Florestall, 2008). Subsequently, many bodies have had to define sandwiches for various, mostly legal, reasons. For example, New York State taxes sandwiches with a list of inclusive terms including bagels, burritos, croissants, gyros, burgers, hotdogs, paninis, wraps, and pittas (New York State, 2019). This all seems like a silly point to make, but it's really important. The words we use matter. Yet, for an item that we can see, touch, smell, and taste, we can't come up with a consistent use of the term. How does this fare for considering terms referring to psychological constructs – hypothetical things that don't "exist" anywhere but are labels of behaviours and psychological processes that are useful for improving understanding of ourselves.

Unsurprisingly, defining a psychological construct like EI has been problematic. Negotiating what EI is, and what it is not, remains an intense ongoing discussion in the academic literature. The scope of the construct is commonly referred to as the content domain of the construct. What are its central components and how can it be interpreted from a theoretical perspective? Only then can we begin to map out how it relates to other constructs – its nomological network.

EI was originally defined as the cognitive abilities required to "monitor one's own and others' feelings and emotions, to discriminate among them and to use this information to guide one's thinking and actions" (Salovey & Mayer, 1990, p. 189). This was subsequently expanded by Goleman to include a variety of constructs including motivation, empathy, social skills, happiness, and achievement-orientation, amongst others (Bar-On 1997; Goleman 1996). Goleman's book *Emotional Intelligence: Why It Can Matter More than IQ* follows me around to this day – I even found it in a villa in Limoux when on holiday with family! Even my mum had a copy (until *I* took it away). Such was the popularity of this work, and the diversity in definitions provided, that various groups,

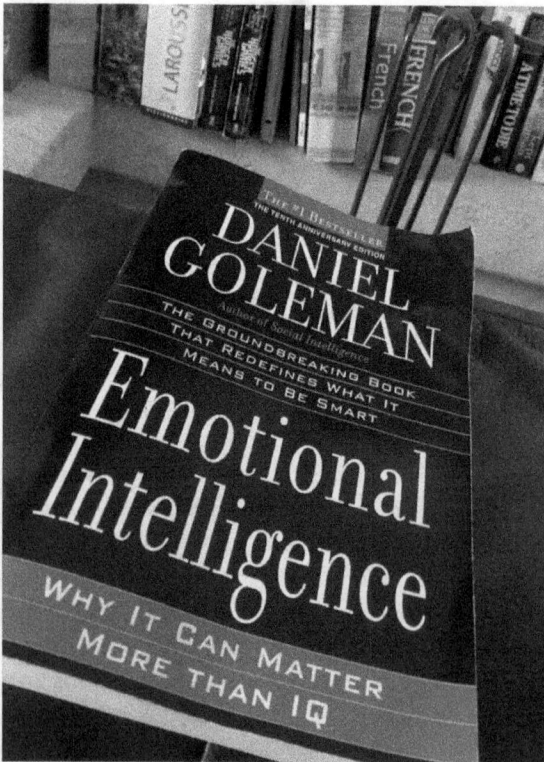

Figure 3.1 Photographic evidence that you can't even escape the universal appeal of *Emotional Intelligence* by going on holiday

including academics, now consider EI to represent a wide range of social and emotional qualities, with no clear consensuses emerging (Evans, 2020).

Within the academic literature, there is a broad sense that current models differentiate between EI as a cognitive ability (also termed Ability EI), a collection of traits (also termed Trait EI), and emotion regulation (goal-orientated behaviours and cognitions to change emotions of self or others) (Hughes & Evans, 2018). Let me talk you through them a little more. Ability EI is commonly conceived as the result of three broad cognitive abilities. First is the ability to recognise specific emotions. Here, it commonly taps into an old body of literature looking at how emotions can be universal. For example, we're on holiday and we don't know the language, but we can communicate our emotional states through our facial movements, and they will probably be easily recognised. Do this with me now. Raise the inner parts of your eyebrows and lower the outer parts of your eyebrows. Turn the corner of your lips downward. Now look in the mirror. You look ridiculous. You also look sad. Most individuals can recognise this pretty easily. The second ability is emotion understanding and represents an individual's understanding of how emotions can develop. For example, we have a friend who has bought a new Christmas jumper – we might anticipate them to feel … excited? Happy? The third ability is emotion management and represents understanding of how you can change the emotions you (or another) experience. Essentially, can you choose appropriate and effective emotion regulation strategies based upon an understanding of their likely consequences in that specific context. For example, your friend just got told that wearing Christmas jumpers in April is inappropriate at work and is sad – how could you help them? Here you might choose to invite them to a mid-April Christmas celebration, encourage them to comply with the organisation's request, or to "fight the power" by returning the following day wearing novelty antlers. There are significant differences in the emotional consequences of these actions, so choices represent your intelligence in appreciating which is best for what you want to feel and achieve in that situation.

Trait EI is a broad term used to describe a wide number of affect-related traits. Personality traits manifest on a continuum – we can be extremely gregarious and socially orientated, or we can be shy and prefer the company of ourselves. This particular trait is called extraversion, and we all sit somewhere on this continuum. Trait EI is used as a label to represent a wide variety of traits with a social or emotional focus upon which we all vary. There is no set list of traits included within Trait EI models, this tends to vary on the specific model or questionnaire adopted, but can include traits such as happiness, empathy, emotion expression, self-esteem, and self-awareness. For example, we can all think of a colleague or friend who lacks a little tact in social situations and whose behaviour we sometimes have funny ways of justifying to ourselves or others as acceptable and just part of their idiosyncrasies. The diversity of psychological traits included within the models of Trait EI is high, and means many of the conclusions drawn from the research conducted in this field are often measure-specific (i.e. results depend upon what constellation of traits you have included).

There's been a lot of discussion about what the third category of EI models represents. It first started off as "competency EI" and/or "mixed EI". I'm sorry, but if you just throw all sorts of different psychological ideas into a pot – motivations, traits, abilities, self-perceptions, and others, and give it a label then you can't claim to be capturing a well-defined or robust construct. Instead, when doing my PhD, I often found that content of EI models which couldn't be prescribed to either ability or trait models were often actually very behavioural in focus (Hughes & Evans, 2018). As such, I consider Emotion Regulation as the third approach to EI. Here, we consider the identification, selection, and implementation of strategies, whether observable behaviours or specific cognitive techniques, used to change the emotions of ourselves or others towards our goals. This can include substance use and humour to support a frustrated colleague, or venting and rumination to help us cope, amongst many others. The range of behavioural and cognitive strategies included is quite diverse, and whilst there are a number of attempts to introduce a hierarchy or structure, e.g. adaptive vs maladaptive strategies (Southward et al., 2019), their impact and success is based upon a range of factors including the quality of implementation and context of use. Similar to Trait EI, I see emotion regulation used as a broad label to capture a wide range of constructs, where a more specific strategy-specific approach is needed.

It's worth noting that whilst I propose the ER model to represent a meaningful extension to the trait–ability divide often propagated, this three-strand approach hasn't yet been consistently adopted in the EI literature and many misconceptions, mistakes, and mis-judged ideas continue to be disseminated. One of my favourite phrases in the academic literature is "jingle-jangle". When I drop the phrase into conversations with friends and family, they ask me to stop talking about Christmas songs, knowing full-well that asking me for more information will unleash a rant about the fragility of psychological knowledge. To keep it brief, it can refer to using the same label to represent different constructs (jingle fallacy) and different labels to represent the same constructs (jangle fallacy). In particular, there has been difficulty integrating ability-based definitions into models of cognitive ability (Evans et al. 2020) and having the term "Trait EI" represent a rebranding of various existing personality traits (Pérez-González & Sanchez-Ruiz 2014). Such is the confusion, that EI seems to be used interchangeably for a wide range of constructs united by nothing more than an emotional or social orientation.

Using a term (EI) that can refer to any number of psychological constructs, from motivation to happiness, from emotion recognition to trait assertiveness, is clearly likely to lead to confusion. If we were to compile a list of all the different constructs perceived to be EI, it would not be difficult to claim relationships between EI and any given outcome – I could just cherry-pick which of the EI constructs I would like. The constructs being united under the EI label are substantively different. Whilst it is generally quite easy to group them into cognitive ability, trait, and emotion regulation categories, even then there are nuances within these. For example, let's say you measure EI as defined by three scales on assertiveness, happiness, and empathy. Current conventions would see us add up the scores on each of these to create a total EI score to then use to predict outcomes. What would that score really represent? Your approach to EI might have links to outcomes, but it makes it really difficult to work out what is being referred to, and what might be driving any effects observed. Let's say it could predict job performance – do we know which of the three components are important? Progress has undoubtedly been made in refining various perspectives from which EI can be interpreted, but, in reality, it continues to have a massive definitional problem. For example, when conducting a meta-analysis on the

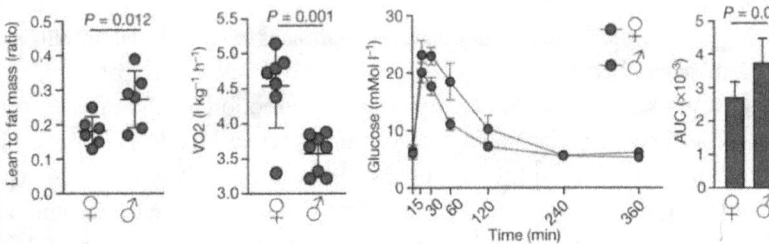

Figure 3.2 In mice? A retweet from @justsaysinmice discussing the differences between the male and female immune system. Copyright of @jamesheathers

impact of EI teaching upon medical students, Cherry et al. (2012) widened the definition of EI to include empathy, mindfulness, empathetic communication style, compassion, and sensitivity, leading to ambiguous conclusions as to what could be attributable to what.

There is a Twitter account (@JustSaysInMice) which responds to articles making claims about biomedical research conducted on mice but a) doesn't clarify that it was based upon mice, or b) infers the conclusions can apply to humans, with the words "IN MICE". See Figure 3.2 for an example. I am currently exhausting any self-restraint I have left not to create a similar account called @ButWhatIsEI to highlight the number and strength of claims published about EI without any real critical insight into what the term is actually referring to.

Assumption 2: We Know How to Measure EI

If EI is to be defined as a trait, then we need a self-rated typical-performance test. For example, I can ask you, to what extent you agree with the following statement: "I normally feel confident in tackling stressful situations". You might respond on a Likert scale ranging from 1 (Strongly Agree) to 7 (Strongly Disagree). This is a very common format for personality measurement and is widely used for selection purposes, particularly with respect to conscientiousness, as this is a strong predictor of performance (Barrick & Mount, 1991), although the value might be somewhat over-exaggerated (Kepes & McDaniel, 2015).

Alternatively, if you consider EI to represent cognitive abilities, you require a maximum-performance paradigm where there is a right and wrong answer. For example, "Tom has been talking about emotional intelligence for 30 minutes and I really need to pee. What emotion am I likely to be experiencing?" Here you might respond to various categories: Anger, Frustration, Surprise, or Shame. Again, this sort of testing is common for assessment purposes and is normally used in context of cognitive ability testing and numerical/verbal reasoning.

If we adopt the emotion regulation approach to emotional intelligence, we might assess behaviour in a specific scenario or context – role-playing or through a work preview task, perhaps. Typically, emotion regulation is captured using a Likert scale similar to Trait EI, capturing general tendencies for specific approaches, or situational judgement test. For example, "You have just had a tense meeting where you needed to negotiate various sensitive topics, and have 20 minutes of the working day left. What would you do with your time?" Here, responses might represent different emotion regulation strategies: catch up with a colleague informally (social support searching), carry on with your to-do list for the day (persistence), leave work early and reflect upon the experience with a friend (venting/reflection), or create a list of things that need to be done (planning). This sort of measurement is less common during selection processes, which is unfortunate. The thing with behaviour is that it directly drives outcomes – personality, intelligence, and many other psychological constructs are more "distal" or "upstream" predictors – they may be considered the early determinants of outcomes, but in principle they drive outcomes through behaviours (Hughes & Evans, 2018). As such, capturing behaviours (cognitive or physical) really seems like an under-utilised opportunity to facilitate selection. The same is true for development – personality is malleable but tends to be quite predictable. Personality can change over time, particularly through meaningful life events, but the whole value in studying personality is that it remains relatively consistent across time and situation. Training based upon personality is there-fore limited, whereby training people to use different behaviours tends to report more consistent impacts. As such, emotion regulation approaches hold untapped potential to facilitate selection activities and decision-making.

EI measures adopt pre-existing and commonly adopted measurement approaches within selection. As such, these different types of measurement are not in-of-themselves problematic. Unfortunately, there often seems to be a dis-connect in how they are applied which makes them problematic. In principle, there should be a relatively simple process during the selection and recruitment of a candidate:

Conduct a job analysis -> compile selection criteria -> identify psycho-logical constructs of benefit -> measure these specific constructs

For example, I am recruiting a sales assistant. I should do a job analysis, and identify that, amongst other things, being able to interact with customers in a positive and engaging way would contribute to up-selling and thus individual, team, and organisational success. I might suggest that an effective individual would be positive and able to build relationships easily. I might therefore con-sider trait happiness an important psychological construct to capture and adopt a trait happiness assessment (in addition to measures of other central competen-cies such as numerical reasoning). Sounds simple, but there are so many ways in which this process can go awry. For example, if the role has a social component, it would be easy to just state you require high EI – this causes problems because it doesn't clarify exactly what EI qualities would be necessary, and thus what is being measured might not be the central criteria by which you wish to differen-tiate candidates. Trait happiness is useful here, would self-esteem be similarly effective for this purpose?

Many of the most popular assessments of EI are controlled by test publishers who tend to encourage looking at "total" scores, rather than the specific facets of interest, and have very little interest in the theoretical grounding of the construct. For example, by making their own "model" of EI to provide a unique selling point to differentiate from competitors, they include any number of different constructs, sometimes measured in ways which are counter to their underlying theory. For example, a popular approach is to capture self-rated perceptions of abilities. Unfortunately, these are not effectively capturing either ability or self-perceptions. Furthermore, there is also the possibility that you might capture the same thing in different ways, e.g. if you are interested in traits that are captured by both Trait EI and personality assessments, e.g. extraversion – the overlap is larger than one might expect and due to the jangle fallacy and secrecy of proprietary measurement, it is often difficult to tell. This might make you put greater (false) confidence in a decision because you perceive two separate criteria to be supporting the same decision, when the reason behind the similarity is because of the underlying similarity in psychological characteristics being measured.

Measurement of EI is possible, but will only be as good as the definition. If I know exactly what it is – if I can appreciate what differentiates individuals who are high and low – I can create an assessment of it that directly and explicitly represents that exact definition. I can then use these measures in specific contexts where they are needed. Unfortunately, EI is not well defined, and often represents a diverse collection of constructs which themselves are often ill-defined. As such, the measurement of EI is as problematic as the definition of EI, and whilst possible, is not necessarily advised, particularly for applied purposes due to the use of "total" scores.

Assumption 3: We Can Measure EI in a Robust and Bias-Free Way

So, EI measurement is possible, but is it robust and legally defensible? Let's just assume for a minute that we're happy with the definition of EI (we're not). We first should have a look at the quality of the data the measures produce. Generally, the quality of evidence supporting use of measures is basic (O'Connor et al., 2019). A major issue in this field is that many of the most common measures adopted are proprietary (e.g. the Trait Emotional Intelligence Questionnaire (TEIQue) and Mayer-Salovey-Caruso Emotional Intelligence Test (MSCEIT)). They are behind paywalls and under the control of commercial enterprises. As such, gauging the extent to which they are reliable (they capture consistent responding) and valid (they capture what they claim to capture) is difficult. We ideally want to produce a body of quality evidence to encourage use of a certain measure, and we would want this to come from a diverse range of independent groups of researchers. Unfortunately, this rarely happens and there are a number of barriers preventing it: the onus is placed upon researchers to a) pay for the measures (and often the training to use them), b) have the will and initiative to run validation studies, and c) gain gatekeeper approval from the test publishers to do so. The latter is a particular problem given that agreement to use different tests from different publishers within the same study to compare efficacy, and for the purpose of providing critical insight into their value, are unlikely to be particularly positively received or encouraged.

On the contrary, test publishers are motivated by demonstrating strong relationships to outcomes, not robust theory development and testing of the nomological net to ensure the constructs captured are distinct and robust. As such, the published reviews of evidence for their value are likely to be distorted. Indeed, reviews of the value of such measures are well-represented by tests of predictive validity (that is, how well they can predict outcomes). There are plenty of studies correlating different models of EI with various outcomes (and this is particularly lucrative given the number of constructs included within these models). For example, there are several studies looking at the relationship between EI and orgasm frequency (Burri et al., 2009; Kamranpour et al. 2019; Silva et al. 2016). Not even kidding – I told you EI was a sexy topic!

Furthermore, there are plenty of analyses that do not require any further data collection except the responses to the items themselves (e.g. testing whether responses to each item are similar to responses on others: internal reliability). What's often missing here is the trickier data to collect which provides a more accurate assessment of their value. For example, there is a deficit of studies looking at how these measures relate to measures of similar and different constructs (convergent/divergent validity) to work out the exact novelty of content in EI models when compared to existing well-studied models, e.g. in personality. The same could be said for test-retest reliability, where we consider the consistency of responses across time (thereby providing information as to whether measurement is consistent and whether the qualities captured represent a trait or a state, etc.). Furthermore, there are no examples where test publishers have worked with "competitors" to work out what aspect of their specific model provides the greatest incremental value. To avoid those types of discussions is to reduce a key central part of scientific development, and in an area where it is so much needed.

So, the theory issue inherent to current EI research continues to hamper our use of EI in selection practices. This is true not just for validation of measures to make them suitable for this purpose, but also in communication about them. Building upon our issues with the underlying theory of the various strains of EI, it is difficult to know what any of the evidence is referring to. This is especially true of any time-strapped practitioner, or indeed anyone who hasn't spent a substantive amount of time engaging with the various ongoing critical debates. As such, any attempt to collate findings is likely to conflate different traits, abilities, and behaviours, meaning that conclusions are likely imprecise and biased towards claiming value. The jingle-jangle in use of terms, and more broadly the substantive and extreme claims made about EI, make building coherent bodies of evidence to inform practice extremely difficult.

Evidence evaluating each measure continues to grow with each study conducted, however, we should acknowledge that responses to measures for the purposes of research and selection may differ. In one, individuals volunteer to provide information towards improving societies' understanding of psychological life as humans. In the other, individuals are actively motivated to demonstrate the vividness of colours in their plumage and compete against others to provide themselves in the best possible light. Under these different conditions, if I was asked "I normally feel confident in tackling stressful situations" should I expect to respond the same?

There is a very small but growing body of evidence looking at the extent to which measures of EI, particularly those using self-report paradigms, are vulnerable to these types of bias (Day and Carroll 2008; Mesmer-Magnus et al. 2006). We should be particularly weary because the questions are often about emotion and are heavily loaded towards positivity. To paraphrase a few items from a popular Trait EI test: "I am well-respected for my calmness…", "I am confident in my strengths…". Would these items be fit for use in selection? This issue is not contained to the trait approach to EI. Some of the most dramatic findings found in the emotion regulation literature come from strategies that would be inappropriate to ask in this context – "I use alcohol to cope with daily stressors…", "I pray when I experience difficulty…". Individuals already tend to under-report alcohol consumption and drug use (e.g. Stockwell et al., 2016) so asking about this, particularly in contexts where there are various reasons to answer positively, is unlikely to be fruitful. As there will be strong motivation incited to effect response patterns, we should expect socially desirable responding to contribute to some level of measurement error when using self-report EI measures for this purpose.

Given the interest in use of EI for recruitment, there have been a few studies which have provided evidence on this specific use. Positively, Iliescu et al. (2012) used data collected from 178 Romanian graduates to claim that EI, in this case defined by the MSCEIT, which adopts the ability-approach, is considered a fair basis for selection. Participants rated the "fairness" of the eight different tasks included in this measure on a 5-point Likert scale, with mean results ranging from 2.4 to 3.5. This has been used to support claims of holding "face validity" for use in selection – the weakest type of evidence, but nevertheless some evidence to suggest that it is subjectively evaluated by test-takers as relevant in this context. Of note, individuals with greater EI abilities in this study were also more likely to suggest the use of MSCEIT as fair in selection (r = .38). You can draw your own conclusions about that!

Against this work, there are several papers that encourage caution in the application of EI-based selection, particularly with current EI measures. For example, there seems to be some small but significant differences in the perceptions surrounding, and successful completion of, ability-based EI test scores between individuals who identify as Black and White (Whitman et al., 2014). Furthermore, it appears that individuals can purposely alter their per-formance/scores on both the (ability-based) MSCEIT and ("Mixed EI") EQ-I measures to fit a job description (Nicholls et al., 2012), with this effect further replicated with other self-report measures (Christiansen et al., 2010). There is also preliminary evidence using the (trait/self-reported ability) WLEIS assessment to suggest that norms developed during research will not be suitable for recruitment/selection purposes (Lievens et al., 2011). I think at this stage we probably don't know enough about any possible adverse impacts and how they differ across theories and models of EI to inform use for this purpose.

Assumption 4: We Know EI Can Predict Desirable Outcomes

The most common source of justification for use of EI for selection is that EI is a predictor of job performance. Therefore, if you select someone with the highest EI you are maximising the probability that this individual will be brilliant in their job. A meta-analysis by O'Boyle et al. (2011) provided pretty encouraging support for this proposition, claiming that all theoretical models of EI could predict "equally well". This work is commonly cited as a justification for implementing EI in organisations, and funnily-enough, if you try to look at the paper on Google Scholar, you get redirected to a copy hosted by an EI-based training company website. Slick.

As noted earlier, there are studies looking at the relationships between all sorts of outcomes and EI models, with plenty in the work context. For example, job satisfaction, organisational commitment, turnover intentions, organisational citizenship behaviours, counterproductive work behaviours… (Miao et al., 2017a; 2017b). I could go on all day listing outcomes relevant to organisations. All are important variables to successful business. All "statistically significant" relationships. I can apply EI within organisations, just you watch me.

Before we do that, let's just try one pressure test of the idea that it would be useful. Let's control for some of the other things we think might overlap with our EI measurement. If we're saying EI is more important than cognitive ability, or indeed some aspects may be part of cognitive ability (e.g. Evans et al., 2020), then it should still predict performance over and above it. This is what is known as incremental predictive validity. Revisiting the relationship to job performance, Joseph et al., (2015) looked at "mixed EI" but controlled for Ability EI, self-efficacy, and self-rated performance, personality, and general mental ability. The results: the relationship is practically zero. The conclusion: "mixed" EI is unlikely to be much more than a combination of things we already know much about.

As you can tell, the ongoing issues surrounding content domain have deeply impacted our ability to draw clear conclusions on the value of EI. Historically, there has been a lot of energy placed into examining the incremental predictive validity of a single approach to EI, or to competitively comparing each of the approaches (e.g. Brackett & Mayer 2003). This has led to contradictory and inconsistent findings, with much confusion surrounding the consequences of EI, and a lack of consensus on what constitutes robust theory and measurement. As it stands, EI correlates with a lot of outcomes, but the extent to which it does after controlling for well-known psychological constructs is questionable.

Assumption 5: We Know EI Can Predict Desirable Outcomes Beyond Current Practices

So, let's suppose that we know what EI is (we don't), we can measure it robustly and without bias (we can't), and it predicts outcomes above and beyond that of other constructs (it doesn't). One might suggest that if standard intelligence or personality tests can form part of recruitment strategies, then why shouldn't EI be thrown into that mix too? A fair question.

We need to have a look at the evidence of EI-based selection in action. There should be studies that have a look at how selection decisions can be improved through the inclusion of EI measures, just as there have been for assessment centres, ability tests, and semi-structured interviews (e.g. Robertson & Smith, 2001). No such evidence exists. Far from finding robust evidence to justify the use of EI for recruitment/selection, the vast majority of papers I have systematically searched for were either not relevant, or provided cross-sectional data on the degree to which EI can predict interview performance (Fox & Spector, 2000; Kluemper, 2008) or job performance (Downey et al., 2011; Iliescu et al. 2012). This is not compelling evidence to include EI in selection decisions and shouldn't encourage anyone to change their practices.

Time to Down Tools?

If I were writing a fancy journal article, I would summarise this work as encouraging extreme caution in the application of EI for recruitment and selection. But I'm not. And so, this is my response: *stop it!* Above, we have looked at the evidence behind five clear assumptions for using EI in selection, and the evidence base for the most fundamental – a clear definition – is inadequate. Anyone strongly encouraging the use of EI-based selection is doing so based upon naivety or anecdotal evidence driven by greed. Whilst aspects of intelligence and personality (and thus EI) may continue to support selection, EI measures are not yet fit for this purpose.

It's not even that the evidence is insufficient to support application of EI in this way. It's dangerous. One key field encouraging the recognition of EI is healthcare (Cadman & Brewer, 2001). Here, EI has been positioned as a "vital prerequisite". It's often associated with the emotional capabilities required from the role – to cope with the personal distress it causes and to provide a better "service" to those health workers support (read: bedside manner). I enjoy interacting with health workers and have experienced many such interactions through the birth of my two children – I am grateful for everything health professionals do. I want them to be psychologically safe in their role, but do I really care about whether they smile at exactly the right points in the conversation, or do I care more that they are clinically competent? A minimum level of emotional competency would be of benefit to prevent burnout, compassion fatigue, and all the other emotional demands of the role, but do they need to have a *very* high EI score? Would I want this to be prioritised over clinical competence? I am confused as to what a high score would even mean. On the basis of most psychological constructs, being on any extreme is typically problematic – not conscientious enough and you can't structure your time or meet basic deadlines. Too conscientious and you are so fixed by rules and doing things in a certain way that you miss other opportunities for creativity or flexibility. There is a happy middle ground. So, does using EI as a way to pick the best candidate from a pool of individuals help? Not in my book (quite literally now). Could it, when defined in certain ways, help remove individuals from the candidate pool that might struggle with the emotional demands of the role? Possibly. Even then, there's just not enough evidence for me to provide anything more than a best guess in this domain. It would be dangerous. And yet this is what is being disseminated on a daily basis by a variety of commercial organisations.

I think there is also another risk. In providing more "toned down" conclusions, or not completely shutting down misleading or extreme claims, we may be contributing to ongoing misuse of EI by not clearly condemning misinformation. There are many organisations, papers, and individuals that are keen to proclaim the benefits of EI with bombast. A lack of direct contradiction of any extreme or unsupported claims may be seen to some as insufficiently critical as to minimise confidence in their conclusions. As such, attitudes towards EI may be difficult to change, which may perpetuate exaggerations and misconceptions. If a claim is made about EI which is exaggerated, untrue, or simply unclear, it should be challenged and disrupted until quality evidence is provided in accordance with the strength of claim. Maybe I do need that @ButWhatIsEI after all…

References

Bar-On, R. (1997). *BarOn emotional quotient inventory*. Multi-health systems.

Barrick, M. R., & Mount, M. K. (1991). The big five personality dimensions and job performance: A meta-analysis. *Personnel Psychology, 44*(1), 1–26.

Brackett, M. A., & Mayer, J. D. (2003). Convergent, discriminant, and incremental validity of competing measures of emotional intelligence. *Personality and Social Psychology Bulletin, 29*(9), 1147–1158.

Burri, A. V., Cherkas, L. M., & Spector, T. D. (2009). Emotional intelligence and its association with orgasmic frequency in women. *Journal of Sexual Medicine, 6*(7), 1930–1937.

Cadman, C., & Brewer, J. (2001). Emotional intelligence: A vital prerequisite for recruitment in nursing. *Journal of Nursing Management, 9*(6), 321–324.

CareerBuilder (2011). *Seventy-One Percent of Employers Say They Value Emotional Intelligence over IQ, According to CareerBuilder Survey*. Accessible: www.careerbuilder.com/share/aboutus/pressreleasesdetail.aspx?id=pr652&sd=8/18/2011&ed=08/18/2011

Cherry, M. G., Fletcher, I., O'Sullivan, H., & Shaw, N. (2012). What impact do structured educational sessions to increase emotional intelligence have on medical students? BEME Guide No. 17. *Medical Teacher, 34*(1), 11–19.

Christiansen, N. D., Janovics, J. E., & Siers, B. P. (2010). Emotional Intelligence in Selection Contexts: Measurement method, criterion-related validity, and vulnerability to response distortion. *International Journal of Selection and Assessment, 18*(1), 87–101.

Day, A. L., & Carroll, S. A. (2008). Faking emotional intelligence (EI): Comparing response distortion on ability and trait-based EI measures. *Journal of Organizational Behavior, 29*(6), 761–784.

Downey, L. A., Lee, B., & Stough, C. (2011). Recruitment consultant revenue: Relationships with IQ, personality, and emotional intelligence. *International Journal of Selection and Assessment, 19*(3), 280–286.

Evans, T. R. (2020). Diversity in perceptions of emotional intelligence. Working Paper.

Evans, T. R., Hughes, D. J., & Steptoe-Warren, G. (2020). A conceptual replication of emotional intelligence as a second-stratum factor of intelligence. *Emotion, 20*(3), 507–512.

Florestall, M. (2008). Is a burrito a sandwich? Exploring race, class, and culture in contracts. *Michigan Journal of Race and Law*: https://repository.law.umich.edu/mjrl/vol14/iss1/1

Fox, S., & Spector, P. E. (2000). Relations of emotional intelligence, practical intelligence, general intelligence, and trait affectivity with interview outcomes: It's not all just 'G'. *Journal of Organizational Behavior, 21*(2), 203–220.

Goleman, D. (1996) *Emotional Intelligence: Why It Can Matter More than IQ*. London: Bloomsbury.

Hughes, D. J., & Evans, T. R. (2016) Comment: Trait EI moderates the relationship between Ability EI and emotion regulation. *Emotion Review, 8*(4), 331–332.

Hughes, D. J., & Evans, T. R. (2018). Putting 'emotional intelligences' in their place: Introducing the integrated model of affect-related individual differences. *Frontiers in Psychology, 9,* 2155.

Iliescu, D., Ilie, A., Ispas, D., & Ion, A. (2012) Emotional intelligence in personnel selection: Applicant reactions, criterion, and incremental validity. *International Journal of Selection and Assessment, 20*(3), 347–358.

Joseph, D. L., Jin, J., Newman, D. A., & O'Boyle, E. H. (2015). Why does self-reported emotional intelligence predict job performance? A meta-analytic investigation of Mixed EI. *Journal of Applied Psychology, 100*(2), 298–342.

Kamranpour, S. B., Tarahi, M. J., Kohan, S., & Alizadeh, S. (2019). Relationship of emotional intelligence with sexual function in females. *Journal of Holistic Nursing and Midwifery, 29*(2), 65–72.

Kepes, S., & McDaniel, M. A. (2015). The validity of conscientiousness is overestimated in the prediction of job performance. *PLoS One, 10*(10), e0141468.

Kluemper, D. H. (2008) Trait emotional intelligence: The impact of core-self evaluations and social desirability. *Personality and Individual Differences, 44*(6), 1402–1412.

Lievens, F., Klehe, U. C., & Libbrecht, N. (2011). Applicant versus employee scores on self-report emotional intelligence measures. *Journal of Personnel Psychology, 10,* 89–95

Mesmer-Magnus, J., Viswesvaran, C., Deshpande, S., & Joseph, J. (2006) Social desirability: The role of over-claiming, self-esteem, and emotional intelligence. *Psychology Science, 48*(3), 336–356.

Miao, C., Humphrey, R. H., & Qian, S. (2017a). A meta-analysis of emotional intelligence and work attitudes. *Journal of Occupational and Organizational Psychology, 90*(2), 177–202.

Miao, C., Humphrey, R. H., & Qian, S. (2017b). Are the emotionally intelligent good citizens or counterproductive? A meta-analysis of emotional intelligence and its relationships with organizational citizenship behavior and counterproductive work behavior. *Personality and Individual Differences, 116,* 144–156.

New York State (2019). *Sandwiches. Tax Bulletin ST-835 (TB-ST-835).* Accessible: www.tax.ny.gov/pubs_and_bulls/tg_bulletins/st/sandwiches.htm

Nicholls, S., Wegener, M., Bay, D., & Cook, G. L. (2012). Emotional intelligence tests: Potential impacts on the hiring process for accounting students. *Accounting Education, 21*(1), 75–95.

O'Boyle, E. J., Humphrey, R. H., Pollack, J. M., Hawver, T. H., & Story, P. A. (2011) The relation between emotional intelligence and job performance: A meta-analysis. *Journal of Organizational Behavior, 32*(5), 788–818.

O'Connor, P. J., Hill, A., Kaya, M., & Martin, B. (2019). The measurement of emotional intelligence: A critical review of the literature and recommendations for researchers and practitioners. *Frontiers in Psychology, 10,* 1116.

Pérez-González, J., & Sanchez-Ruiz, M. (2014) Trait emotional intelligence anchored within the Big Five, Big Two and Big One frameworks. *Personality and Individual Differences, 65,* 53–58.

Robertson, I. T., & Smith, M. (2001). Personnel selection. *Journal of Occupational and Organizational Psychology, 74*(4), 441–472.

Salovey, P., & Mayer, J. D. (1990). Emotional intelligence. *Imagination, Cognition, and Personality, 9,* 185–211.

Silva, P., Pereira, H., Esgalhado, G., Monteiro, S., Afonso, R. M., & Loureiro, M. (2016). Emotional intelligence, sexual functioning, and subjective sexual well-being in Portuguese adults. *Journal of Education, Society and Behavioural Science, 15*(1), 1–11.

Southward, M. W., Heiy, J. E., & Cheavens, J. S. (2019). Emotions as context: Do the naturalistic effects of emotion regulation strategies depend on the regulated emotion? *Journal of Social and Clinical Psychology*, *38*(6), 451–474.

Stockwell, T., Zhao, J., Greenfield, T., Li, J., Livingston, M., & Meng, Y. (2016). Estimating under-and over-reporting of drinking in national surveys of alcohol consumption: Identification of consistent biases across four English-speaking countries. *Addiction*, *111*(7), 1203–1213.

Watkin, C. (2000). Developing emotional intelligence. *International Journal of Selection and Assessment*, *2*, 89–92.

Whitman, D. S., Kraus, E., & Van Rooy, D. L. (2014). Emotional intelligence among Black and White job applicants: Examining differences in test performance and test reactions. *International Journal of Selection and Assessment*, *22*(2), 199–210.

Zeidner, M., Matthews, G., & Roberts, R. D. (2004) Emotional intelligence in the workplace: A critical review. *Applied Psychology*, *53*(3), 371–399.

Diversity Training 4

Racism is an issue that casts a dark shadow over everything we as humans do. Racism undermines a united and effective society and every opportunity to challenge it should be taken. Unfortunately, many attempts to challenge racism in organisations amount to little more than a publicity stunt, or increased demand upon those who suffer most from its destructive consequences. We all have a responsibility to fight racism, and that includes organisations.

As HR plays a major role in recruitment, culture, climate, and managing conflict, HR has a particularly important responsibility in challenging the rampant interpersonal and structural racism prevalent in organisations. In addition to any obvious moral motivations, there is a substantive body of literature which argues for the value of diversity within organisations for innovation, productivity, and recruitment (e.g. Robertson, 2019). Indeed, there are a number of popular culture tropes which can be easily found online surrounding the percentage gains in a number of outcomes – individual, team, and organisational – from prioritising diversity within teams. The evidence behind such claims are often questionable and it is often difficult to untangle the moral bias that may be present, however, the evidence against homogeneity in teams, e.g. through group-think (Janis, 1982), where the desire for conformity in the group results in poor decision-making, is clear enough in direction to encourage diversity.

Diversity can take many forms, and whilst often considered in context of race or sex, can more accurately refer to the composition of an organisation or group with respect to its differences in both observable and unobservable characteristics and social group memberships (Schneider & Northcraft, 1999). Diversity is a fundamental asset to societies and organisations and one central

DOI: 10.4324/9781003035794-4

practice within organisations is to recruit based on, give training about, or increase appreciation of, diversity.

A few years ago, Starbucks, the popular coffeeshop chain, closed its doors to the public for diversity training, following the arrest of two black men who were placed in handcuffs, due to calls to the police by staff because the men didn't order anything. Facing strong media backlash for claims of racism, Starbucks delivered four hours of training to all staff. Choosing to close more than 8,000 stores is surely a strong statement against racism, and that alone was likely to be a beneficial strategic move to recover some reputational damage, but did it do any real good? Is a compulsory one-off four-hour session enough to re-educate individuals on their implicit biases?

Saving me from making any questionably libellous claims about this specific case, the data and outcomes from Starbuck's intervention have not been released. Phew. Career thus far still intact, let's look at what is available to help us determine whether such work is likely to be successful – a not insubstantial body of academic literature, starting with a basis of what such training might entail and how it's expected to work.

Diversity training is typically defined as "a distinct set of instructional programmes aimed at facilitating positive intergroup interactions, reducing prejudice and discrimination, and enhancing the skills, knowledge, and motivation of participants to interact with diverse others" (Bezrukova et al., 2016, p. 1228). Workplace diversity training is widely adopted (Ryan et al., 2002), and aims to harness the benefits of differences to commercial advantage by fostering greater employee understanding of diversity, subsequent legislation, and the self, and encouraging more inclusive behaviour (Tipper, 2004). If not at least a little cynical, some secondary outcomes might also include reputational benefits and reduced legal conflicts (Aghazadeh, 2004).

Given that the definition of diversity training offered is quite broad and could refer to a range of actions, we turn to theory to help structure our thoughts. There are a number of useful psychological theories that have been applied to diversity training. For example, the Theory of Planned Behaviour (Ajzen, 1991). Here, attitudes (e.g. acknowledging that racism is a problem), subjective norms (e.g. explicit expectations to contribute to initiatives challenging structural racism), and perceived behavioural control (e.g. space in workload to implement) are seen to drive behavioural intentions. It is these intentions which subsequently inform behaviour. The Theory of Planned Behaviour offers a useful framework to begin differentiating between approaches to diversity training, and can also help with how we consider evaluating such works (Wiethoff, 2004). As such, lets drill down into a little more detail of the different components of attitudes.

A prominent perspective taught in nearly all psychology degrees, whether explicitly or indirectly, is that attitudes can have affective, behavioural, and cognitive components. Attempts to differentiate approaches to diversity training made by such tricomponent models have been presented in various guises (e.g. Kandola, 2009; Kulik & Roberson, 2008) and seem particularly meaningful as the training methodology, focus, and outcomes should differ. For example, we might expect a behavioural training intervention to be more practice-orientated, and evaluated directly based upon behaviour change, whereas a cognitive intervention might be more content-driven and be assessed through a test of knowledge. The three approaches to diversity training will now be evaluated in context of their empirical support.

Cognitive Approach

The cognitive approach to diversity training intends to change an individual's understanding of diversity or raise awareness about their level of bias. This training is designed to give trainees information about diversity-based laws, the benefits of diversity, or challenge misconceptions about specific social groups. In terms of application, this sort of approach is the lowest hanging fruit. These sorts of interventions can be delivered in a very traditional training format, either online or face-to-face, and are unlikely to really rock the boat in causing distress or extreme responses. These interventions are often framed in context of legal considerations and so often can be easier to implement. The main strengths of the cognitive-based approach are that it can be relatively simple to design. Best-practice principles can be taken from the broader training field, and learning can be easily tested and reinforced. Training needs assessments have been suggested to be of particular benefit in targeting important knowledge-gaps in individuals, teams, and organisations (Roberson et al., 2003) – as with recruitment and selection (see Chapter 3), you need to know exactly what is needed to be able to be effective.

So, generally, does the cognitive approach to diversity training work? Unlike the other approaches to diversity training, cognitive-based approaches typically report modest yet maintained long-term impacts upon knowledge (Bezrukova et al., 2016). This is exactly as you might expect. As with any other fact-based knowledge (termed "crystallised intelligence" in the psychology literature), you know it (and might remember it) if you are taught it, but you are unlikely to work it out through rules of logic (Kulik & Roberson, 2008). For example, if you are taught the different futures of King Henry VIII's wives, you might have a chance of remembering it (Divorced, Beheaded, Died, Divorced, Beheaded,

Survived!). This sort of intervention is pretty easy to evaluate – just ask them questions based upon content you intend for them to learn.

Seems too good to be true? Bingo! Scientists are protesting daily with figures about the worsening of climate change, the number of animals and plants reported as extinct, the growing inequality between the rich and poor, the growing rise of right-wing extremism, and financial conflict of interests and corruption in politics. Would me telling you this change how you are going to spend your day? I would love it if we all took action to challenge these threats to our society and wellbeing, but the answer is likely to be "no". (Other acceptable answers include: "No, I will be too engrossed in your book, Tom".) What we know often has relatively small impacts upon our behaviour. As such, despite having modest impacts upon knowledge (Bezrukova et al., 2016), cognitive-based interventions are flawed when adopted as an isolated intervention, as there is little evidence to suggest that knowledge leads to behavioural change as strongly as originally theoretically proposed (e.g. Nishiuchi et al., 2007; Rodriguez & Walls, 2000; Shavitt, 1990). This is particularly true for long-term behaviour change due to a lack of longitudinal evidence (Alhejji et al., 2016; Chang et al., 2019). Action is based upon a variety of contributing factors, including the likely outcomes of such behaviour, whether the outcomes are big or small, and whether it impacts you personally, or the wider team/group/organisation/society, etc. Motivation to enact knowledge at work is most likely to occur in context of an incentive/reward structure, and supportive organisational climate, however, there is still relatively little empirical or theoretical structure to demonstrate how this process might best occur (Bell & Kravitz, 2008; Paluck & Green, 2009). All in all, it doesn't really look good, does it? We might expect that people might learn something from these interventions, but if we need that to translate diversity into action, this sort of intervention alone is unfortunately not enough.

To maximise the likelihood of making a difference, cognitive-based diversity training should be implemented in context of a wider integrated diversity policy (Bezrukova et al., 2012). Congruency between practice and culture is important. For example, some of my own previous research found that positive feedback was more strongly associated with performance when found in a feedback-seeing culture (Evans & Dobrosielska, 2019). The literature surrounding practice-culture congruency is pretty consistent in arguing for greater benefits to behaviours/interventions in environments that are supportive of the goals. With regard to diversity training, it should be implemented in context of a culture that is explicitly supportive and facilitative of diversity (Sanchez & Medkik, 2004). Otherwise, this sort of diversity training can become a tick-box exercise which is less likely to be implemented and does a disservice to all those it tries to serve.

Diversity training, contrary to a broader "diversity management" term, does not require any broader organisational changes to structures, decision-making, or culture (Richard et al., 2000; Wentling & Palmer-Rivas, 1999). This is clearly problematic and is echoed by Godard (2014) who raised concerns surrounding the "psychologization" of human resources. Diversity training practices are contingent upon agency and do nothing to acknowledge or challenge the role of organisational barriers, which often represent a key obstacle to more inclusive practices (Noon, 2018; Sukhera et al., 2018a). As such, there is an inherent tension between training designed to increase individual responsibility and accountability (Kernahan & Davis, 2007), and the commonly cited organisational barriers to more inclusive structures, systems, and processes. For example, there is longitudinal evidence to suggest that implicit bias training leads to frustration surrounding the organisational constraints to inclusivity and equality (Sukhera et al., 2018a). So, this sort of training might even do much greater harm than good.

With my researcher hat on, there is only one complication with attempting to achieve culture change and evaluate intervention impact concurrently – it would make it difficult to disentangle what effects are attributable to the training specifically, restricting clarity of evaluative works. For example, the training itself might not be of benefit, but it might provide a clear signal that diversity is more important. That would probably not be captured positively in any evaluation of the intervention, but it would be of value for the organisation in the long-run. This would perhaps lead me to be less likely to run such an intervention in the future because of the lack of "results" observed. Regardless of this complication, organisational norms represent a vital aspect of change in inclusivity, and a more holistic approach to diversity seems likely to be most effective (Pless & Maak, 2004).

Affect

The second approach to diversity training is that of affect. Far from the knowledge-sharing experiences of cognitive-based diversity training, here we are purposely intending participants to be reflective and to present them with a more striking and memorable experience upon which changes might be made. Consider the boat truly rocked here. Interventions of this nature typically include activities to elicit strong emotional dissonance from trainees. I have two examples.

First up is called the "Walking Through White Privilege" activity (McIntosh, 1988). You and your fellow trainees line up at the "starting line" and the instructor reads through a number of questions and instructions for movement to start the race to the finish line. Take a step forward if either of your parents had a white-collar job. Take a step backwards if you were raised by only one parent/guardian. Take a step forward if you had more than 50 books in your house when growing up. Take a step back if you have ever read a book where someone with a similar background to you was positioned in a degrading or humiliating role based upon that background. Cue those with privilege standing at the front of the room, "winning", and those with multiple identities with less privilege standing behind the starting line. A devastating metaphor for the current culture.

The second common example of this affect-based training is the brown-eyes/blue-eyes activity (Weiner & Wright, 1973). Martin Luther King was killed on the April 4, 1968. The next day, children attended Jane Elliott's class and asked her why. Her response is now a famous activity in training about discrimination. Children with brown eyes were branded using fabric and were considered the privileged group, given additional rights and power, e.g. access to the water fountain and gym, extra lunch and playtime, whilst the children with blue eyes were expected to sit at the back of the classroom and segregate themselves. After initial resistance, the interactions became hostile, and outcomes of the class diverged. The following day, roles were reversed, yet responses were less intense. The activity closed with a written reflection of their experience. This type of experience was considered one of the central drivers of modern diversity training and similar frameworks for team training are regularly adopted to counter prejudice and racism to this date.

If even the thought of completing these exercises makes you feel awkward, you are not alone, and that is the exact point. Affective approaches are typically designed to cause "uncomfortable feelings about power, privilege and professional effectiveness" (Goggins & Dowcett, 2011, p. 71) towards subsequent behavioural change. In contrast to a simple sit-down lecture on the benefits of diversity for performance and creativity, we can expect that these activities might cause tension, extreme responses, and more intense personal reflection.

Diversity is often considered a matter of emotion (Ashkanasy et al., 2002; Brewis, 2017), with diversity matters frequently causing strong and varied emotional responses (Finn & Chattopadhyay, 2000). Most research focusses on negative emotional consequences of diversity and considers them proxy for conflict (Garcia-Prieto et al., 2003). Indeed, even being encouraged to attend diversity training has been associated with aversive emotional reactions (Sanchez & Medkik, 2004); Do they think I am racist? Am I racist? Do I need to be doing something about this? However, these emotional responses appear to represent a function of appraisal, as the positivity of response towards diversity training can be altered by how the training is communicated about and framed (Holladay et al., 2003).

Understanding the various emotional demands (also referred to as "emotional labour" in the academic literature; Bassett-Jones, 2005) and the processes of regulation adopted in response to these activities is important. Affect-based diversity training assumes that trainees are appropriately skilled to manage the emotional dissonance caused. Without convincing evidence for the presence of sufficient emotional competency, inciting an emotional response appears to be a haphazard approach to diversity training. For example, let's consider the "walking through privilege" activity discussed above. If you are standing at the front having "won" the race, you are likely *and are expected* to be experiencing some level of embarrassment and shame. This could even cause anger at those standing behind you for highlighting your privilege – an outcome completely at odds with the intentions of the training. Similarly, if you are standing at the back you have had to disclose a number of personal circumstances which may have been unfair, traumatic or otherwise, and you have been used as an example to create a learning experience for those with privilege who have not had to endure the same level of hardship or complexity in circumstances. Consider intersectionality also, for example, how black women hold different experiences to those of black men, or white women.

Furthermore, affect-based diversity training assumes the trainers are also competent! Running these activities requires very careful management to create the opportunities for learning required to drive positive outcomes. They require competence in affect-related individual differences to manage effectively (Jordan et al., 2002). This raises all sorts of questions about who should be running this sort of training, in what sort of context and framing, and for what expected outcomes. It certainly feels like it would be more impactful, but it seems more unclear whether it might meet the desired ends.

A more structured perspective on diversity training surrounds implicit/ unconscious bias. This is to tackle times when we unconsciously attribute particular qualities to a member of a certain group. A classic example is when white police officers attribute greater likelihoods of criminality or violence to black suspects, the consequences of which can be seen in statistics surrounding stop and search and deaths in custody, both of which may contribute to lower confidence in the police and reporting to/supporting the police and disproportionate representation within the whole criminal justice system.

Implicit bias activities, popularised by their recent widespread application by Starbucks and through the Implicit Association Test (Greenwald et al., 1998), are a common example of affect-based diversity training. Here the task is to make individuals explicitly aware of these "unconscious" biases, intending to cause dissonance between the idealised and actual self which could be resolved through more inclusive behaviour (Sukhera et al., 2018b). Being confronted with one's own biases elicits a complex blend of emotions (Todd et al., 2010).

Understandable. If a "scientific" test calls you racist or sexist, then you must be ... right? The latest review argues that this strategy impacts awareness of biases but not behaviour, although this conclusion is perhaps a little limited as behaviour is infrequently effectively assessed as an outcome (Atewologun et al., 2018). Implicit bias interventions frequently report counterproductive outcomes, and whilst stated that the reason why is "unclear" (Atewologun et al., 2018), it seems likely that the lack of theory and mixed emotional competence of trainees plays a significant role. Indeed a recent meta-analysis specifically focussed on interventions to change implicit measures suggested they are often inconsistent, and produce "trivial changes in behaviour" (Forscher et al., 2019).

The second main recommendation to be more impactful is therefore to adopt theory-informed diversity training (Paluck, 2006; Smith et al., 2006). Such practices would be concurrent with earlier recommendations and would include matching the training design with the outcomes measured, i.e. cognitive, affective or behavioural (Kraiger et al., 1993). Training objectives are often not explicitly stated (Bezrukova et al., 2012) and in practice, evaluation mainly focusses upon trainees' self-reported attitudes towards the training as assessed (directly) after the implementation (Rohmann et al., 2017), if at all (Pendry et al., 2007). Theory development will be particularly fruitful in uniting perspectives to demonstrate the processes by which distal antecedents such as emotions can impact inclusive behaviour. Treating these approaches as capturing different parts of the same process may be beneficial to negotiate the disconnect between the majority of training which is knowledge, awareness, or affective in nature, and the expectation for concrete organisational outcomes (e.g. Rodriguez & Walls, 2000).

Greater theory-informed training, particularly surrounding social identity and affect, could help drive more consistent outcomes and a more robust understanding. Developments in Social Identity Theory (Tajfel & Turner, 1979) applied to diversity training provide an important impetus for improving the efficacy of affective approaches (Foldy, 2003; Schneider & Northcraft, 1999). The central argument of this theory is that our concept of self is based upon our group membership (indeed try to describe yourself without groupings – I am a human, I am a man, I am a hater of Marmite) and thus we work hard to make our group positive and distinct to make ourselves look and feel good. This leads to in-group favouritism and out-group discrimination. Recent theory argues that the social groups elicited during training, and subsequent membership or attitudes towards such groups, can impact the individual and team response to, and thus efficacy of, diversity training (Garcia-Prieto et al., 2003; Tran et al., 2011). This theory-informed development is of interest as it suggests social identity processes are part of the mechanisms by which differential responses to training, particularly those with strong affective components, can be understood. Such works have inspired the development of Social Identity Theory-based training, for example changing social identity salience, with some very early supporting evidence (Ehrke et al., 2014). Contrary to other emotive approaches, the primary value of Social Identity Theory-informed training lies in framing inclusivity as positive, minimising the evocation of negative personal emotional states such as guilt and defensiveness, and providing a robust theoretical framework from which its impacts can be structured and understood (Pendry et al., 2007). Maybe there is some light in the tunnel for diversity training after all?

Behaviour

The final approach to diversity training is that of skills- or behaviour-based training. Here, training intends to support skill development and reinforcement to support trainees to better negotiate diversity and inclusion when in heterogenous groups (Carnevale & Stone, 1994). Such skills can include cross-cultural understanding and intercultural communication (Treven & Treven, 2007), and training sessions often focus upon using practical activities such as simulations or role-plays (e.g. Bush & Ingham, 2001). The skills-based approach to diversity training is promising because it can directly impact behavioural practice, which is a proximal factor to outcomes (i.e. it's a closer predictor of behaviour than more distal factors such as personality/intelligence), and can draw from best practices in skill development facilitation, including behavioural modelling, practicing, and feedback (McDonald-Mann, 1998).

I'm sure you weren't expecting me to sing its praises though. There are several inconsistencies surrounding the skills-based approach to diversity training. The skills-based approach makes assumptions that trainees have the relevant distal antecedents of competency to understand when and how to apply such behaviours in practice. This assumption may help to account for the training transfer gap. Indeed, a wide range of organisational training initiatives report "learning" having taken place, but very few evaluate and have evidenced subsequent changes in practices. There is little research examining behavioural outcomes to diversity training, and that which does exist have commonly reported small and temporary effects (Bezrukova et al., 2016). Without also understanding the cognitive and affective antecedents of appropriate implementation, skills-based training interventions are likely to be of limited impact.

Many papers examining skills-based approaches to diversity training adopt a competency perspective (e.g. Holmes, 2004) whereby any number of skill types can be considered under the diversity management umbrella. Therefore, the lines between what constitutes general training, e.g. communication, and diversity training, e.g. intercultural communication, is often unclear. This state represents the jingle-jangle fallacy (Thorndike, 1904), whereby training capturing similar skills is referred to with different titles (jingle), and similar training is labelled differently (jangle). Without work to resolve such confusion, it becomes difficult for practitioners to identify which are the most appropriate skills to train and how best to do so. In this respect, needs assessments have again been proposed to help focus both content and evaluation of diversity training (Roberson et al., 2003).

Similar to most work on competencies, there is often relatively poor evaluations of skills-based diversity training due to the lack of theoretical clarity. Most behavioural interventions have been evaluated based upon post-training attitudes rather than behaviours (e.g. Hanover & Cellar, 1998), relying upon more immediate self-reported perceptions rather than relevant longitudinal behavioural outcomes (Kulik & Roberson, 2008). This is pretty poor evidence. Remember a time when you got a new gadget for Christmas? At the time, you are learning all its new cool functions and thinking about all the ways in which you can use it to make your life more exciting and easier, then six months later it's found itself buried back in its box, lonely and attracting dust at speed (see also: gym membership). These competency interventions are heavily commercialised and often lack any theoretical basis or robust evaluation. The proliferation of these atheoretical diversity training sessions and measurement tools provided by proprietary organisations, with little transparency in practice, has likely led to inconsistent evaluations and cherry-picked dissemination of outcomes (Grand et al., 2018).

The third main recommendation is therefore encouraging more rigorous and transparent academic and practitioner work on diversity training evaluation (Nguyen, 2014). In contrast to evidence-based management (Dobbin & Kalev, 2017), exploration of real-world diversity training shows practice often follows very poor implementation standards (Hite & McDonald, 2006). Such is the extent of this, that Bell and Kravitz (2008) suggest that there is no research-practice gap because there is insufficient research to inform any clear applications. Ouch. To develop a body of quality evidence upon which to inform practice, more robust evidence is needed (Nguyen, 2014). There is scope to improve implementation by drawing more upon related fields, e.g. best practices in training, diversity education (King et al., 2010), and Human Resource Management (Theodorakopoulos & Budhwar, 2015). For example, Pendry and Driscoll (2011) detail many sensible recommendations including deriving testable predictions and assessing both short-term and long-term impacts. Going beyond such guidelines, applied research should also adopt preregistered designs to prevent partial reporting of, or cherry-picked, outcomes (Evans et al., 2021), and open data to support external verification and secondary analyses exploring contextual factors (Weston et al., 2019).

Evidence

Recommendations for practice are only as valuable as the quality of evidence supporting them. Given the limited understanding of the processes and outcomes of each approach to diversity training, and the third recommendation to improve training evaluation, it seems to be of significant benefit to examine the quality of the literature which has informed these recommendations to determine their likely value.

The most comprehensive source of evidence for informing recommendations I have discussed thus far has been that of a meta-analysis (Bezrukova et al., 2016). A meta-analysis is an attempt to identify and synthesise all previous works on a given topic – in this case diversity training effectiveness. By collating many studies looking at the same thing, we minimise reliance upon any single finding (which may be due to chance, bad practices, or otherwise), and look instead at what the general trend of the literature might tell us. This way we might secure a more robust estimate of what the typical effect might be. For example, if there are a wide range of results (some studies reporting negative impacts, some reporting null effects (i.e. no impact), and some studies reporting positive impacts), this might tell us a number of things. One might be that the training effectiveness is highly variable and without consistency/consensus on good practice. Another might be that there are some things we don't know about that might impact the type of results we expect, e.g., differences between cognitive and affect-based diversity training, which are causing the differences in outcomes. The meta-analysis is an attempt to synthesise all the available research into a clearer picture and estimate of what is going on.

The meta-analysis by Bezrukova et al. (2016) synthesised 260 independent studies evaluating diversity training, with a total of 29,407 participants. They concluded that diversity training can be of benefit to training outcomes ($g = .38$), particularly on participant reactions ($g = .61$), cognitive learning ($g = .57$) and behavioural learning ($g = .48$). The "g" referred to here represents the Hedges g – a measure of effect size. The bigger the "g", the stronger impact the intervention had upon outcomes. Broadly speaking, a g of .2 would be considered a small impact, .5 a moderate impact, and .8 a large impact (Cohen, 1988). For example, a g of -.9 would mean that diversity training dramatically *decreased* the outcome, whether that be performance, attitudes, or understanding. A g of .10 would suggest diversity training is associated with very modest increases upon outcomes assessed. Based upon the meta-analysis, it looks like diversity training can meet training outcomes to a modest extent.

As this meta-analysis combined data from educational and organisational studies, we're going to re-analyse the data, this time only looking at the 64 studies which reported organisational interventions. The average effect size was $g = .42$, slightly but not significantly higher than that found in educational contexts ($g = .36$). The effect of the interventions ranged from $g = -.46$ (a moderate negative impact) to $g = 2.07$ (a MASSIVE positive impact). This is quite a range. I want to consider one factor which may be of relevance – sample size.

Here, sample sizes of the individual studies varied from seven participants (seven! *seven?!*) to 462 ($M = 74$). That is to say, in a systematic review of all the available academic literature evaluating impacts of workplace diversity training, the average sample is of 74 people. I'm sure we all have lists of people which we dislike longer than this! Would you trust this literature to inform your organisation's strategy?!

Smaller sample sizes are problematic because with fewer data points, it is much more difficult to provide a precise estimate. They often tend to report more variable effect sizes; that is, they are unable to make confident claims about the size of an effect. This is not inherently problematic – sometimes providing a guesstimate of an effect is useful, for example, to determine whether something might have a positive or negative, a tiny effect or massive effect – but even these broad conclusions should be approached with caution when holding such small samples. The major reason why this is likely to be problematic is because studies that report a positive ("statistically significant") effect are far more likely to be published than those with a null (no effect) or negative effect. We call this publication bias (Dickersin & Min, 1993). This is important, because when considered alongside the high variability, and lack of precision in estimates of effects, these small samples can distort our understanding by providing a misleading representation on the true size of effect – most often exaggerating them.

So, let's do a little digging. Let's first consider whether the smaller samples were more likely to report larger effect sizes. I ran a simple spearman's correlation and found exactly that ($r = -.41$, $p < .001$; see Figure 4.1). This is a common conclusion to draw, and very similar relationships have been identified elsewhere (Schäfer & Schwarz, 2019). I have created a scatterplot of the data in Figure 4.1 – each dot is a study, and you can see there is a general trend of data highlighted by the straight grey line. This tells us that the studies with higher sample sizes were generally associated with smaller effects. For those looking carefully, it does look like the Johnson et al. (2009) paper, which has a sample size of 462, slightly distorts the relationship, however, if I remove this study and re-run analyses, they look very similar and the relationship does not significantly differ ($r = .39$, p < .001). These results might suggest that publication bias

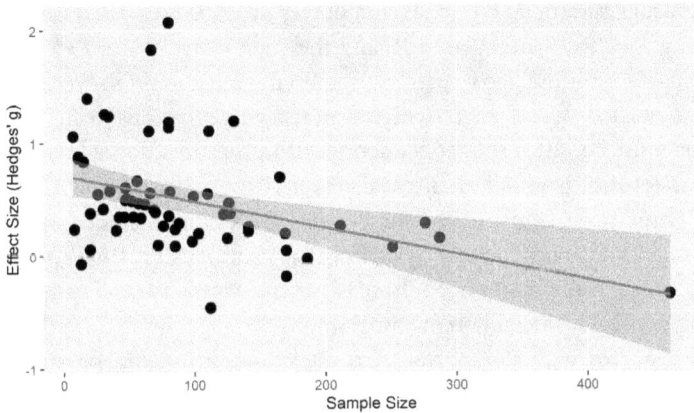

Figure 4.1 Relationship between effect size and sample size

has likely led to an over-estimated effect size, limited by the number of studies with weak or non-significant effects not published (Levine et al., 2009; Slavin & Smith, 2009). Indeed, the main effect reported from the combination of education and workplace studies reduced in strength by almost half ($g = .20$) when the original authors accounted for publication bias. This tells us we should be careful. It suggests that generally diversity training has very small effects upon outcomes.

It's not looking good and it's not going to get any better unfortunately. So, our critique thus far has been that sample size is low, and that various biases are likely to be artificially inflating the perceived benefits of diversity training. What sample size is big enough? How do we know? We're going to tackle this question by looking at power. Unfortunately, this does not require any capes or masks (i.e. they are optional. If you are sitting down reading this in a cape and mask, that's OK. In fact, tweet me about it – @ThomasRhysEvans. I'd love to see it).

Power ranges from 0 to 1 and refers to the extent (probability) that we can find an effect if there is an effect to be found. The greater the power, the lower the likelihood that we are saying there isn't an effect when there is one. This is known as a type-2 error or "false-negative". In short, we need high power to be confident in applying the recommendations of a study. Normally, we accept .8 or 80% power: that represents a 20% chance that we are saying there is no effect of diversity training when there is one.

Sample size, effect size, p-value (normally .05) and power are all inter-related and we can calculate any one of these things from the other three. So, let's have a look at the data again. I want to know, what is the sample size needed to detect an effect of $g = .20$ (as was reported above after controlling for publication bias), and otherwise usual parameters (p < .05 and power at .8). Power analysis was conducted using the "Pwr" package in R, and the code – if you want to take a look – is available with the accompanying materials (https://osf.io/ytkad/). The sample size needed? 199. If we go with recent recommendations to increase power to .9 for more robust results (Chambers, 2013), this jumps to 264. How many studies meet this, from all of the available academic literature available to this point? Three studies. Just three. On average, the studies included in the meta-analysis had 23% power to robustly identify the more conservative g = .20 effect size. I think we really might need those capes and masks after all.

We can analyse the data in a different way though – let's see the size of effects we could have reported with 80% power from the studies included. For simplicity, I am going to consider the studies with the highest sample size and thus greatest possibility to detect smaller effects. The Johnson et al. (2009) paper has the power to detect sizes as small as .13. The Taylor-Ritzler et al. (2008) paper could detect small .17 effects. Re-analysing the data from Combs and Luthans (2007), they could detect a small-to-moderate effect of .36. We have just considered the three largest studies, and already one of these does not have sufficient power to detect the expected size of effect. Detecting big effects is easy. We might expect to see large differences in disposable income between those who shop in Waitrose and those who shop in Asda. Detecting smaller differences, e.g. the differences in impact of one cup of tea versus two cups of tea on memory ability, is difficult and requires much larger samples and more precise measurement. Translating this to diversity training, do we expect brief sessions to cause large effects? Probably not. Especially when we look at outcomes which are broader or rely upon a number of factors, such as performance. In which case, we need to have much larger studies that are capable of identifying these small effects, should they cause them.

As a whole, these secondary analyses of the Bezrukova et al. (2016) data suggest the quality of evidence in the field is poor and thus caution should be exercised when drawing recommendations from them. Such conclusions echo repeated criticisms of the field with respect to small samples and cross-sectional methodologies incapable of drawing causal conclusions (Alhejji et al., 2016; Chang et al., 2019). Imprecise and suboptimal designs and measurement practices mean little is clear about what works, when, why, and where (Bell & Kravitz, 2008; Paluck & Green, 2009). As such, there is little evidence to inform practice (Curtis & Dreachslin, 2008) with acknowledgement that most recommendations represent "best guesses" or intuition (Kalev et al., 2006; Kravitz, 2007). There are a number of strategies widely disseminated to support implementation, for example, the Organisational Diversity Learning Framework (Fujimoto & Härtel, 2017) and AGEM recommendations (Cocchiara et al., 2010), however these are based upon mostly poor-quality evidence.

Not content with just accepting their word, there is another twist in the tale. After doing some more detailed analyses for this book, I discovered a number of errors with the Bezrukova et al. (2016) meta-analysis we just discussed. To pick two examples, firstly let's have a look at the paper with the largest sample (462) by Johnson et al. (2009). They originally reported a moderate positive effect of diversity training – not a moderate negative effect as reported in the meta-analysis. There had been a mistake in the interpretation of low outcome scores as problematic rather than desirable. In a second example, one of the papers presented in the manuscript violates the inclusion criteria. Inclusion criteria essentially dictate what papers a meta-analysis will include, for example, they have to be in a workplace setting or must have a certain study design. The study design criteria for inclusion in this meta-analysis was that of a pre-post comparison, use of relevant control group post-intervention, or both. One paper by Holladay and Quiñones (2008) does not meet either criteria. This work instead compares the effectiveness of two different intervention groups (framed to focus on similarities or differences). As post-intervention differences between these groups would not have been a clear assessment of the impact of diversity training itself, but rather differences between different types of diversity training intervention, its inclusion was inappropriate. I have since been in discussion with some of the authors (who are incredibly lovely!) and we are working on a response paper considering why such errors occur and what strategies might facilitate more reproducible meta-analyses. I hope this work will go some way to correct the record, but this does little to change the wider problems with this body of literature. The changes to effect size broadly suggest a larger effect than reported, so the evidence for diversity training is more encouraging than original presented, but nevertheless the conclusion stands: we don't know enough about diversity training to implement it well.

Following the meta-analysis by Bezrukova et al. (2016), there have been a number of developments, most notably a preregistered field experiment (Chang et al., 2019; $n = 3016$). Here, small and mixed effects were reported from different one-hour online-delivered diversity training sessions on bias. Attitudinal improvements were found most clearly within workers from different cultures, and behavioural changes were most strongly noted in those with pro-diversity attitudes pre-intervention. These findings constitute preliminary evidence for informing decisions as to whether this approach to training should be voluntary or compulsory, and to whom. Representing an ecologically-valid intervention, preregistered analysis plan and large sample size, Chang et al. (2019) provides a convincing quality benchmark for future research to better understand the various dynamics by which the efficacy of diversity training can be improved.

Whilst we have been very critical of the current state of understanding, it seems misguided to stop doing something about these issues altogether.

Diversity training, and diversity management initiatives more broadly, are a signal to employees that diversity is a valued priority (Sanchez & Medkik, 2004), and whilst not its primary focus, this outcome is normally good in of itself. So, we should be doing something about racism, diversity, and inclusivity, but what should we be doing? The truth is, I don't know. We've looked at three approaches to diversity training – cognitive, affective, and behavioural. Across all three there is relatively poor understanding of the processes and outcomes of such training approaches. Based upon what we have discussed, if you are going to use diversity training, it should be theory-informed, robustly designed and evaluated, and implemented in context of a wider integrated diversity/inclusivity-management policy. It should be seen as an experimental intervention, not a clear solution to any issues. By looking closely at the existing literature, we can see academic understanding of diversity training has low power, and likely produces exaggerated estimates of training impact. As such, all recommendations based upon this body of evidence should be considered tentatively.

References

Aghazadeh, S. M. (2004). Managing workforce diversity as an essential resource for improving organizational performance. *International Journal of Productivity and Performance Management, 53*(6), 521–531.

Ajzen, I. (1991). The theory of planned behavior. *Organizational Behavior and Human Decision Processes, 50*(2), 179–211.

Alhejji, H., Garavan, T., Carbery, R., O'Brien, F., & McGuire, D. (2016). Diversity training programme outcomes: A systematic review. *Human Resource Development Quarterly, 27*(1), 95–149.

Ashkanasy, N. M., Härtel, C. E., & Daus, C. S. (2002). Diversity and emotion: The new frontiers in organizational behavior research. *Journal of Management, 28*(3), 307–338.

Atewologun, D., Cornish, T., & Tresh, F. (2018). *Unconscious bias training: An assessment of the evidence for effectiveness.* Equality and Human Rights Commission Research Report Series. Accessible: https://warwick.ac.uk/services/ldc/researchers/resource_bank/unconscious_bias/ub_an_assessment_of_evidence_for_effectiveness.pdf

Bassett-Jones, N. (2005). The paradox of diversity management, creativity and innovation. *Creativity and Innovation Management, 14*(2), 169–175.

Bell, M. P., & Kravitz, D. A. (2008). From the guest co-editors: What do we know and need to learn about diversity education and training? *Academy of Management Learning & Education, 7*(3), 301–308.

Bezrukova, K., Jehn, K. A., & Spell, C. S. (2012). Reviewing diversity training: Where we have been and where we should go. *Academy of Management Learning & Education, 11*(2), 207–227.

Bezrukova, K., Spell, C. S., Perry, J. L., & Jehn, K. A. (2016). A meta-analytical integration of over 40 years of research on diversity training evaluation. *Psychological Bulletin, 142*(11), 1227–1274.

Brewis, D. N. (2017). Social justice 'lite'? Using emotion for moral reasoning in diversity practice. *Gender, Work & Organization, 24*(5), 519–532.

Bush, V. D., & Ingram, T. N. (2001). Building and assessing cultural diversity skills: Implications for sales training. *Industrial Marketing Management, 30*(1), 65–76.

Carnevale, A. P., & Stone, S. C. (1994). Diversity beyond the golden rule. *Training & Development, 48*(10), 22–40.

Chambers, C. D. (2013). Registered reports: A new publishing initiative at Cortex. *Cortex, 49*(3), 609–610.

Chang, E. H., Milkman, K. L., Gromet, D. M., Rebele, R. W., Massey, C., Duckworth, A. L., & Grant, A. M. (2019). The mixed effects of online diversity training. *Proceedings of the National Academy of Sciences, 116*(16), 7778–7783.

Cocchiara, F. K., Connerley, M. L., & Bell, M. P. (2010). "A GEM" for increasing the effectiveness of diversity training. *Human Resource Management, 49*(6), 1089–1106.

Cohen, J. (1988). *Statistical power analysis for the behavioral sciences.* Hillsdale, NJ: Erlbaum.

Combs, G. M., & Luthans, F. (2007). Diversity training: Analysis of the impact of self-efficacy. *Human Resource Development Quarterly, 18*, 91–120. Accessible: http://dx.doi.org/10.1002/hrdq.1193

Curtis, F. E., & Dreachslin, J. L. (2008). Integrative literature review: Diversity management interventions and organizational performance: A synthesis of current literature. *Human Resource Development Review, 7*(1), 107–134.

Dickersin, K., & Min, Y. I. (1993) Publication bias: The problem that won't go away. *Annals of the New York Academy of Sciences, 703*, 135–146

Dobbin, F., & Kalev, A. (2017). Are diversity programs merely ceremonial? Evidence-free institutionalization, in R. Greenwood, C. Oliver, T. B. Lawrence, & R. E. Meyer (Eds.), *The SAGE handbook of organizational institutionalism.* London: Sage, 808–828.

Ehrke, F., Berthold, A., & Steffens, M. C. (2014). How diversity training can change attitudes: Increasing perceived complexity of superordinate groups to improve intergroup relations. *Journal of Experimental Social Psychology, 53*, 193–206.

Evans, T. R. (2019). *Preregistration of Applied Research and Practice.* Presented at the UK Open Science Working Group Conference (OSWG19), April 11, 2019.

Evans, T. R., and Dobrosielska, A. (2019). Feedback-seeking culture moderates the relationship between positive feedback and task performance. *Current Psychology, 40*(7), 3401–3408.

Evans, T. R., Branney, P., Clements, A., & Hatton, E. (2021). Improving evidence-based practice through preregistration of applied research: Barriers and recommendations. *Accountability in Research*, 1–21.

Finn, C., & Chattopadhyay, P. (2000). Managing emotions in diverse work teams: an affective events perspective. *Academy of Management Proceedings, 2000*(1), D1–D6.

Foldy, E. (2003). "Managing" diversity: Power and identity in organizations. In I. Aaltio-Marjosola, & A. Mills (Eds.), *Gender, identities and the cultures of organizations,* London: Routledge.

Forscher, P. S., Lai, C. K., Axt, J. R., Ebersole, C. R., Herman, M., Devine, P. G., & Nosek, B. A. (2019). A meta-analysis of procedures to change implicit measures. *Journal of Personality and Social Psychology, 117*(3), 522–559.

Fujimoto, Y., & EJ Härtel, C. (2017). Organizational diversity learning framework: going beyond diversity training programs. *Personnel Review, 46*(6), 1120–1141.

Garcia-Prieto, P., Bellard, E., & Schneider, S. C. (2003). Experiencing diversity, conflict, and emotions in teams. *Applied Psychology, 52*(3), 413–440.

Godard, J. (2014). The psychologisation of employment relations? *Human Resource Management Journal, 24*(1), 1–18.

Goggins II, L., & Dowcett, E. (2011). Beyond introduction: The need for competency in diversity training. *International Journal of Diversity in Organisations, Communities & Nations, 11*(2), 67–74

Grand, J. A., Rogelberg, S. G., Allen, T. D., Landis, R. S., Reynolds, D. H., Scott, J. C., ... & Truxillo, D. M. (2018). A systems-based approach to fostering robust science in industrial-organizational psychology. *Industrial and Organizational Psychology, 11*(1), 4–42.

Greenwald, A. G., McGhee, D. E., & Schwartz, J. L. (1998). Measuring individual differences in implicit cognition: the implicit association test. *Journal of Personality and Social Psychology, 74*(6), 1464.

Hanover, J. M., & Cellar, D. F. (1998). Environmental factors and the effectiveness of work-force diversity training. *Human Resource Development Quarterly, 9*(2), 105–124.

Hite, L. M., & McDonald, K. S. (2006). Diversity training pitfalls and possibilities: An exploration of small and mid-size US organizations. *Human Resource Development International, 9*(3), 365–377.

Holladay, C. L., Knight, J. L., Paige, D. L., & Quiñones, M. A. (2003). The influence of framing on attitudes toward diversity training. *Human Resource Development Quarterly, 14*(3), 245–263.

Holladay, C. L., & Quiñones, M. A. (2008). The influence of training focus and trainer characteristics on diversity training effectiveness. *Academy of Management Learning & Education, 7*(3), 343–354.

Holmes, T. A. (2004). Designing and facilitating performance-based diversity training. *Performance Improvement, 43*(5), 13–19.

Hughes, D. J., & Evans, T. R. (2018). Putting 'Emotional Intelligences' in Their Place: Introducing the Integrated Model of Affect-Related Individual Differences. *Frontiers in Psychology, 9*, 2155.

Janis, I. L. (1982). *Groupthink: Psychological studies of policy decisions and fiascoes*. Boston, MA: Houghton Mifflin.

Johnson, L. M., Antle, B. F., & Barbee, A. P. (2009). Addressing disproportionality and disparity in child welfare: Evaluation of an anti-racism training for community service providers. *Children and Youth Services Review, 31*, 688–696.

Jordan, P. J., Ashkanasy, N. M., Härtel, C. E., & Hooper, G. S. (2002). Workgroup emotional intelligence: Scale development and relationship to team process effectiveness and goal focus. *Human Resource Management Review, 12*(2), 195–214.

Kalev, A., Dobbin, F., & Kelly, E. (2006). Best practices or best guesses? Assessing the efficacy of corporate affirmative action and diversity policies. *American Sociological Review, 71*(4), 589–617.

Kandola, B. (2009). *The value of difference: Eliminating bias in organisations*. Oxford: Pearn Kandola.

Kernahan, C., & Davis, T. (2007). Changing perspective: How learning about racism influences student awareness and emotion. *Teaching of Psychology, 34*(1), 49–52.

King Jr, J. E., Bell, M. P., & Lawrence, E. (2009). Religion as an aspect of workplace diversity: An examination of the US context and a call for international research. *Journal of Management, Spirituality and Religion, 6*(1), 43–57.

King, E. B., Gulick, L. M., & Avery, D. R. (2010). The divide between diversity training and diversity education: Integrating best practices. *Journal of Management Education, 34*(6), 891–906.

Kraiger, K., Ford, J. K., & Salas, E. (1993). Application of cognitive, skill-based, and affective theories of learning outcomes to new methods of training evaluation. *Journal of Applied Psychology, 78*(2), 311–328.

Kravitz, D. A. (2007). Can we take the guesswork out of diversity practice selection? *Academy of Management Perspectives, 21*(2), 80–81.

Kulik, C. T., & Roberson, L. (2008). Common goals and golden opportunities: Evaluations of diversity education in academic and organizational settings. *Academy of Management Learning & Education, 7*(3), 309–331.

Levine, T. R., Asada, K. J., & Carpenter, C. (2009). Sample sizes and effect sizes are negatively correlated in meta analyses: Evidence and implications of a publication bias against nonsignificant findings. *Communication Monographs, 76*(3), 286–302.

McDonald-Mann, D.G. (1998). Skill-based training. In C. D. McCauley, R. S. Moxley, & E. Van Velsor (Eds.), *The center for creative leadership: Handbook of leadership development*. San Francisco: Jossey-Bass, pp. 106–126.

McIntosh, P. (1988). White privilege and male privilege: A personal account of coming to see correspondences through work in women's studies. Accessible: http//seamonkey.ed.asu. edu/~meisaac/emc598gunpacking.html

Nguyen, S. (2014). The critical role of research in diversity training: How research contributes to an evidence-based approach to diversity training. *Development and Learning in Organizations: An International Journal, 28*(4), 15–17.

Nishiuchi, K., Tsutsumi, A., Takao, S., Mineyama, S., & Kawakami, N. (2007). Effects of an education program for stress reduction on supervisor knowledge, attitudes, and behavior in the workplace: A randomized controlled trial. *Journal of Occupational Health, 49*(3), 190–198.

Noon, M. (2018). Pointless diversity training: Unconscious bias, new racism and agency. *Work, Employment and Society, 32*(1), 198–209.

Paluck, E. L. (2006). Diversity training and intergroup contact: A call to action research. *Journal of Social Issues, 62*(3), 577–595.

Paluck, E. L., & Green, D. P. (2009). Prejudice reduction: What works? A review and assessment of research and practice. *Annual Review of Psychology, 60*, 339–367.

Pendry, L. F., & Driscoll, D. M. (2011). Five guiding principles to help improve diversity-training assessment. *Training and Management Development Methods, 25*(2), 1–19.

Pendry, L. F., Driscoll, D. M., & Field, S. C. (2007). Diversity training: Putting theory into practice. *Journal of Occupational and Organizational Psychology, 80*(1), 27–50.

Pless, N., & Maak, T. (2004). Building an inclusive diversity culture: Principles, processes and practice. *Journal of Business Ethics, 54*(2), 129–147.

Richard, O. C., Fubara, E. I., & Castillo, M. N. (2000). The impact of explanations and demographic group membership: Reactions to diversity initiatives. *Journal of Applied Social Psychology, 30*(5), 1039–1055

Roberson, L., Kulik, C. T., & Pepper, M. B. (2003). Using needs assessment to resolve controversies in diversity training design. *Group & Organization Management, 28*(1), 148–174.

Roberson, Q. M. (2019). Diversity in the workplace: A review, synthesis, and future research agenda. *Annual Review of Organizational Psychology and Organizational Behavior, 6*, 69–88.

Rodriguez, R. R., & Walls, N. E. (2000). Culturally educated questioning: Toward a skills-based approach in multicultural counselor training. *Applied and Preventive Psychology, 9*(2), 89–99.

Rohmann, A., Froncek, B., Mazziotta, A., & Piper, V. (2017). Current evaluation practices of diversity trainers in German-speaking countries. *International Journal of Training Research*, 15(2), 148–159.

Ryan, J., Hawdon, J., & Branick, A. (2002). The political economy of diversity: Diversity programs in fortune 500 companies. *Sociological Research Online*, 7(1), 1–15.

Sanchez, J. I., & Medkik, N. (2004). The effects of diversity awareness training on differential treatment. *Group & Organization Management*, 29(4), 517–536.

Schäfer, T., & Schwarz, M. A. (2019). The meaningfulness of effect sizes in psychological research: Differences between sub-disciplines and the impact of potential biases. *Frontiers in Psychology*, 10, 813.

Schneider, S. K., & Northcraft, G. B. (1999). Three social dilemmas of workforce diversity in organizations: A social identity perspective. *Human Relations*, 52(11), 1445–1467.

Shavitt, S. (1990). The role of attitude objects in attitude functions. *Journal of Experimental Social Psychology*, 26, 124–148.

Slavin, R., & Smith, D. (2009). The relationship between sample sizes and effect sizes in systematic reviews in education. *Educational Evaluation and Policy Analysis*, 31(4), 500–506.

Smith, T. B., Constantine, M. G., Dunn, T. W., Dinehart, J. M., & Montoya, J. A. (2006). Multicultural education in the mental health professions: A meta-analytic review. *Journal of Counselling Psychology*, 53(1), 132–145.

Sukhera, J., Milne, A., Teunissen, P. W., Lingard, L., & Watling, C. (2018a). Adaptive reinventing: implicit bias and the co-construction of social change. *Advances in Health Sciences Education*, 23(3), 587–599.

Sukhera, J., Milne, A., Teunissen, P. W., Lingard, L., & Watling, C. (2018b). The actual versus idealized self: Exploring responses to feedback about implicit bias in health professionals. *Academic Medicine*, 93(4), 623–629.

Tajfel, H., & Turner, J. C. (1979). An integrative theory of intergroup conflict. In W. G. Austin, & S. Worchel. (Eds.) *The Social Psychology of Intergroup Relations*. Monterey, CA: Brooks/ Cole, pp. 33–47.

Taylor-Ritzler, T., Balcazar, F., Dimpfl, S., Suarez-Balcazar, Y., Willis, C., & Schiff, R. (2008). Cultural competence training with organizations serving people with disabilities from diverse cultural backgrounds. *Journal of Vocational Rehabilitation*, 29(2), 77–91.

Theodorakopoulos, N., & Budhwar, P. (2015). Guest editors' introduction – Diversity and inclusion in different work settings: Emerging patterns, challenges, and research agenda. *Human Resource Management*, 54(2), 177–197.

Thorndike, E. L. (1904). *An Introduction to the Theory of Mental and Social Measurements*. New York: The Science Press.

Tipper, J. (2004). How to increase diversity through your recruitment practices. *Industrial and Commercial Training*, 36(4), 158–161.

Todd, N. R., Spanierman, L. B., & Aber, M. S. (2010). White students reflecting on whiteness: Understanding emotional responses. *Journal of Diversity in Higher Education*, 3(2), 97–110.

Tran, V., Garcia-Prieto, P., & Schneider, S. C. (2011). The role of social identity, appraisal, and emotion in determining responses to diversity management. *Human Relations*, 64(2), 161–176.

Treven, S., & Treven, U. (2007). Training in diversity management. *Journal of Diversity Management*, 2(1), 1–7.

Weiner, M. J., & Wright, F. E. (1973). Effects of undergoing arbitrary discrimination upon subsequent attitudes toward a minority group. *Journal of Applied Social Psychology, 3,* 94–102.

Wentling, R. M., & Palma-Rivas, N. (1999). Components of effective diversity training programmes. *International Journal of Training and Development, 3*(3), 215–226.

Weston, S. J., Ritchie, S. J., Rohrer, J. M., & Przybylski, A. K. (2019). Recommendations for increasing the transparency of analysis of preexisting data sets. *Advances in Methods and Practices in Psychological Science, 2*(3), 214–227.

Wiethoff, C. (2004). Motivation to learn and diversity training: Application of the theory of planned behavior. *Human Resource Development Quarterly, 15*(3), 263–278.

Workplace Stress Interventions

5

ping you have one new email! OK, let's just have a quick look. Oh, it's from the wellbeing group, great. It's International Men's Day so it's probably raising awareness about suicide in men… Wait. No. They can't seriously be suggesting this… You have got to be kidding me… A knitting session to deal with general stress. Don't forget to bring your needles! I mean, where do I start on this?

I would love to claim that this chapter is not a direct result of these types of initiatives filling my inbox, but that would be an absolute lie. Employee wellbeing should be a central priority of every organisation and I hope this chapter is going to convince you why wellbeing initiatives need to be positioned as an organisational responsibility focussed more upon structural and holistic-level support and change. I am sick of my friends being told they need to be more "resilient" when more often than not what they are really being told is: we don't know how – or don't have the intention or resources available – to support you. Business are not autonomous units: they are ideas and values framed to unite individuals towards certain outcomes. People matter. They should be prioritised as such.

The Basics

The field of stress management interventions captures any and all activities or programmes initiated by an organisation primarily to reduce stressors directly or reduce the impact of stressors upon employees (Ivancevich et al., 1990). To appreciate the diversity and nuances in academic work on such stress interventions, we should acknowledge the different types, foci, approaches, and

DOI: 10.4324/9781003035794-5

evaluation strategies to stress intervention. Differentiation upon this basis can be useful to draw consensuses and patterns from findings within a diverse body of evidence.

Workplace stress interventions are often categorised into three classifications: primary, secondary, or tertiary. Primary interventions are those designed to minimise stress before they even happen: a preventative measure. For example, if the job is known to be emotionally demanding, organisations might want to recruit on the basis of superior emotion management competencies (see Chapter 3 for more on this). Secondary interventions are those designed to dampen the intensity of stress once it has happened, helping individuals to manage their stress experience, and often acting as damage-limitation to avoid negative experiences from escalating. For example, secondary interventions might include yoga, mindfulness, or resilience training. Oh, and knitting. Finally, tertiary training captures more dramatic actions that are designed to support those whose work have been compromised by their experience of stress and to return them to manageable levels. Tertiary interventions might include providing counselling services or individualised support to specific individuals. This differentiation has sometimes been captured as focussing on the individual, the individual-organisation interface, and the organisation, respectively (DeFrank & Cooper, 1987). Although there are some meaningful differences between such definitions, e.g. tertiary referring to either more dramatic support or organisational change, these are not clear boundaries and I therefore discuss this using the former.

These three intervention types can also be differentiated as to whether they focus upon individual-focussed or organisational-focussed initiatives. Whilst we have given examples above of individual-focussed initiatives, we can also consider action at the same levels orientated towards organisational functioning, and we might imagine that doing so might help develop more structural and thus long-term change. For example, a primary organisational intervention might be to offer flexible working arrangements to mitigate the consequences to work–life balance. A secondary organisational intervention might include participative decision-making groups, implementing mentoring programmes, or increasing role clarity or autonomy. Finally, tertiary organisational interventions can include restructuring job roles, changing the work environment, or offering training to reduce strain.

Based upon this model, we can (relatively) easily group interventions into six different categories. This isn't just an academic activity either, we might reasonably expect meaningful differences between such intervention types, based upon their focus on preventing, managing, or correcting stress responses. However, we shouldn't expect homogenous findings within groups. We should also acknowledge the substantive differences in form between interventions within these categories. For example, we can say "exercise" is a secondary individual-focussed intervention, but this could be inclusive of a group walk, yoga session, walking meetings and using stairs instead of lifts, amongst other activities. We wouldn't expect these interventions to all have the same impact on stress, and so we should expect differences in outcomes regardless of any shared categorisation. This gives an early sign to expect that differences are likely to be plentiful, and that close attention will be needed to inform adoption of any specific intervention.

The Evidence

What Is Considered to Work?

Given the importance of managing stress in the workforce in this increasingly competitive and demanding employment market, the body of evidence informing stress management interventions has been steadily increasing. This is particularly true for secondary individual-level, and primary organization-level, interventions (Holman et al., 2018). Research tends to focus on individual-level interventions because they are more prevalent in use and because organisation-focussed interventions tend to have a number of outcomes so may less frequently get classified as a stress management intervention to be easily identified within systematic reviews. As a result, a small number of consistent conclusions have been drawn. For example, in a systematic review of systematic reviews (yeah sorry, we can be a weird bunch), Pieper et al. (2019) concluded that programmes with more than one component were more effective than stand-alone interventions (Holman et al., 2018; Richardson & Rothstein, 2008; van der Klink et al. 2001). This work suggests that, similar to the conclusion on diversity training in the previous chapter, a consistent and multifaceted strategy is likely to be more effective than one-off or knee-jerk short-term strategy. Richardson and Rothstein (2008) provide further evidence to reinforce such conclusions, suggesting that the effects of multiple interventions increase over time and their effects are longer lasting. Undertaking a range of initiatives that are designed to provide a supporting environment, and send a clear message to employees that their health and wellbeing is important, is more likely to produce the type of outcomes intended for such initiatives. It sounds obvious but the financial demands upon such practices are often considered a barrier rather than an investment opportunity to secure an engaged and committed workforce.

The review by Pieper et al. (2019) also suggested that mindfulness-based stress reduction and cognitive-behavioural training interventions have value in minimising stress levels and improving wellbeing. Cognitive-behavioural interventions are designed to change thought patterns and problematic behaviours and subsequently reinforce more positive and active coping methods. Such interventions initially received substantive support (e.g. Bhui et al., 2012; Richardson & Rothstein, 2008; van der Klink et al., 2001), suggesting moderate effects on wellbeing, although more recent evidence suggests the quality of work is poor and the expected outcomes are more modest and equivalent to other types of interventions (Dalgaard et al., 2017; Ruotsalainen et al., 2015). Specifically, Dalgaard et al. found no significant effects of the intervention on stress when participants with significant stress complaints were randomly allocated to either six sessions with a psychologist over 16 weeks, or two control groups.

Another common secondary individual-level intervention studied is the use of relaxation or mindfulness techniques. Modest effects have been noted by previous meta-analyses (Holman et al., 2018; Richardson & Rothstein, 2008; van der Klink et al., 2001). Indeed, a recent systematic review of the evidence suggested mindfulness-based stress reduction reported promising potential to improve stress and a range of other mental health indices (Janssen et al., 2018). However, it is also worth noting that the research quality is low with only two of the 23 studies identified evaluated as "high quality". A key priority of the broader body of evidence on mindfulness and relaxation will be to identify the exact mechanisms behind the effect – is it the breathing? Is it the heightened awareness? We should be looking for where the effect can be greatest, although this will probably be problematic given the diversity in actions captured under the "mindfulness" term (Eby et al., 2019).

The evidence for organisation-level interventions is even more disparate and thus problematic for drawing robust conclusions. An early narrative review of organisation-level interventions from Briner and Reynolds (1999) suggested interventions like job redesign often had no effect on stress, and where effects were reported they were often small and led to both positive and negative impacts. To some extent this should be expected – whilst individual-level interventions are often focussed on changing perceptions of stress directly, organisational strategies change the systems these individuals work in – the levels of demand or resources available to them – so we should expect "mixed" results where some outcomes increase and others decrease.

A workplace is like a spider's web. There's lots of interacting strands, some fundamental to the stability of the web, some less so, and if we make a single change to one strand, it has knock-on consequences to the others. Some might bear more weight or importance, and others might lose some, or fall away completely. When we make changes in the workplace, we make changes to the composition of the web, and in doing so we impact a number of different aspects of the role and our appraisal of it. Changes will impact some factors directly, and others more so indirectly. As such, we should expect a range of outcomes from a single organisational change, with it unlikely to cause a consistent positive or negative effect. As such, studies adopting organisational interventions for stress are expected to produce some "messier" findings to interpret.

Whilst the early review on organisation-level interventions was highly sceptical, and similar conclusions have been recently drawn (e.g. Holman et al., 2018), there are some reasons to be cautiously optimistic for their value (Semmer, 2003). For example, in the Pieper et al. (2019) review of systematic reviews, peer supervision and flexible work time was associated with lower stress and burnout symptoms. Fundamentally, organisation-focussed initiatives represent an opportunity to make direct changes to the problematic factors being experienced (Riva & Chinyio, 2018). If an individual is experiencing burnout because of work-life conflicts, then making flexible working arrangements available is likely to provide an opportunity to that individual to manage their stressors more effectively.

There is now also a growing appreciation for the role of implementation quality and employee participation in the success of organisation-level interventions (Holman et al., 2018). Let me give you an example. In a previous job, all members of staff were asked to come up with a wellbeing target as part of their annual performance appraisal. We were explicitly encouraged to take our own wellbeing as a personal (rather than organisational) responsibility and thus the onus for managing to meet that target was on us. Now, you could attempt to defend this policy by suggesting it's about creating individualised action plans. That by being self-made and explicit I was more likely to follow it and achieve it. That it made wellbeing an important discussion point in the performance evaluation process. To me, that was a weak act of responsibility displacement. We were encouraged to treat our wellbeing like a tick-box exercise and a priority on-par with our others demands, e.g. student satisfaction ratings. I know which of the two that particular employer would want me to prioritise. The target created was not going to be fed back to higher management to identify stressors and to facilitate interventions, it was going to be sent to our managers to "approve" it. It represented no commitment or substantive action from the organisation, it was communicated poorly, and subsequently, adoption was highly variable. This scenario highlights how the success of an organisation-level intervention is at least partially dependent upon how it is implemented and how staff are supported to participate. Furthermore, this scenario highlights the risk of placing the burden of stress management on individuals. It excuses poor work conditions or structurally driven stressors, places the greatest burden on those most likely to need support, and does not acknowledge differences between individuals by assuming that each individual has the same level of awareness, skills, capacity, and intention to act on wellbeing demands.

In sum, whilst there is a limited body of evidence to draw upon, there do appear to be a few areas of consensus from the literature to inform practice. Notably, there seems to be great variability in the sizes of effect these interventions hold (Holman et al., 2018). This could be considered problematic and representative of a scattergun approach to building evidence in this field, but this is actually to be expected given the diversity of approaches available within the field. The diversity in effects is not problematic and the body of evidence shouldn't be criticised based upon this. This doesn't mean that the literature can't be critically viewed though...

Study Design and the Role of Randomised Control Trials

Throughout this text we have discussed a number of different research designs recognising that they offer different levels of quality of evidence towards improving practice. A popular metaphor for this quality difference is the evidence hierarchy (see Figure 5.1) where the quality of work increases as you go up the hierarchy and the prevalence in use of the design type typically decreases. The hierarchy isn't quite so useful to identify the value of any given individual study. For example, an experimental study with a robust pre-post design with control group might represent a trustworthy basis of evidence whereby a meta-analysis might be useless if the studies analysed are all of poor quality (also known as "garbage in, garbage out"). It nevertheless provides us with a broad judgement on the value of certain designs however, which may be useful when evaluating the literature as a whole.

Evaluating the quality of evidence available, it is widely agreed that studies in the field of stress management are inconclusive and largely based upon the lowest levels of the evidence hierarchy: anecdotes, testimonials, and case-study designs (Briner & Reynolds, 1999; Ivancevich et al., 1990; Richardson & Rothstein, 2008).

Many of the workplace stress intervention evaluations described above are experimental designs. Some studies have one group and researchers tested them before and after on their stress outcome (called pre-post design). Some have two groups, one of which doesn't engage in the intervention (control group), and researchers compare their post-intervention stress scores (control group design). Some use both an intervention and control group, test both before and after, and compare the pre-post intervention change between groups. The latter design is the most robust for drawing conclusions as it allows us to examine change (by pre-post change) but also consider the role of maturation, change, or contextual factors (by comparison to control). The latter design is unfortunately the least common (Tetrick & Winslow, 2015).

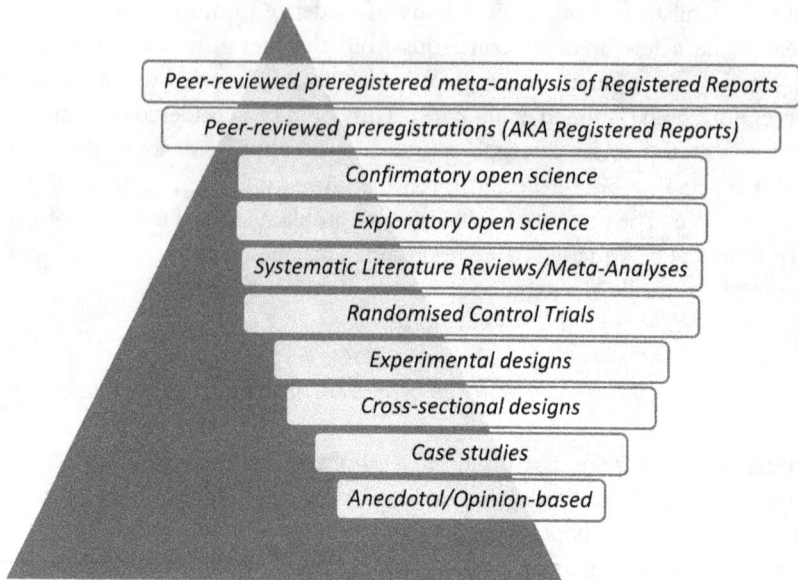

Figure 5.1 The inverse relationship between design quality and prevalence

Prior to the replication/credibility crisis, one of the most sought-after designs was that of randomised control trial (RCT). We sometimes hear about some RCTs on the news in relation to things like vaccine development. A randomised control trial is like the pre-post control trial described above, but better. Firstly, we randomise participants to the different groups (e.g. intervention vs waiting conditions). The benefit of this randomisation is the lack of systematic differences between groups. Imagine we allocated one intervention to one organisation and asked a different organisation not to do anything about wellbeing different to normal. Ignoring the obvious ethical issue, what we have here is allocation bias – factors that might impact the outcomes we are interested in will not be similarly shared between the two groups. For example, one group might be facing redundancy or have higher workloads, meaning that the change in stress is unlikely to be comparable between groups.

Whilst randomisation itself is relatively easy, in practice there are several barriers to conducting effective RCTs (Holman et al., 2018). We should first acknowledge that there are ethical problems with giving an intervention to only some of those who might benefit from it. This is sometimes mitigated through a waiting-list design where some receive the intervention but only after the outcomes are captured from the intervention group. There are also practical considerations as to whether the interventions can be delivered effectively to some individuals possibly scattered across different geographical or business areas. Online is easy, but one-on-one or physical interventions can be demanding on resources. We might also find it difficult to either recruit participants when there is a probability of being allocated into the control group (is it worth my time to complete their questionnaires if I might not even be doing anything?), or to find those who are equivalent enough to make the comparison between them and the intervention group meaningful. There are clear reasons why RCTs are not the standard. Furthermore, being allocated into a control group might, in of itself, influence the outcomes captured, as participants get a sense of whether they have been lucky or not (Nabe-Nielson et al., 2015).

The complexity of effective RCT design does not justify its rarity, because they produce higher-quality evidence and there are a number of workarounds (Tetrick & Winslow, 2015). For example, we can identify comparison groups which are not necessarily as highly matched as we might intend from more "academic" or experimental work, but which might provide an adequate assessment of longitudinal changes in outcomes. For example, we could match participants into equivalent pairs, e.g. two stressed males roughly 35 years old, and then randomise one of each pair to undertake the intervention. There are also several design choices we could make to make it more practical. For example, we can test different intervention groups with different interventions. Here, we can still draw clear conclusions about the intervention efficacy because we have both pre- and post-intervention measurements. A similar design choice could be a factorial design whereby participants are randomly allocated to different kinds of interventions, e.g. they may take part in intervention 1, 2, both, or none. Having multiple intervention types can be suboptimal when drawing conclusions about whether the interventions improve upon existing practices when they don't have a traditional non-active control group, although these concerns can be partially mitigated through use of an active control (where they do as similar as possible activities as to the intervention group, just with the "active ingredient" removed). In extreme circumstances, a waiting-list design where all participants end the study having taken part can be particularly useful in these circumstances and can be more popular with organisations. In addition to these complications, akin to many other fields we discuss in this book, there are many issues with consistently and effectively reporting RCTs (O'Shea et al., 2016). In sum, they are difficult to run, and difficult to report transparently. They are still immensely valuable however, particularly when preregistered, so they sometimes just require a little creativity to be achievable.

Second, RCTs frequently (but not always) "mask" or anonymise. Historically this has been termed "blinding", although we're going to avoid use of that term. It's highly unusual and difficult in the types of research we have been discussing above, where we allocate one group or business a certain intervention and another we ask just to complete the stress questionnaires pre-post but not to act. In RCTs we aim to "mask" as many people involved in the process as possible. Not in the pandemic way, but in a way where those involved don't know who is in which group. This could mean the participants, the researcher, the statistician running the data analysis, basically anyone who might be able to introduce bias through their involvement. As discussed in Chapter 2 in context of having external analysts, it's of benefit to have individuals who are uninterested – or, even better, uninformed – completing the work to minimise biased outcomes driven by subjectivity.

Concealment of allocation is of benefit to minimise bias, but obviously there are limits. For example, in an RCT on stress management, participants are likely to know whether they are in an active group or not. We're asking them to do some knitting every week, or we're only asking them to complete some outcome measures in six months' time. So, we can't always mask our participants. But we can mask most others – the businesses themselves so they do not make decisions based upon their grouping, e.g. give those who are in the intervention group more work because they can now "cope with more". We can mask the researchers so that they put equal effort into collecting data from participants – prompting them to engage in activities and complete any outcome measures similarly. We can also mask the analysts, so group A and group B mean nothing more than letters and there is no expectation to say one is different or better than the other.

So, RCTS have often been referred to as the "gold standard" in research, representing much higher up the evidence hierarchy than the more common pre-post design. Likely due to a combination of the researcher investment, organisational buy-in, and practicalities associated with randomisation and masking, they are extremely rare in organisational studies broadly, and workplace stress interventions specifically (Tetrick & Winslow, 2015). There are a few pockets of evidence, e.g. for "mindfulness" (Bartlett et al., 2019), however, these are mostly limited and are unlikely to represent conclusive and convincing blueprints for success.

There are also several additional concerns surrounding RCTs which require consideration. For example, most RCTs focus upon the outcomes of interventions, but fail to consider that we might also be interested in the processes involved which drive such outcomes (Cox et al., 2007). Interventions are often treated as this black box – you pop in an organisational issue, the box represents your intervention, and the issue comes out the other side resolved. Work framed in this way has limited value for informing future understanding and practice. One method to design this out might be to collect data on a variety of outcomes throughout the process. For example, implementing an organisation-level structural change to improve stress might require regular measurement of a number of indices to determine what is working, when, and why. In this context we might regularly monitor indices of attitudes, well-being and behaviour. Furthermore, we should also be considering the quality of implementation, and whether the strength of outcome to be expected varies with different practices in implementation. We often assume that interventions will have uniform effects without consideration for quality implementation, e.g. the need for support in other areas which might arise by undertaking the intervention, public commitment made by managers to support the intervention, or indeed an individual's attitudes and engagement with the work. It's even possible for us to examine this by building in evaluations of each stage of the process (Nielsen & Abildgaard, 2013). Waiting to the end of an intervention to claim it has failed suggests a lack of engagement with these ideas. Success or failure could be determined by the quality of the design or implementation, or it could be having effects on certain intermediate outcomes but not to the "success" criteria or to the desired outcomes within the given timeframe. As such, not only is there a deficit of quality RCTs examining the impact of stress interventions, there is also a deficit of studies to provide insight into the black box – the processes underpinning their impact and if/how the quality of implementation may impact them (Holman et al. 2018).

Evidence Quality

Independent of intervention study design, there does appear to be a quality issue. Systematic reviews are currently incapable of drawing conclusions about "(a) which outcomes are affected by which types of interventions and/or activities, (b) for whom an intervention type or specific intervention activity is most beneficial, and (c) the specific causal mechanisms underlying the effectiveness of interventions" (Tetrick & Winslow, 2015). In sum, they tell us very little.

I have a particular issue with the lack of attention upon whether the intentions effectively engage and produce positive long-term changes for the particular group of individuals who would benefit from them most. This is particularly salient for me as it is not complex to evaluate statistically, but demonstrates a problematic lack of priorities. For example, see Figure 5.2 for the results of two interventions on self-perceptions of stress management. They had the identical "effect" if we looked at the change from mean pre-intervention scores (7.5) to post-intervention scores (9), but in reality, they had very different effects. On the left, it looks like our intervention had a small effect on the group as a whole, with greatest increases seen for those with the highest scores before the intervention started. On the right, the intervention was highly effective for those who started with low stress management scores, but appears to have reduced

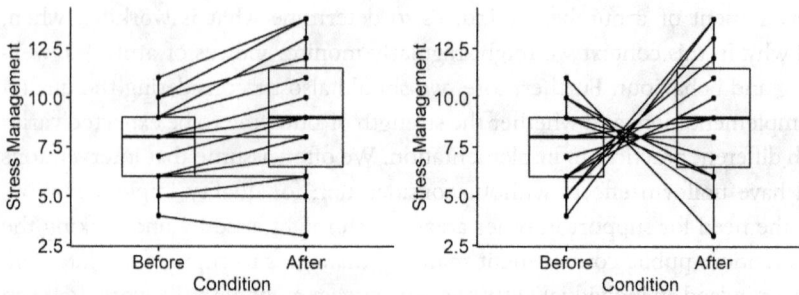

Figure 5.2 Results from two stress management interventions

scores in those who were initially high. Not difficult to create, but dramatically different outcomes. Would you want to run either of these interventions?

Bunce and Stephenson (2000) evaluated the reporting quality of studies and found that they infrequently detailed the sample or intervention appropriately, held generally insufficient sample sizes, and changes attributed to interventions were infrequently robust or meaningful in practice. In essence, studies were so poorly reported that there was little hope in attempting to replicate or generalise the results to other groups. In their own words, "at present the quality of reporting and research design is such that it is difficult to form an impression of what type of SMI (stress management intervention) is appropriate to whom, and in what circumstances" (p. 197).

I consider replicability to be one of the biggest barriers to impact in this field and is something I highlight consistently as a peer-reviewer of intervention-based studies. Yes, you can evaluate an intervention, you might even do a good job, but unless you share the materials and content of the intervention, it's pointless. Journal word counts are too small for you to report everything in enough detail as to replicate it. So, all I know from your paper is that whatever you did might have been good. I have no hope in attempting to run a similar or identical intervention and have little-to-no understanding of how it could be implemented, e.g. sometimes the framing of interventions can have an impact upon engagement and effectiveness (Holladay et al., 2003). When you phrase it like this, it all seems pretty futile.

In-depth examination of the individual studies conducted unfortunately does not paint a prettier picture. Most studies rely upon only self-report measures, with few measuring objective stress through physiological or real-world outcomes (e.g. sick days or referrals to Occupational Health) (Tetrick & Winslow, 2015). Furthermore, there is almost exclusive use of organisations with WEIRD (Western, Educated, Industrialised, Rich, and Democratic) populations (Henrich et al., 2010). The result of which is a body of evidence which is highly contextualised by Western Europe/North American culture, with little consideration for the generalisability of intervention claims (Tetrick & Winslow, 2015). This is not different from the broader field of psychology, but fails to consider the possibility for learning from considering cross-cultural similarities. Excluding the use of a fairly homogenous population to draw from, the study of stress management has attracted high levels of diversity in foci of studies, whether that be in the setting or context, aspects of the intervention, or the sample of interest. As such there is a sporadic, fragmented, and inconsistent mass of studies, which cannot be compared or combined, and thus a questionable body of evidence upon which decisions can be based (Pieper et al., 2019). Not to make it even worse, but even the reviews of the research lack the level of criticality discussed here, and tend to represent moderate quality syntheses (Pieper et al., 2019). For example, the paper excitingly titled "Workplace Stress Management Interventions: What Works Best?" by Sidle (2008) is not much more than a summary of a previous review (Richardson & Rothstein, 2008) we have discussed.

Theory

There's something else I would also like to highlight – a lack of theory. I go on about this quite a lot (see also Chapters 3, 4, and 6). A theory provides a structure and a focus to support intervention design and implementation. A theory provides a framework to allow researchers to establish consensuses, identify limits to its generalisability (e.g. does it only work for certain groups of individuals or outcomes measured in certain ways?) and more broadly develops our understanding and practices. The Job Demands-Resources (JD-R: Schaufeli & Bakker, 2004) model is one of the most commonly adopted theories for stress intervention research (e.g. Tetrick & Winslow, 2015). There are a number of different conceptualisations, but broadly speaking this collection of models argues that the interaction between job demands and job resources (defined however you want) determines your strain and engagement, and these then predict positive and negative workplace outcomes. The interaction between high demands and low resources is considered particularly problematic for burnout. This has an intuitive appeal – by finding the balance between demands upon us and the resources we have to manage them, we can find opportunities to better support individuals to achieve their goals. A strength and weakness of this model is that what is defined as a demand or resource is ultimately individualistic and thus tautologically based. Let's have a look at the original definition of job demands – "aspects of the job that require sustained physical and/or psychological (i.e., cognitive or emotional) effort and are therefore associated with certain physiological and/or psychological costs" (Schaufeli & Bakker, 2004: 296). By definition, job demands are things that have psychological costs ... that is, things that would lead you to disengage, reduce your performance, and/ or be exhausted. These are several common definitional qualities of burnout. Now let's have a look at exhaustion, a central component of burnout: a consequence of extended exposure to specific job demands like intense physical, affective, and cognitive strain (Demerouti et al., 2003). A relationship between demands and burnout is therefore not surprising. They are part of the same process.

Furthermore, what constitutes one individual's demand might constitute another's resource. For example, having control, or having other people reliant upon you. As such, there is no way you can apply this model in the same way across individuals. It's good to acknowledge that these things can be interpreted differently by different individuals, but this makes drawing more generalisable conclusions somewhat more complex. This also makes it very difficult to falsify – to provide evidence to the contrary and ultimately the conclusion seems to be that balancing demands upon staff with the support to complete their goals determines their stress levels. This tells us little about how this process works, and what aspects of the process are most susceptible to intervention (Schaufeli & Taris, 2014).

The consequence of such an individualised model is that "off-the-shelf" stress interventions are unlikely to be successful. To be effective we need to target the problematic demands and identify resource opportunities, acknowledging that what constitutes these categories for each individual person will be unique. There are two consequences of this: a) personalised interventions are likely to be the most effective, and b) the opportunity for wider interventions are facilitated by shared demands/resources. For example, we might expect some similarities of demands within the same organisation. For example, if stress levels across an organisation are high and employees report intense workloads, the organisation could consider increasing the number of days of leave for each staff, thereby facilitating more resources, or increase the number of staff available to complete the work, thereby decreasing the demands upon each individual. Real-world issues aren't always quite so simple, but you can see why organisations can tend to place the emphasis on an individual's psychological resources rather than the organisation's demands ... £££.

Most of the evidence for the relationships claimed by the JD-R comes from cross-sectional correlational work. As the JD-R model aims to make predictions, cross-sectional evidence is redundant when aiming to produce robust evidence to evaluate the theory. As such, Lesener et al. (2018) provided a meta-analytical look at longitudinal research conducted using the JD-R. Their analyses suggest the relationships proposed by the model are robust, i.e. demands predicts later burnout, and resources predict later burnout and engagement ratings. From the 74 relevant studies meeting their criteria, they also rated various aspects of the studies, including study design and method of analysis, from insufficient, sufficient, good to very good. Studies could be considered "high-quality" if they were rated sufficient or greater in all five criteria. Only 29 studies met these criteria, however, results were highly similar regardless of quality ranking. This provides initial evidence to suggest that the JD-R may be a fruitful framework to facilitate understanding and changing workplace stress, but that evidence quality is likely to remain a significant barrier to the development of robust intervention guidelines.

Recommendations

Based upon the complexities of study design, quality, and theory, there are few practices, if any, that can be recommended confidently. Such is the state of affairs that Pieper et al. (2019) have argued that there is insufficient quality evidence to recommend even a single specific intervention or programme that should be widely implemented. That is not to say that we shouldn't be acting upon stress and running interventions and following the evidence (even if poorer quality than preferred), just that there is not enough evidence to draw conclusive recommendations with a confident expectation of success. Indeed, the current body of evidence, although fragmented, has driven a number of tentative recommendations applicable to most general stress management practices. Whilst built from a suboptimal evidence base, they provide some useful guidelines.

The first priority for organisations interested in stress management interventions is to assess the extent of action required. This stage is so important because it moves the organisation from a state of bystandership and passivity to one of awareness and readiness. This can come in various names and forms, but reflects a needs, risk or stress audit (Jacobs et al., 2018). By comprehensively assessing the demands and stressors of all levels and groups within the workforce, organisations can identify both the groups and specific individuals in need of support and more accurately identify the particular sources and causes of stress to manage. Furthermore, it reflects an opportunity to raise awareness about broader issues, e.g. around culture, and more localised issues.

Following identification of the needs or risks for the workforce, the interventions proposed should be assessed for how realistic implementation would be. For financial and practical reasons, interventions should be prioritised to maximise resource use. Strategies which facilitate meaningful and long-term changes in daily work practices are highly desirable (Leka & Cox

2008). Furthermore, the plan should also have built-in flexibility to manage the unique demands of the context. This might mean changing or altering the interventions implemented depending upon the specific groups of interest (Pieper et al., 2019). For example, altering mindfulness session timings to negotiate the different demands across different departments within an organisation.

When deciding upon the nature of interventions, the existing literature encourages adoption of interventions that have more than a single component (Pieper et al., 2019). Initiatives to acknowledge specific dates – International Men's Day for example – are all very well and good, but without any meaningful changes they are likely to be nothing more than a token gesture and could be cynically viewed as opportunistic identity management. Any review concluding that communal knitting is an inclusive and effective intervention to tackle workplace stress is to be immediately shredded. Meaningful stress management doesn't happen through a one-off intervention, but instead through structurally embedding numerous changes to the day-to-day activities of the individuals within the organisation (Leka & Cox, 2008). Responding effectively to the risk assessment, whether it be a need for immediate tertiary interventions or ongoing preventative work, is in combining and committing to both organisational and individual-level changes (Jacobs et al., 2018). As noted earlier, organisations have a tendency to produce individual-level interventions rather than at the organisational-level, which also suggests there is a missed opportunity to maximise the likelihood of positive change by embedding meaningful long-term change to organisations through organisational interventions (Pieper et al., 2019). Developing this more comprehensive intervention strategy, where primary, secondary, and tertiary initiatives can be applied in a complementary and focussed approach to identified deficits in stress management, is more likely to drive sustained and positive outcomes that can benefit both organisations and the individuals within them (Leka & Cox, 2008).

A comprehensive stress management plan requires investment and ongoing commitment. For example, it requires a substantive financial and resource investment from the organisation to ensure that responsibility, planning, and project management are embedded into the workload of the relevant staff members (Jacobs et al., 2018). It also requires regular re-evaluation to identify the efficacy of each component of the plan, and to ensure that they have led to long-term change embedded into the culture and strategy of the organisation. For example, if a tertiary-level intervention has been successful in rehabilitating stressed employees into the workforce, a secondary-level intervention to maintain manageable levels of stress, or a formalised action plan to identify and support other individuals in similar situations of high-stress, are the logical next processes to be planned.

So, we have discussed lots about plans, but let's now consider the people. Many academics have considered "organisational readiness for change" an important component to success, but what does that even mean? I can only see this as relevant if we look at the individuals within the organisation. Meaningful stress interventions can involve substantive change (Pieper et al., 2019), and this can be emotionally demanding (see Chapter 6). As discussed above, individual engagement with interventions is fundamental to their impact. Stress management interventions therefore require substantive individual investment and an individual's readiness or resistance to such changes can determine the consequences of such plans. Identifying ways to secure engagement, commitment, and support should be a vital consideration (Leka & Cox 2008).

One approach to this might be to secure the buy-in and support of all levels of management. At the highest level, management has the authority to financially invest in stress management and to push wellbeing as a central priority. Given the level of investment required, this commitment can often be the greatest barrier to action. Middle-managers are central in translating senior management commitment into day-to-day change, and thus can also represent a strong source of resistance. They have an important role in implementing such initiatives and monitoring engagement to provide feedback, role-modelling, and leadership over any subsequent issues the interventions may raise (Jacobs et al., 2018). They can support the work to secure ongoing and meaningful improvements in daily practices and thus culture.

A second approach is to focus on securing the commitment of those whom the interventions are designed to serve. One approach to ensuring commitment and buy-in from employees is to adopt a participative approach to stress management planning (Pieper et al., 2019). Employee involvement should start with the risk assessment, treating them as subject matter experts as to what the major stressors might be, what changes might be helpful, and what success would look like. It establishes respect, demonstrates commitment from management, and encourages the individuals to hold an active voice. The latter, in of itself, might be positive for stress by fostering empowerment and control and minimising uncertainty or resistance (Jacobs et al., 2018). If the first they hear about the intervention is in an email to ask them to engage then many opportunities to maximise impact and engagement have been missed. Communication is important, and being a respected partner and co-contributor to these projects is likely to contribute to the efficacy of the interventions. The need for such work to be acknowledged in workloads is, I'm hoping, obvious, to avoid the double-burden of placing additional work upon the individuals who are currently experiencing the greatest issues.

So, What Can We Do Now?

Unfortunately, based on the literature reviewed, it's clear that there is no "go-to" intervention or action guaranteed to secure successful stress reduction or prevention. However, we should not, and cannot, fail to act on the issues surrounding workplace stress. It's important that organisations take responsibility for their role in creating safe working environments, framing stress management as an important responsibility to all parties. There are several different ways that stress can be managed, whether that be encouraging individuals to take action or to implement structural change, or focussing upon stress prevention, reduction, or management. There is no one single ticket to success in any of these streams; this would involve the combination of different elements from robust designs and evaluations, context-specific decision-making, and quality implementation. This isn't an easy ask, but this is an investment and target worth aiming for.

I encourage practitioners and HR working in stress and wellbeing to question their current practices. At what point in the process do you involve employees? Do you know where the issues lie or how stressed your workforce really are? Have you focussed resources to meet their need (with respect to primary, secondary, and tertiary interventions)? What evidence is informing your specific intervention type? How much of your actions are encouraging employees to take action and how much are focussed upon organisational changes? How do you assess "success" and who makes that judgement? You don't have to address all the recommendations described above simultaneously, but small changes to reframe the discussion in these ways might open up more opportunities for more meaningful changes to the stress – and thus wellbeing and productivity – of staff.

Opportunities for academic-industry collaborations should be embraced wherever possible. I particularly encourage academics to adopt more rigorous designs and to evaluate the quality and relevance of the existing bodies of evidence with greater scrutiny when deciding the specific type of intervention to plan. Most reviews suggest the quality of current evidence informing any given practice is weak. Throughout this chapter we have discussed different types of evidence and I encourage all future works to preregister their work (see Chapter 7 for overview and guidance) and to carefully consider the design of their work to maximise value. We can quickly improve upon the quality of most existing works by beginning to build in more nuanced assessments of both the processes and outcomes of stress management interventions and by being creative when coming up with appropriate control groups for RCT (or similar) designs. A more future-orientated priority of the field should be to synthesise these more robust evidence sources towards a more coherent body of evidence as to what works, for who, and how. Science is mostly cumulative so all efforts towards this goal represent steps in the right direction. We should get organised and begin to develop pockets of high-quality evidence, prioritising those areas with the greatest capacity for real-world positive change.

I encourage you, yes, you reader, as a fellow human, to reflect upon the themes of the chapter – responsibility and voice; what could you do to encourage/maintain a psychologically safe working climate for yourself and your colleagues? This doesn't always have to be a massive resource drain, you could support change in all manner of small ways: communicating wellbeing as a priority, encouraging and supporting structural change, providing emotional support to colleagues, and, most importantly, pushing back on aimless initiatives designed to do little more than provide management a claim of having done something.

Time to get knitting everyone – don't forget your needles!

References

Bartlett, L., Martin, A., Neil, A. L., Memish, K., Otahal, P., Kilpatrick, M., & Sanderson, K. (2019). A systematic review and meta-analysis of workplace mindfulness training randomized controlled trials. *Journal of Occupational Health Psychology, 24*(1), 108–126.

Bhui, K. S., Dinos, S., Stansfeld, S. A., & White, P. D. (2012). A synthesis of the evidence for managing stress at work: A review of the reviews reporting on anxiety, depression, and absenteeism. *Journal of Environmental and Public Health, 2012,* 515874.

Briner, R. B., & Reynolds, S. (1999). The costs, benefits, and limitations of organizational level stress interventions. *Journal of Organizational Behavior, 20*(5), 647–664.

Bunce, D., & Stephenson, K. (2000). Statistical considerations in the interpretation of research on occupational stress management interventions. *Work & Stress, 14*(3), 197–212.

Cox, T., Karanika, M., Griffiths, A., & Houdmont, J. (2007). Evaluating organizational-level work stress interventions: Beyond traditional methods. *Work & Stress, 21*(4), 348–362.

Dalgaard, V. L., Andersen, L. P. S., Andersen, J. H., Willert, M. V., Carstensen, O., & Glasscock, D. J. (2017). Work-focused cognitive behavioral intervention for psychological complaints in patients on sick leave due to work-related stress: Results from a randomized controlled trial. *Journal of Negative Results in Biomedicine, 16*(1), 13.

DeFrank, R. S., & Cooper, C. L. (1987). Worksite stress management interventions: Their effectiveness and conceptualisation. *Journal of Managerial Psychology, 2*(1), 4–10.

Demerouti, E., Bakker, A. B., Vardakou, I., & Kantas, A. (2003). The convergent validity of two burnout instruments: A multitrait-multimethod analysis. *European Journal of Psychological Assessment, 19*(1), 12–23.

Eby, L. T., Allen, T. D., Conley, K. M., Williamson, R. L., Henderson, T. G., & Mancini, V. S. (2019). Mindfulness-based training interventions for employees: A qualitative review of the literature. *Human Resource Management Review, 29*(2), 156–178.

Henrich, J., Heine, S. J., & Norenzayan, A. (2010). The weirdest people in the world? *Behavioral and Brain Sciences, 33*(2–3), 61–83.

Holladay, C. L., Knight, J. L., Paige, D. L., & Quiñones, M. A. (2003). The influence of framing on attitudes toward diversity training. *Human Resource Development Quarterly, 14*(3), 245–263.

Holman, D., Johnson, S., & O'Connor, E. (2018). Stress management interventions: Improving subjective psychological well-being in the workplace. In E. Diener, S. Oishi, & L. Tay (Eds.), *Handbook of well-being*. Salt Lake City, UT: DEF Publishers.

Ivancevich, J. M., Matteson, M. T., Freedman, S. M., & Phillips, J. S. (1990). Worksite stress management interventions. *American Psychologist, 45*(2), 252–261.

Jacobs, S., Johnson, S., & Hassell, K. (2018). Managing workplace stress in community pharmacy organisations: Lessons from a review of the wider stress management and prevention literature. *International Journal of Pharmacy Practice, 26*(1), 28–38.

Janssen, M., Heerkens, Y., Kuijer, W., Van Der Heijden, B., & Engels, J. (2018). Effects of Mindfulness-Based Stress Reduction on employees' mental health: A systematic review. *PLoS One, 13*(1), e0191332.

Leka, S., & Cox, T. (2008). Best practice in work-related stress management interventions. Accessible: www.prima-ef.org/uploads/1/1/0/2/11022736/09_english.pdf.

Lesener, T., Gusy, B., & Wolter, C. (2018). The job demands-resources model: A meta-analytic review of longitudinal studies. *Work & Stress,* 1–28. https://doi.org/10.1080/02678373.2018.1529065

Nabe-Nielsen, K., Persson, R., Nielsen, K., Olsen, O., Carneiro, I.G., Garde, A.H. (2015). Perspectives on Randomization and Readiness for Change in a Workplace Intervention Study. In: Karanika-Murray, M., Biron, C. (eds) *Derailed Organizational Interventions for Stress and Well-Being*. Springer, Dordrecht. Accessible: https://doi.org/10.1007/978-94-017-9867-9_23

Nielsen, K., & Abildgaard, J. S. (2013). Organizational interventions: A research-based framework for the evaluation of both process and effects. *Work & Stress, 27*(3), 278–297.

O'Shea, D., O'Connell, B. H., & Gallagher, S. (2016). Randomised controlled trials in WOHP interventions: A review and guidelines for use. *Applied Psychology, 65*(2), 190–222.

Pieper, C., Schröer, S., & Eilerts, A-L. (2019). Evidence of workplace interventions: A systematic review of systematic reviews. *International Journal of Environmental Research and Public Health, 16*(19), 3553.

Richardson, K. M., & Rothstein, H. R. (2008). Effects of occupational stress management intervention programs: A meta-analysis. *Journal of Occupational Health Psychology, 13*(1), 69–93.

Riva, S., & Chinyio, E. (2018). Stress factors and stress management interventions: The heuristic of "bottom up" an update from a systematic review. *Occupational Health Science, 2*(2), 127–155.

Ruotsalainen, J. H., Verbeek, J. H., Mariné, A., & Consol, S. (2015). Preventing occupational stress in healthcare workers (Review) summary of findings for the main comparison. *Cochrane Database of Systematic Reviews, 4,* CD002892. https://doi.org/10.1002/14651858.CD002892.pub5

Schaufeli, W. B., & Bakker, A. B. (2004). Job demands, job resources, and their relationship with burnout and engagement: A multi-sample study. *Journal of Organizational Behavior, 25*(3), 293–315.

Schaufeli, W. B., & Taris, T. W. (2014). A critical review of the job demands-resources model: Implications for improving work and health. In G. F. Bauer, & O. Hämmig (Eds.), *Bridging occupational, organizational and public health: A transdisciplinary approach* (pp. 43–68). Springer Science + Business Media. Accessible: https://doi.org/10.1007/978-94-007-5640-3_4

Semmer, N. K. (2003). Job stress interventions and organization of work. In J. C. Quick, & L. E. Tetrick (Eds.), *Handbook of occupational health psychology* (pp. 325–353). American Psychological Association. Accessible: https://doi.org/10.1037/10474-016

Sidle, S. D. (2008). Workplace stress management interventions: What works best? *Academy of Management Perspectives, 22*(3), 111–112.

Tetrick, L. E., & Winslow, C. J. (2015). Workplace stress management interventions and health promotion. *Annual Review of Organizational Psychology and Organizational Behaviour, 2*(1), 583–603.

Van der Klink, J. J., Blonk, R. W., Schene, A. H., & Van Dijk, F. J. (2001). The benefits of interventions for work-related stress. *American Journal of Public Health, 91*(2), 270–276.

Organisational Change Initiatives **6**

We all need to change. We could be healthier, happier, more efficient, greener, fairer, and more compassionate, but changing is often long, slow, and difficult. Trying to get a group of individuals within an organisation to change, particularly when challenging well-entrenched processes and practices, is especially difficult. In every workplace, I have been told: "oh the system is a bit clunky, and we've talked about getting it sorted, but it's actually manageable once you go through it all a few times". I then waste hours of precious time attempting to execute a simple task. It's hardly then surprising that the trope of organisational change is that of extremely high rates of failure. Pick up any Organisational Development or HR magazine and you're likely to read about how difficult and unlikely it is that you can effectively drive change. There are many individuals, groups, and organisations who are happy to bring expertise which might increase the likelihood for a cost, but are they especially useful?

First up, we should acknowledge the inherent need to change, and potential value for an organisation to do so. We must. It's just not an option. Just as climate change threatens to destroy the world as we know it unless we act, organisations need to be regularly changing to survive (Branson, 2008). This all comes at a cost. There's the obvious direct process costs and also the opportunity costs of pursuing one direction rather than another (Jacobs et al., 2013; Mellert et al., 2015). Change also has a human cost: Castillo et al., 2018; Helpap & Bekmeier-Feuerhahn, 2016). It causes a wide array of emotions, some of which can help drive the change and maximise the opportunities to do things differently (Tsaousis & Vakola, 2018) and some of which feed self-perceptions of inadequacy and insecurity, compromising mental health and driving resistance to change (Harvey et al., 2017). Representing costly work of primary

DOI: 10.4324/9781003035794-6

importance to maintaining profitability, it is unsurprising to see a wide number of experts, consultants, organisations, services, products, and indeed academic literature, focussed on the topic. So, do any of these things help stack the odds of success in our favour?

Can Change Be Successful?

The bar starts low. Every estimate commonly disseminated seems to suggest that the vast majority of change initiatives fail to secure their intended outcomes (Balogun & Hailey, 2008). Industry surveys over the last three decades have consistently reported low success. For example, an industry survey in 1992 claimed only 37% of change initiatives from across 300 electronic companies were successful in resolving quality deficits by 10%. Subsequent survey estimates have ranged from 10% to 30% (Beer & Nohria, 2000; Raps, 2004). Contrary to my initial expectations, academic research estimates have converged on similar estimates (19%: Smith, 2003 and 25%: Mourier & Smith, 2001). A review by Smith (2002) reported a general 33% success rate, but stated that this changes dramatically according to who measures the change and the type of change attempted. Success was much more likely when restructuring and downsizing (46%) than culture change (19%). Unsurprisingly, success was also more likely when captured by the leaders or senior organisational representatives than when rated by those working at lower levels of the organisation. Clearly, there might be more going on than is represented by a simple yet worrying percentage.

A single estimate of change success is fruitless beyond highlighting a broad theme of difficulty (Hughes, 2011). We know that the effectiveness of any given change is affected by several factors, including the design and approach of the change and the ways we chose to evaluate them. As has been the theme of this book, we should also question the quality of evidence informing such estimates. Unsurprisingly, the quality of work is low (Burnes, 2011). Hughes (2011) discusses the origin of the commonly cited 70% failure figure, and how despite the lack of any rigorous evidence, this has been proliferated across industry communications (clearly motivated by financial initiatives to support change), but also academic circles (and no-one knows why!). Whilst some estimates are based upon no data at all, estimates are most commonly based upon personal and superficial analyses (Guimaraes & Armstrong, 1998) and subsequently represent questionable evidence (Burnes, 2011).

We can also question the question – what percentage of change initiatives fail or succeed? The question makes a number of assumptions (Hassard, 1995). First, it assumes the change has one outcome that has been pre-specified, clearly articulated, and is capable of being measured objectively. It shouldn't matter who makes the final judgement as they would always come to the same outcome – success or failure. That's not to say that change initiatives can't have an array of outcomes, just that there is one central objective driver. Second, it assumes that the reasons for success or failure can be controlled such that we can make a clear statement of the impact of change. If the change wasn't the driver of the outcome, then it can't be deemed a success or failure. We must be able to provide an objective causal claim that different outcomes were experienced specifically because of that action. Finally, it implies that the difference between failure and success is meaningful, and binary/dichotomous – there is a failure or success, right or wrong, 0 or 1, with no middle grounding. For example, it would mean that an improvement of 9% against a target of 10% would make the change initiative a failure. Might still save the company millions in stress days, productivity, speed of processing, motivation, opportunity identification, etc., but still a failure because it didn't hit the benchmark.

So perhaps it's not sensible to even try to calculate success rates. Given the complexity, it's likely to be more misleading than anything, and really gives us little more than a broad guide for our expectations. Work is messy, change is messy, and perhaps we need to better acknowledge the chaos of change through different approaches and perspectives? (Cao & McHugh, 2005; Pettigrew et al., 2001; Sturdy & Grey, 2003). What is clear however, is that attempts to make changes with an organisation can have a multitude of effects and there is a role for understanding what factors may contribute to such outcomes to better our understanding and practice (Burnes, 2011).

The Evidence

Change encapsulates a lot of different actions, so we must first clarify our focus in order to differentiate the evidence for different actions. Change is described as "the process of continually renewing an organization's direction, structure, and capabilities to serve the ever-changing needs of external and internal customers" (Moran & Brightman, 2001, p. 111). Change can take the form of small incremental adjustments, like process and product refinements, or can represent grand-scale ongoing developments, like mergers and takeovers. Change can be a purposeful, planned activity, or it can emerge from other activities within and outside of the organisation (Al-Haddad & Kotnour, 2015; Todnem By, 2005). There are quite a few calls to introduce taxonomies or frameworks to differentiate these different types of approaches, but there's often very little agreement on the labels for different types of change and little evidence to support meaningful differentiation (Todnem By, 2005). Here, our friend jingle-jangle returns again. Is this change initiative the same as another because they are both termed "transformational" change (jingle fallacy)? Are continuous and incremental change types different because they are labelled as such (jangle fallacy)? As such, change becomes hard to categorise or code, because change is ongoing and particularly because the nature and type of change in the same initiative can fluctuate over time (Van de Ven & Sun, 2011).

Similar concerns have been raised over the lack of clarity in outcomes and change methods adopted (Al-Haddad & Kotnour, 2015). The majority of change models share highly similar content and provide few new insights capable of driving improved practice (Bamford & Forrester, 2003; Rosenbaum et al., 2018). As a whole, there is little shared language or consensus to resolve such inconsistencies across definitions, models, and approaches (Burnes, 2011; Weick & Quinn, 1999). The academic field of organisational change is doing little to provide a coherent and convincing body of evidence upon which practice decisions can be made (Burnes, 2004; Todnem By, 2005).

So, what do we know? Mosadeghrad and Ansarian (2014) ran a systematic literature review to identify common barriers to organisational change success. Looking at work published between 1980 and 2011 they reported only 56 empirical papers capable of providing insight. The central findings of the review were a list of 55 barriers to change, themed as strategic (e.g. poor management), procedural (e.g. inappropriate methods of implementation), human resources (e.g. lack of employee involvement), contextual (e.g. employee trust in senior management), and structural barriers (e.g. lack of financial support). It turns out that the a) model or tool of change, b) implementation, and c) environment in which its initiated can all contribute to the outcomes of change. Hardly a surprise. If only we knew all these factors that influenced results, we could use it as a checklist, right? Trust in manager, check. Finances, check. Boom! Guaranteed outcome. Unfortunately, we don't know what works, where, and why.

One way around this is referred to as the contingency approach. This has been applied to a number of fields and the basic principle is that there is no one rule to win every game. Structural, situational, contextual factors drive what the best decision would be. This was originally framed within management terms – that managers need to act differently depending upon their relationship with each employee to maximise outcomes. For some individuals they need to invest in relationship-building, whereas for others they need to prioritise task-orientated developments. This idea has subsequently infiltrated and become dominant within the organisational change literature (Burnes & Jackson, 2011; Dunphy & Stace, 1993; Jacobs et al., 2013; Jansson, 2013; Sturdy & Grey, 2003; Todnem By, 2005; Van de Ven & Sun, 2011). Of course, this makes sense – there's no blueprint for success, so consider a number of factors to influence your approach. Such a model can help identify broad trends, when some decisions on change work better in certain circumstances in others. For example, some change initiatives are going to be more preferable within a merger than a takeover. However, this model relies upon a lot of information to work out what works best. For example, if we take just two factors – whether the market is crashing or booming, and whether the change is planned or naturally occurs. We might imagine that the four scenarios possible all might require different strategies to manage optimally.

Now let's acknowledge that it's not possible to categorise things so simplistically, the market can be in various states of change, and there are multiple different ways in which we could differentiate change. If we can process the larger range of potential scenarios, then we can begin to acknowledge that there are a vast number of factors to consider beyond these two. In principle, if we had data on all these possible decision points, we could effectively map out how effective different actions are in different scenarios. It would be a perfect contingency model. As should be pretty clear, we do not have that body of evidence. This model makes the assumption that we know what works, when, and how. We do not. As has been noted by the work by Mosadeghrad and Ansarian (2014), we barely know the range of factors to consider which might facilitate or prevent positive outcomes, let alone how such factors interact or what outcomes could be expected in any given combination. What have researchers been doing this whole time to help? Are there nevertheless nuggets of insight available to extract from the sporadic literature and are they based on convincing research? Let's dive a little deeper to explore whether following evidence-based recommendations for change can help.

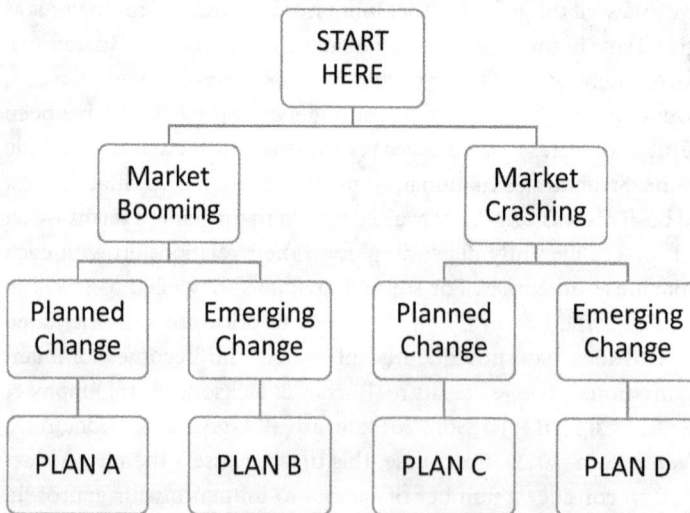

Figure 6.1 All complex things can become a flowchart eventually…

The Value of Evidence-Based Practice

The job of academics and practitioners is to effectively evaluate a variety of sources of evidence and use them to inform the practices they recommend or initiate. It can be difficult, but the key is to balance the evidence from real-world organisations' evaluating practices with the theoretical and empirical evidence collected by academics, alongside one's own experience and reflections, to extract maximum value from the opportunity. This is evidence-based practice: "conscientious, explicit and judicious use of the best available evidence ... to increase the likelihood of a favorable outcome" (Barends et al., 2014, p. 4). The best evidence-based practice is based upon various sources of really high-quality data (Kepes et al., 2014). Recommendations based upon evidence are only as good as the evidence used to inform them. Evidence-based practice informed by poor evidence is suboptimal at best and at worst can be misleading and counterproductive.

The quality of evidence available within organisational change is predominantly low and not suitable for informing practice recommendations (Raineri, 2011). This should hardly be surprising to readers, or indeed to practitioners, because there have been a number of serious critiques of the field which have spanned several decades (e.g. Macy & Izumi, 1993). Empirical work on change has tended to make assumptions which make conclusions less convincing, and analyses are typically based upon simplistic and superficial analyses rather than in-depth rigorous work (Doyle, 2002; Guimaraes & Armstrong, 1998). Such is the extent of the weaknesses of the body of evidence, Edmonstone (1995, p. 16) reported that subsequent attempts to facilitate successful change evidence "fundamental flaws". There seems to be substantive concerns of evidence quality in many different approaches to change (e.g. Buchanan et al., 2005), and little robust empirical evidence to support any given theory, approach, or practice (Guimaraes & Armstrong, 1998; Todnem By, 2005).

The majority of works are case reports or cross-sectional surveys (Kepes et al., 2014). Case studies are stories about a single change initiative, which is too often imprecise about what conclusions can generalise. Cross-sectional surveys, those which capture outcomes at a single point in time, are infrequently insightful of a process that is so fundamentally enmeshed with time. Barends et al. (2014a) conducted a systematic literature review to identify all sources of evidence on change interventions and reported that of the 563 academic studies reported, 77% used these design types. Some papers (e.g. Austin & Ciaassen, 2008; Newhouse et al., 2007) even claimed to adopt evidence-based practices but failed to rigorously evaluate their organisational change initiative. Of the other studies, only 10 reported pre-test-post-test designs – those where outcomes were assessed before and after and where participants were allocated to a change initiative or not (a control group). These types of study are so valuable because they tell us two things. Pre-post measurements tell us whether something has changed from time 1 to time 2 (and sometimes multiple other time points!). However, these studies don't tell us much about why an outcome changed, and it would be misleading to state it was necessarily the intervention. The control group is therefore a useful strategy as, if it represents a very similar or equivalent group with the only difference being the intervention, we can make more confidence claims about the likelihood of the intervention driving the pre-post change in outcomes. These study designs are super useful for drawing causal conclusions about the value of a given intervention, and so it is disappointing to see so little uptake. The popularity of poor evaluation methods is a strong driver of the quality of evidence available from which we can inform decision-making (Packard & Shih, 2014).

You might think some of this is a little dramatic, so let's just look at some of the more prominent theory-based discussions in the field. Perhaps it's just the empirical work that's poor? If you were to go on any course on change management, you will find individuals bouncing on the balls of their feet in excitement to talk about Lewin's model/theory of change. It's one of the most widely cited, discussed, taught, and applied models. They will tell you it makes change an easy three-step process. First, we "unfreeze" an old behaviour or approach. Second, we "move" or "change" our approach. Third, we "refreeze" to normalise and embed the change. It's that easy (I don't need to provide a lengthy critique of why such an oversimplification is problematic here do I?) and has become so embedded within discourse of change that it is considered by many to represent the fundamental processes within change (Cummings et al., 2016). Unfortunately, Lewin didn't really propose such a model. It's been distorted over time and doesn't represent his contribution especially well (Cummings et al., 2016). The unfreeze-change-refreeze step model has nevertheless been popular despite such misattributions and has inspired a number of developments in the field.

A similar model was proposed by Kotter (1996), this time with eight stages. Again, this has been widely praised (Appelbaum et al., 2012) and applied due to its structured nature and accessibility (e.g. King et al., 2017). Much of the initial evidence evaluating Kotter's model was collected by Kotter. We only need to go back to Chapter 2 to see why evaluating our own work might be problematic – the IKEA effect, flexibility in processes and interpretations, incentives that encourage positive findings… Unfortunately, there has been little robust evaluation since. Predominantly, this model is used after interventions have taken place to help structure discussions as to what happened and is relatively infrequently used as the guiding structure to inform strategic decision-making (Appelbaum et al. 2012).

1. Establish a sense of urgency.
2. Creating the guiding coalition.
3. Develop a vision and strategy.
4. Communicate the vision.
5. Empower action towards the vision.
6. Generate short-term improvements.
7. Consolidate improvements.
8. Anchor new approach to the culture.

There are loads of these kinds of models for structured stages of change. Indeed, any change consultancy organisation is likely to have their own, perhaps with a cool acronym, infographic, and general spiel about how it gives structure and support and makes it all easier to negotiate. Rosenbaum et al. (2018) looked at 13 academic process-based models and unfortunately found little novel insight. They came to the conclusion that they all share overlap with the original three-step model from Lewin (1947) and whilst they may add some little acknowledgement of various procedural steps to support change, they are generally very similar in scope and value.

In representing a relatively homogenous group of theories, and subsequent models and tools, where the assumptions are fundamentally the same, there has been relatively minimal diversity in techniques offered to practitioners as a result (Bamford & Forrester, 2003). These types of models are offered as a set of checkpoints through unchartered lands. Traverse through the desert dunes to the river, down into the forest, then across the hills. Unfortunately, change is infrequently a linear process where you travel from A to B. These don't do justice to the complexity of the change process in practice. There is often back and forth, deviations from plans, resistance to actions, and readjustments of priorities and targets. There are a number of published case studies which evidence the problematic simplicity of thinking of change as a set of linear steps to follow (e.g. Hackman, 2017; Pollack & Pollack, 2015). This rational approach, thinking of "neat linear prescriptions on how to best manage change" fails to acknowledge the reality that managing change is a "complex muddied political process consisting of competing histories and ongoing multiple change narratives which may vie for dominance" (Dawson, 2003, p. 37).

The two models discussed, that of Lewin and Kotter, are dominant within discussions from academics and practitioners alike, but they are also fantastic examples of how the process of change has been reduced to simplistic yet frequently contradictory guidelines for implementation (Appelbaum et al., 2012). Of course, there are alternatives. Not all theories and models of change frame it like a set of milestones to meet. However, they are infrequently accompanied with evidence and very rarely constitute robust or convincing bodies of evidence

(Bamford & Forrester, 2003; Todnem By, 2005). It therefore seems reasonable to suggest that academic theories currently provide no valid theoretical structure or support to implementing effective change (Todnem By, 2005).

The evidence to inform organisational change is poor (Packard & Shih, 2014; Stouten et al., 2018), but this isn't really any different to many other HR and management fields (e.g. Chapters 3–5; Barends et al., 2017; Kepes et al., 2014; Rousseau, 2006; Rynes et al., 2002). Academics have spent a long time creating inadequate and irrelevant theories accompanied by weak evidence, which are of little value to practitioners, and practitioners have been creating and adapting many strategies to help drive change successfully in the field but have had fewer avenues to disseminate good practices. This is called the academic–practitioner divide and is well reported in the field of organisational change (e.g. Applebaum et al., 2012; Buchanan, 1993; Saka, 2003; Stouten et al., 2018). One fundamental barrier is the lack of shared language and diversification of terms, approaches, and tools, which have done little to "translate current research into a format usable by practitioners" (Applebaum et al., 2012, p. 764). They have different mental representations of change – documents created by academics tend to emphasise theories, frameworks, and models, whereas practitioners focus upon teams, individuals, and the practical actions taken to facilitate change (Pollack, 2015). This disconnect is a lose-lose situation. Practitioners have no consensus. This means there are lots of different typologies, theories, models, and approaches, with little coherent conclusions as to which, where, and when they should be enacted. Instead, the majority have clutched on to well-meaning but simplistic theories, that are far more descriptive of change than actively inspiring action. The minority have spun in different directions attempting to provide a niche or novel strategy and end up either pursuing an approach with insufficient evidence to be convincing, or by making slight deviations towards the same faulty assumptions of the majority. Without any clear conclusions, practitioners are mostly left to their own devices in deciding their approach to action. Indeed, with no coherent evidence base, it's easy to justify any approach because their small piece of evidence, whether academic or from personal experience, is better than none. Unfortunately, that personal experience or case-study evidence is low-quality and almost certainly limited (Shaw, 2019). Such is the extent of this reliance upon past experience that Shaw (2019) accused practitioners of "plagiarising" methods and practices as an attempt to manage costs. Looking for the best practice in each specific context is costly, but given that we have established that one key does not fit all locks, this is clearly sub-optimal. Furthermore, this deviates from what we should all be attempting to do – evidence-based practice. Practitioners aren't using evidence-based practice, making decisions through conscientious, explicit, and judicious use of the best available evidence from multiple sources (Kepes et al., 2014) and I can hardly blame them – the evidence quality is poor, and both theories and empirical conclusions do not reflect convincing bases for action.

So, here we are again, doubting absolutely everything. And rightfully so. The majority of evidence in this field is based upon problematic cross-sectional or case-study designs, and has been post-hoc interpreted through simplistic and unquestioned theoretical models. Evaluations of change seem particularly poorly designed and leave us with few clear conclusions as to how to inform practice. As such, practitioners most often apply models and practices based upon their previous experiences, which were likely original drawn from the post-hoc theories and poor-quality cross-sectional and case-study evaluation studies noted. This relationship becomes tautologically justified, whereby their continued and yet unquestioned use continues into further work. Evidence-based practice is just not enough to help drive change at the moment – until we have a better quality of evidence capable of drawing causal and convincing claims on the consequences of any given action or approach, success will remain haphazardly achieved.

Moving Forward to Improve Evidence Quality

Enough doom and gloom. There is some potential good news to extract from this. Firstly, academics are getting better and better at effectively evaluating and synthesising evidence quality. There are a growing number of new tools and statistical approaches available to identify statistical errors (e.g. StatCheck (Rife et al., 2016) and GRIM (Brown & Heathers, 2017)), synthesise existing evidence transparently (e.g. the NIRO project, Topor et al., under review) and evaluate evidence according to its relevance to practice (IJzerman et al., 2020). The existing evidence base is highly questionable, but if there are any lessons to learn, we are getting better at finding and evaluating them. These sorts of initiatives give me hope that whilst the evidence quality may be poor, it is not completely redundant.

Second, the academic–practitioner divide is malleable. Academics are getting much better at disseminating results to the communities which they support. There are many who are becoming louder and louder in public spaces, predominantly through the medium of social media and other such technology-driven media. My personal favourite examples of such are the annual Royal Institution Christmas Lectures (www.rigb.org/christmas-lectures), but they are more commonly found on Twitter (say hello, @ThomasRhysEvans), Tik-Tok, and others. Some of the most useful and widely received educational content is available via YouTube and some of the most influential works in business contexts can be found on LinkedIn. In addition to becoming louder, academics are also becoming more influential in practice contexts. Part of this is due to the current university strategy to focus on knowledge exchange and "impact". Many universities have recently been changing their priorities to better acknowledge individuals for driving real-world societal change, so this dramatic change in reward/incentive structures is likely to only help cross-pollinate ideas across work boundaries and facilitate wider engagement between communities. I strongly believe that together we are stronger (see Chapter 8), so I imagine this will be instrumental in developing more practical models and theories, and more rigorous evaluation of interventions.

Third, we can improve evidence quality using understanding of research methods and practices that are currently available. We know why evidence quality is currently assessed as poor, and what we could do about it if we were sufficiently motivated. One of the greatest constraints to meaningful recommendations has been the type of study design adopted to evaluate organisational change. As cross-sectional works and case studies have been the majority, and continue to increase in number dramatically (Barends et al., 2014a), wider adoption of more robust longitudinal work is crucial if we are to better understand the various processes involved in driving change and drawing casual conclusions (Jose, 2016; Maxwell & Cole, 2007; Selig & Preacher, 2009). These sorts of designs are rare for a reason – they often require much greater investment and planning, financial incentives to collect data from individuals across multiple time points, and more complex analytical strategies. All in all, they are difficult (Pettigrew, 1990). Difficulty doesn't justify their relative absence however (Barends et al., 2014a; 2014b). Change occurs over time, and there is a clear need for studies that can present convincing causal claims for the implications of adopting one strategy over others. No number of cross-sectional studies or case studies is going to provide us that evidence, so academics should be designing high-quality longitudinal works, and collaborating where they have insufficient resources alone. We'll discuss more of this nature of work in Chapter 8.

There are alternatives, should there be too many barriers to longitudinal work. One exciting opportunity is the application of replication studies to identify clearer consensuses in findings (Barends et al., 2014b; Hamlin, 2018). Replication studies are not able to draw a clear line between robust and erroneous results (Smaldino & McElreath, 2016), but they are beneficial for providing doubt or confidence in previous bodies of evidence. This is particularly important when acknowledging the number of questionable "novel" results already published and the likelihood that many of these findings are type 1 errors, with researchers reporting an effect when there isn't one (Murayama et al., 2014; Simmons et al., 2011). There are very few research studies that constitute replication studies in the field of HR, and this is indicative of a space where findings are more likely to be extreme or falsified (Fanelli & Loannidis, 2013). Indeed, the field of organisational change management is dominated by one-off studies that have remained unchallenged (Barends et al., 2014a) yet have been widely accepted by academic and practitioner communities. Replications are generally quite rare, with 1 in 1000 papers being replicated (Makel et al., 2012) and typically report modest levels of successful replication (Nosek, 2018).

There are many reasons why replication studies are also problematic, however. For example, let's say the original study had a small sample size and large effect size. Quite common. If we were to plan a replication study, we might plan our sample recruitment based upon projections from this previous work (this is referred to as power analysis). This is good practice but would be likely to lead to a suboptimal result. The big effect size (quite possibly erroneously found) will suggest small numbers of participants are needed to replicate the effect. However, the likelihood is that the original effect size is distorted by the small sample size, and thus a much greater number of participants is actually needed to identify a much smaller effect than expected. Indeed, many replication attempts report effects half the size of the original studies (Camerer et al., 2018; Open Science Collaboration, 2015). Nevertheless, more replication and longitudinal studies, including that of randomised control trials, will be of greatest impact upon practice and should represent a central priority for researchers (Barends et al., 2014).

A final research practice of note is that of preregistration. By (publicly) disclosing key elements of your research (e.g. the design, hypotheses, analyses) before you start collecting data, you could mitigate problematic practices associated with chasing good outcomes rather than good processes. Researchers often change analysis decisions once they have the data so they report statistically significant results (p-hacking) which are more likely to be published (publication bias) (Lakens, 2019; Munafò et al., 2017). Preregistration can contribute towards issues like this, and could be particularly beneficial in the field of organisational change. For example, because of the regularity with which theories are applied to explain and structure findings in a post-hoc rather than intentional manner (Appelbaum et al., 2012), preregistration might support more meaningful theory adoption and development. Similarly, because expected outcomes cannot be changed, omitted, or distorted (e.g. outcome switching), reports might reflect more representative and nuanced assessments of "success" or "failure". More on the value of preregistration is discussed in Chapter 7.

Across all these practices, I have a further few observations. Academics operate within a system that rewards and prioritises finding new shiny results, rather than checking, evaluating, and replicating existing results (Barends et al., 2014a; Munafò et al., 2017). Practitioners too appear to be place excessive emphasis on establishing new projects rather than maintaining, developing, and rigorously evaluating existing ones. Unfortunately, this structural direction doesn't help us in establishing a clear body of evidence from which we can make decisions. A great example of this prioritisation of "new" is in the field of emotional intelligence, and in Chapter 3 I discussed how it has been poorly applied to selection and assessment domains. It too has found its way into the organisational change literature (e.g. Scott-Ladd & Chan, 2004; Vakola et al., 2004). Once again, I have substantive concerns that without a clear and consistent base of theoretical understanding and robust measurement (Evans et al., 2020; Evans & Steptoe-Warren, 2019; Hughes & Evans, 2018), the result is a lot of noise where application may even lead to counterproductive outcomes. I am not against new ideas, nor application of knowledge from one field to another, in fact, this is a core component of scientific progress. However, I do object when this is prioritised amidst a body of evidence that has been heavily criticised for its poor quality and disparate nature. Here, a more focussed and rigorous body of evidence capable of establishing consensuses and consistency is far more useful for application (Cummings, 2004). It is my hope that the business community will one day lose its fascination with buzzwords (Cluley, 2013) and instead ask "what's the quality of evidence like?"

My second observation is that if individuals start running, supporting, and valuing replication, longitudinal, and preregistered research projects, there might be some knock-on consequences for adoption of other good practices. For example, researchers or companies who share materials and data of their projects openly and without any gatekeeping could allow much more rigorous external evaluations (Klein et al., 2018) and could help share learning that practitioners and academics alike would benefit from. Imagine if we had the data from Starbucks' evaluation of the bias training it ran (Chapter 4) – data on that scale would be super valuable and could support a whole number of developments in understanding and practice through secondary analyses (Gilmore et al., 2018; Vazire, 2018). A culture shift towards transparency and rigour would have a dramatic influence on the quality of evidence created through many such pathways. For example, one might hope that the standards of publication would increase. There are many initiatives, such as the "pottery-barn rule", when journals commit to requesting and publishing preregistered replications of studies they have previously published (Srivastava, 2012). The snowballing impact of such initiatives gives me hope that evidence quality in this field will eventually improve and become a fundamental basis for informing action.

These recommendations of replications, preregistration, rejecting novelty, sharing data and materials, etc. may appear disparate, but they represent just some of the changes in practices growing in adoption following the replication crisis and associated events in 2011 (see Chapter 1). Norms are slowly changing to prioritise and reward rigour and transparency, rather than novelty and statistically significant findings. These practices have been united thus far under the title of "open science" which itself is part of a wider "open scholarship" movement that attempts to improve the rigour and accessibility of research, education, and knowledge-exchange initiatives (Tennant et al., 2020). Open scholarship practices represent a smorgasbord of behaviours and actions that are designed to improve the accessibility, transparency, and rigour of research (Vicente-Sáez & Martínez-Fuentes, 2018). Whilst I haven't labelled these practices as open scholarship directly, we've already discussed many different behaviours and practices encapsulated by this term throughout this book – replication, preregistration, open data, etc. It can also include things like open peer review (which can refer to a number of different ways to make peer review a more transparent and accountable practice; Ross-Hellauer, 2017), independent checks of analysis code to ensure the specific numerical outputs can be replicated from the same data (computational reproducibility checks), and much more. These practices cover the entirety of the research cycle and are going to be instrumental in driving research quality (Munafo et al., 2017). Research quality is so important because the value of evidence-based practice is determined by the quality of evidence available (Kepes et al., 2014). A low bar of quality has been set so such norms look likely to have immediate consequences for organisational decision-making. We need to learn from these opportunities to reflect and re-evaluate what we prioritise and what we subsequently do, and there are many low-hanging fruits to maximise the outcomes of that investment.

We'll talk more about the potential of open scholarship practices over the next few chapters. In the meantime, it would be fair to say that they provide us a viable opportunity to correct some of the concerns surrounding data quality towards more effective recommendations for change management (Packard & Shih, 2014; Todnem By, 2005). It's going to take a massive effort from individual researchers and practitioners, alongside substantive changes in organisational structures and systems to normalise and maximise their value, however, we should be reassured that our understanding of change is so good that it won't really be an issue to implement such changes… Oh, wait.

Conclusion

It's been hard to extract any useful recommendations from the literature as to how best implement organisational change. Evidence-based practice is often thought to be the desirable go-to, but it's simply not possible to draw rigorous recommendations from the generally low-quality of evidence currently available. The theories are often descriptive, simplistic, and disconnected from the messy reality of organisational life. The evidence is often from cross-sectional or case-study research, which has extremely limited value for effectively evaluating a complex and dynamic situation, and there are no clear consensuses on practices, perspectives, or even languages suitable for providing a coherent basis of evidence. We're not even very good at appreciating what success or failure might look like. If we want to make evidence-based practice recommendations that increase the likelihood of successful change, we need to dramatically improve the quality of theory, evidence, and discourse surrounding organisational change. Designing longitudinal studies with rigorous evaluation is fundamental. Open scholarship practices like sharing data and running replications may also contribute to such improvements in transparency and credibility. We're quite some way from being able to make meaningful recommendations for practice, however. In the meantime, small incremental improvements to transparency and rigour will make all the difference.

References

Al-Haddad, S., & Kotnour, T. (2015). Integrating the organizational change literature: A model for successful change. *Journal of Organizational Change Management, 28*(2), 234–262.

Allcorn, S., Stein, H. F., & Duncan, C. M. (2018). Organisational change: A longitudinal perspective. *Organisational and Social Dynamics, 18*(2), 273–296.

Appelbaum, S. H., Habashy, S., Malo, J. L., & Shafiq, H. (2012). Back to the future: Revisiting Kotter's 1996 change model. *Journal of Management Development, 31*(8), 764–782.

Austin, M. J., & Ciaassen, J. (2008). Impact of organizational change on organizational culture: Implications for introducing evidence-based practice. *Journal of Evidence-Based Social Work, 5*(1–2), 321–359.

Balogun, J., & Hailey, V. H. (2008). *Exploring strategic change*. Pearson Education.

Bamford, D. R., & Forrester, P. L. (2003). Managing planned and emergent change within an operations management environment. *International Journal of Operations & Production Management, 23*(5), 546–564.

Barends, E., Janssen, B., ten Have, W., & ten Have, S. (2014a). Effects of change interventions: What kind of evidence do we really have? *The Journal of Applied Behavioral Science, 50*(1), 5–27.

Barends, E., Janssen, B., ten Have, W., & ten Have, S. (2014b). Difficult but doable: Increasing the internal validity of organizational change management studies. *The Journal of Applied Behavioral Science, 50*(1), 50–54.

Barends, E., Rousseau, D. M., & Briner, R. B. (2014). *Evidence-based management: The basic principles*. Center for Evidence-Based Management.

Barends, E., Villanueva, J., Rousseau, D. M., Briner, R. B., Jepsen, D. M., Houghton, E., & ten Have, S. (2017). Managerial attitudes and perceived barriers regarding evidence-based practice: An international survey. *PLoS One, 12*: e0184594.

Beer, M. & Nohria, N. (2000) Cracking the code of change. *Harvard Business Review, 78*(2), 133–141.

Branson, C. M. (2008). Achieving organisational change through values alignment. *Journal of Educational Administration, 46*(3), 376–395.

Brown, N. J., & Heathers, J. A. (2017). The GRIM test: A simple technique detects numerous anomalies in the reporting of results in psychology. *Social Psychological and Personality Science, 8*(4), 363–369.

Buchanan, D., (1993). Review of 'A Strategy of Change': Concepts and Controversies in the Management of Change. *Journal of Management Studies, 30*(4), 684–686.

Buchanan, D., Fitzgerald, L., Ketley, D., Gollop, R., Jones, J. L., Lamont, S. S., ... & Whitby, E. (2005). No going back: A review of the literature on sustaining organizational change. *International Journal of Management Reviews, 7*(3), 189–205.

Burnes, B. (2004). *Managing change: A strategic approach to organisational dynamics.* Pearson Education.

Burnes, B. (2011). Introduction: Why does change fail, and what can we do about it? *Journal of Change Management, 11*(4), 445–450.

Burnes, B., & Jackson, P. (2011). Success and failure in organizational change: An exploration of the role of values. *Journal of Change Management, 11*(2), 133–162.

Camerer, C. F., Dreber, A., Holzmeister, F., Ho, T. H., Huber, J., Johannesson, M., ... & Wu, H. (2018). Evaluating the replicability of social science experiments in Nature and Science between 2010 and 2015. *Nature Human Behaviour, 2*(9), 637–644.

Cao, G., & McHugh, M. (2005). A systemic view of change management and its conceptual underpinnings. *Systemic Practice and Action Research, 18*(5), 475–490.

Castillo, C., Fernandez, V., & Sallan, J. M. (2018). The six emotional stages of organizational change. *Journal of Organizational Change Management, 31*(3), 468–493.

Chambers, C. D. (2013). Registered reports: A new publishing initiative at Cortex. *Cortex, 49*(3), 609–610.

Cluley, R. (2013). What makes a management buzzword buzz? *Organization Studies, 34*(1), 33–43.

Cummings, S., Bridgman, T., & Brown, K. G. (2016). Unfreezing change as three steps: Rethinking Kurt Lewin's legacy for change management. *Human Relations, 69*(1), 33–60.

Cummings, T. (2004). Organization development and change. In J. Boonstra (Ed.), *Dynamics of organizational change and learning* (pp. 25–43). Chichester, England: Wiley.

Dawson, P. (2003). Organisational change stories and management research: Facts or fiction. *Journal of Management & Organization, 9*(3), 37–49.

Doyle, M. (2002). From change novice to change expert: Issues of learning, development and support. *Personnel Review, 31*(4), 465–481.

Dunphy, D., & Stace, D. (1993). The strategic management of corporate change. *Human Relations, 46*(8), 905–920.

Edmonstone, J. (1995). Managing change: an emerging new consensus. *Health Manpower Management, 21*(1), 16–19.

Evans, T.R. (2020). Improving evidence quality for organisational change management through open science. *Journal of Organizational Change Management, 33*(2), 367–378.

Evans, T.R., Hughes, D.J., & Steptoe-Warren, G. (2020). A conceptual replication of emotional intelligence as a second-stratum factor of intelligence. *Emotion, 20*(3), 507–512.

Evans, T. R., & Steptoe-Warren, G. (2019). Emotional Intelligence measurement: Misunderstanding and misuse. *Assessment & Development Matters, 7*(1), 9–12.

Fanelli, D., & Ioannidis, J. P. (2013). US studies may overestimate effect sizes in softer research. *Proceedings of the National Academy of Sciences*, 201302997.

Gilmore, R. O., Kennedy, J. L., & Adolph, K. E. (2018). Practical solutions for sharing data and materials from psychological research. *Advances in Methods and Practices in Psychological Science, 1*(1), 121–130.

Guimaraes, T., & Armstrong, C. (1998). Empirically testing the impact of change management effectiveness on company performance. *European Journal of Innovation Management, 1*(2), 74–84.

Hackman, T. (2017). Leading change in action: Reorganizing an academic library department using Kotter's eight stage change model. *Library Leadership & Management, 31*(2), 1–27.

Hamlin, R. G. (2018). Organizational change and development: The case for evidence-based practice. In R. G. Hamlin, A. Ellinger, & J. Jones (Eds.), *Evidence-based initiatives for organizational change and development* (pp. 1–29). Hershey, Pennsylvania: IGI Global

Harvey, S. B., Modini, M., Joyce, S., Milligan-Saville, J. S., Tan, L., Mykletun, A., ... & Mitchell, P. B. (2017). Can work make you mentally ill? A systematic meta-review of work-related risk factors for common mental health problems. *Occupational & Environmental Medicine, 74*(4), 301–310.

Hassard, J. (1995). *Sociology and organization theory: Positivism, paradigms and postmodernity.* Cambridge; Cambridge University Press.

Helpap, S., & Bekmeier-Feuerhahn, S. (2016). Employees' emotions in change: Advancing the sensemaking approach. *Journal of Organizational Change Management, 29*(6), 903–916.

Hughes, D., & Evans, T. R. (2018). Putting 'emotional intelligences' in their place: Introducing the integrated model of affect-related individual differences. *Frontiers in Psychology, 9*, 2155.

Hughes, M. (2011). Do 70% of all organizational change initiatives really fail? *Journal of Change Management, 11*(4), 451–464.

IJzerman, H., Lewis, N. A., Przybylski, A. K., Weinstein, N., DeBruine, L., Ritchie, S. J., ... & Anvari, F. (2020). Use caution when applying behavioural science to policy. *Nature Human Behaviour, 4*(11), 1092–1094.

Jacobs, G., van Witteloostuijn, A., & Christe-Zeyse, J. (2013). A theoretical framework of organizational change. *Journal of Organizational Change Management, 26*(5), 772–792.

Jansson, N. (2013). Organizational change as practice: A critical analysis. *Journal of Organizational Change Management, 26*(6), 1003–1019.

Jose, P. E. (2016). The merits of using longitudinal mediation. *Educational Psychologist, 51*(3–4), 331–341.

Kerr, N. L. (1998). HARKing: Hypothesizing after the results are known. *Personality and Social Psychology Review, 2*(3), 196–217.

Kepes, S., Bennett, A. A., & McDaniel, M. A. (2014). Evidence-based management and the trustworthiness of our cumulative scientific knowledge: Implications for teaching, research, and practice. *Academy of Management Learning & Education, 13*(3), 446–466.

King, S., Hopkins, M., & Cornish, N. (2017). Can models of organizational change help to understand 'success' and 'failure' in community sentences? Applying Kotter's model of organizational change to an Integrated Offender Management case study. *Criminology & Criminal Justice, 18*(3), 273–290.

Klein, O., Hardwicke, T. E., Aust, F., Breuer, J., Danielsson, H., Mohr, A. H., ... & Frank, M. C. (2018). A practical guide for transparency in psychological science. *Collabra: Psychology, 4*(1), 20.

Klein, R. A., Vianello, M., Hasselman, F., Adams, B. G., Adams, R. B., Jr., Alper, S., ... Nosek, B. A. (2018). Many Labs 2: Investigating variation in replicability across sample and setting. *Advances in Methods and Practices in Psychological Science, 1*(4), 443–490.

Kotter, J.P. (1996). *Leading change.* Boston, MA: Harvard Business School Press.

Lakens, D. (2019). The value of preregistration for psychological science: A conceptual analysis. *Japanese Psychological Review, 62*(3), 221–230.

Lewin, K. (1947). Frontiers in group dynamics: Concept, method and reality in social science; social equilibria and social change. *Human Relations, 1*(1), 5–41.

Macy, B. A., & Izumi, H. (1993). Organizational change, design, and work innovation: A meta-analysis of 131 North American field studies – 1961–1991. In R. W. Woodman, & W. A. Pasmore (Eds.), *Research in organizational change and development* (Vol. 7, pp. 235–313). Greenwich, CT: JAI Press.

Makel, M. C., Plucker, J. A., & Hegarty, B. (2012). Replications in psychology research: How often do they really occur? *Perspectives on Psychological Science, 7*(6), 537–542.

Maxwell, S. E., & Cole, D. A. (2007). Bias in cross-sectional analyses of longitudinal mediation. *Psychological Methods, 12*(1), 23–44.

Mellert, L. D., Scherbaum, C., Oliveira, J., & Wilke, B. (2015). Examining the relationship between organizational change and financial loss. *Journal of Organizational Change Management, 28*(1), 59–71.

Moran, J. W., & Brightman, B. K. (2001). Leading organizational change. *Career Development International, 6*(2), 111–119.

Mosadeghrad, A. M., & Ansarian, M. (2014). Why do organisational change programmes fail? *International Journal of Strategic Change Management, 5*(3), 189–218.

Mourier, P., & Smith, M. (2001). *Conquering organisational change.* USA: CEP Press.

Munafò, M. R., Nosek, B. A., Bishop, D. V., Button, K. S., Chambers, C. D., Du Sert, N. P., ... & Ioannidis, J. P. (2017). A manifesto for reproducible science. *Nature Human Behaviour, 1*(1), 0021.

Murayama, K., Pekrun, R., & Fiedler, K. (2014). Research practices that can prevent an inflation of false-positive rates. *Personality and Social Psychology Review, 18*(2), 107–118.

Newhouse, R. P., Dearholt, S., Poe, S., Pugh, L. C., & White, K. M. (2007). Organizational change strategies for evidence-based practice. *Journal of Nursing Administration, 37*(12), 552–557.

Nosek, B. A. (2018). Twitter communication. Accessible: https://twitter.com/BrianNosek/status/1064549892322979840

Nosek, B. A., Spies, J. R., & Motyl, M. (2012). Scientific utopia: II. Restructuring incentives and practices to promote truth over publishability. *Perspectives on Psychological Science, 7*(6), 615–631.

Open Science Collaboration. (2015). Estimating the reproducibility of psychological science. *Science, 349*(6251).

Packard, T., & Shih, A. (2014). Organizational change tactics: The evidence base in the literature. *Journal of Evidence-based Social Work, 11*(5), 498–510.

Pettigrew, A. M. (1990). Longitudinal field research on change: Theory and practice. *Organization Science, 1*(3), 267–292.

Pettigrew, A. M., Woodman, R. W., & Cameron, K. S. (2001). Studying organizational change and development: Challenges for future research. *Academy of management journal*, 44(4), 697–713.

Pollack, J. B. (2015). Understanding the divide between the theory and practice of organisational change. *Organisational Project Management*, 2(1), 35–52.

Pollack, J., & Pollack, R. (2015). Using Kotter's eight stage process to manage an organisational change program: Presentation and practice. *Systemic Practice and Action Research*, 28(1), 51–66.

Raineri, A. B. (2011). Change management practices: Impact on perceived change results. *Journal of Business Research*, 64(3), 266–272.

Raps, A. (2004). Implementing strategy. *Strategic Finance*, 85, 48–53.

Rife, S. C., Nuijten, M. B., & Epskamp, S. (2016). StatCheck: Extract statistics from articles and recompute p-values [web application]. Retrieved from: http://statcheck.io.

Rosenbaum, D., More, E., & Steane, P. (2018). Planned organisational change management: Forward to the past? An exploratory literature review. *Journal of Organizational Change Management*, 31(2), 286–303

Ross-Hellauer T. (2017). What is open peer review? A systematic review [version 2; peer review: 4 approved]. *F1000Research*, 6, 588

Rousseau, D. M. (2006). Is there such a thing as evidence-based management? *Academy of Management Review*, 31, 256–269.

Rynes, S.L., Colbert, A.E., & Brown, K.G. (2002). HR professionals' beliefs about effective human resource practices: correspondence between research and practice. *Human Resource Management*, 41(2), 149–174.

Saka, A. (2003). Internal change agents' view of the management of change problem. *Journal of Organizational Change Management*, 16(5), 480–496.

Schaffer, R. H., & Thomson, H. A. (1992). Successful change programs begin with results. *Harvard Business Review*, 70(1), 80–89.

Scott-Ladd, B., & Chan, C. C. (2004). Emotional intelligence and participation in decision-making: Strategies for promoting organizational learning and change. *Strategic Change*, 13(2), 95–105.

Selig, J. P., & Preacher, K. J. (2009). Mediation models for longitudinal data in developmental research. *Research in Human Development*, 6(2–3), 144–164.

Shaw, D. (2019). Partners and plagiarisers: Dualities in consultants' influence on organisational change projects. *Journal of Organizational Change Management*, 32(1), 51–66.

Simmons, J. P., Nelson, L. D., & Simonsohn, U. (2011). False-positive psychology: Undisclosed flexibility in data collection and analysis allows presenting anything as significant. *Psychological Science*, 22(11), 1359–1366.

Smaldino, P. E., & McElreath, R. (2016). The natural selection of bad science. *Royal Society Open Science*, 3(9), 160384.

Smith, M. E. (2002). Success rates for different types of organizational change. *Performance Improvement*, 41(1), 26–33.

Smith, M. E. (2003). Changing an organisation's culture: Correlates of success and failure. *Leadership & Organization Development Journal*, 24(5), 249–261.

Srivastava, S. (2012, September 27). The hardest science: A Pottery Barn rule for scientific journals [Web log post]. Accessible: https://hardsci.wordpress.com/2012/09/27/a-pottery-barn-rule-for-scientific-journals/

Stouten, J., Rousseau, D. M., & De Cremer, D. (2018). Successful organizational change: Integrating the management practice and scholarly literatures. *Academy of Management Annals, 12*(2), 752–788.

Sturdy, A., & Grey, C. (2003). Beneath and beyond organizational change management: Exploring alternatives. *Organization, 10*(4), 651–662.

Tennant, J. P., Agrawal, R., Baždarić, K., Brassard, D., Crick, T., Dunleavy, D. J., ... & Yarkoni, T. (2020). A tale of two 'opens': Intersections between Free and Open Source Software and Open Scholarship. Accessible: https://doi.org/10.31235/osf.io/2kxq8

Thorndike, E. L. (1904). *An introduction to the theory of mental and social measurements.* New York: The Science Press.

Todnem By, R. (2005). Organisational change management: A critical review. *Journal of Change Management, 5*(4), 369–380.

Topor, M., Pickering, J. S., Mendes, A. B., Bishop, D. V. M., Büttner, F., Mahmoud, M. E., Evans, T. R., Henderson, E. L., Kalandadze, T., Nitschke, F. T., Staaks, J. P. C., van der Akker, O. R., Yeung, S. K., Zaneva, M., Lam, A., Madan, C. R., Moreau, D., O'Mahony, A., Parker, A. J., Riegelman, A., Testerman, A., Westwood, S. J. (under review). *An integrative framework for planning and conducting Non-Intervention, Reproducible, and Open Systematic Reviews (NIRO-SR).* Meta Psychology.

Tsaousis, I., & Vakola, M. (2018). Measuring change recipients' reactions: The development and psychometric evaluation of the CRRE scale. In M. Vakola, & P. Petro (Eds.), *Organizational Change* (pp. 114–127). Routledge.

Vakola, M., Tsaousis, I., & Nikolaou, I. (2004). The role of emotional intelligence and personality variables on attitudes toward organisational change. *Journal of Managerial Psychology, 19*(2), 88–110.

Van de Ven, A. H., & Sun, K. (2011). Breakdowns in implementing models of organization change. *Academy of Management Perspectives, 25*(3), 58–74.

van't Veer, A. E., & Giner-Sorolla, R. (2016). Pre-registration in social psychology: A discussion and suggested template. *Journal of Experimental Social Psychology, 67*, 2–12.

Vazire, S. (2018). Implications of the credibility revolution for productivity, creativity, and progress. *Perspectives on Psychological Science, 13*(4), 411–417.

Vicente-Sáez, R., & Martínez-Fuentes, C. (2018). Open Science now: A systematic literature review for an integrated definition. *Journal of Business Research, 88*, 428–436.

Wagenmakers, E. J., Wetzels, R., Borsboom, D., van der Maas, H. L., & Kievit, R. A. (2012). An agenda for purely confirmatory research. *Perspectives on Psychological Science, 7*(6), 632–638.

Weick, K. E., & Quinn, R. E. (1999). Organizational change and development. *Annual Review of Psychology, 50*(1), 361–386.

Preregistration in Organisations

7

Evidence-based practice is only as good as the quality of evidence being considered. It's hopefully become clear that many current HR practices endorsed as best practice are lacking in robust academic evidence to support. You would be forgiven if you got to this chapter with no hope left about being able to engage in HR in an evidence-informed way. This was how I was originally going to end this book.

Time's up.
Down tools.
Stop.

But I don't think that is entirely fair. Evidence quality can vary dramatically between topics, and we have only covered a few, some very specific and some broad. HR have many functions and so we shouldn't be too quick to draw such grand conclusions. But it would also be unfair to stop the story there. Science as a practice is currently undergoing a revolution and I want to share some of this with you too. If the quality of evidence becomes better, then so too will the expected outcomes from evidence-based practice. Maybe there is hope.

Changes in research norms came rapidly following a number of groups who decided to take a meta-approach to evidence, as we have done in this book, by looking at whether previous findings replicate. The question was, if we used the same (or similar) methods, could we recreate findings reported in other papers? In physics or biology this seems more obvious. For example, if we lick a piece of bread and pop it in a sealed bag for two weeks, would it grow mould? We could test this multiple times with different conditions – keeping it cold outside

DOI: 10.4324/9781003035794-7

or warm inside, different lickers, different types of bread. If mould was consistently observed, then we would call this a robust effect and it would give us greater confidence that this is a "true" finding. If we found mould inconsistently, we would learn more about what specific conditions contribute to mould development. The same occurred in psychology, mostly outside the practice of bread-licking or mould-measuring though.

Replications can come in various shapes and sizes, so let me illustrate this with an example. Let's say I asked lots of my students to participate and I was interested in whether facial indicators of power are correlated with business performance. They came into my lab (I don't yet have one, but my birthday is coming up soon...) and I asked them all to rate photos of Fortune 500 CEOs on how powerful, and how good a manager they were, just based upon looks. I then average the score for each CEO and look at the relationship to the companies' profits as measured in pounds. A fairly simple study and this work does indeed exist – it was a paper originally published by Rule and Ambady in 2008.

So, this facial rating study was one of 100 studies that were chosen for replication as part of the psychology Reproducibility Project led by Brian Nosek and the Open Science Framework team. This study could be replicated in several ways. For the purposes of illustrating the process, we'll discuss replication as either direct or conceptual, but it's normally a continuum based upon the extent of similarity to the previous work (Hüffmeier et al., 2016). A conceptual replication is where we might change the method or analysis to see whether the effect is consistent. We could assess power in a different way. We could assess different types of leaders (maybe political or sports coaches). We could assess performance through income, profits, market share growth, etc. We could look at different facial factors. A direct replication would be using the exact same method and analysing the data in the exact same way. So, three researchers in Virginia, USA, did run a direct replication of this project and found that the effect was no longer statistically significant, although they still reported a positive relationship similar to the original findings (Eggleston et al., 2015). How might we evaluate this? A success in replicating the effect size or a failure to replicate a statistically significant result?

Let's have a look at the bigger picture. The Reproducibility Project (Open Science Collaboration, 2015) was one of the largest replication efforts to date and in general the conclusion of the whole project errs on the side of low replicability. Of the 100 studies in psychology tested, they found effects reported were, on average, half the size of those originally reported. Furthermore, only 36 reported statistically significant results, compared to 97 of the 100 original studies.

There have been several similar replication projects and the conclusions are fairly convergent – replication rates are relatively low. There are lots of issues in the research cycle, as highlighted in Chapter 1, and the consequence is that research is perhaps not as objective and conclusive as commonly perceived. This body of replication work has done much to introduce scepticism towards the quality of evidence academia commonly produces (Anvari & Lakens, 2018). Whilst this might be considered much needed given the state of evidence, and I would encourage healthy scepticism in all contexts, public trust in research could be compromised and hard to recover (Wingen et al., 2020), and this might be problematic for adherence to science-based recommendations, e.g. public health campaigns. I remain positive and hopeful despite low replicability, however. The Reproducibility Project and others have driven a much wider agenda change. These projects have placed robust research practices in the spotlight and popped them right on to the pedestal. In particular, these works have driven much wider knowledge and uptake of the open scholarship movement as a positive force for change.

Open scholarship, also termed open science or open research, is a movement to make every aspect of the research cycle we discussed in the first chapter more rigorous, transparent, and accessible. From my experience, it's (unfortunately) less driven by the big publishing giants and funders who might be interested in higher-quality outputs, but more so by academics, especially early career academics, interested in ensuring that their work is as robust and impactful as is possible, with engagement beyond the pages of the dusty journals.

Whilst academics are not in agreement about the exact definition of open scholarship (although we're getting there, e.g. Parsons et al., 2022), acknowledging that it's quite a morally- and value-loaded term (think: open in what way? do we mean free as in free speech or free beer? Tennant et al., 2020); in practice, open scholarship is simply a number of practices that can take place at various points throughout the research process. A delightful buffet (Bergmann, 2018) of opportunities to improve research transparency and engagement. Key aspects of openness include access, data, evaluation, policy, and tools (Pontika et al., 2015) and can result in open research workflows, open-access publications, open software, and educational resources (Vicente-Sáez & Martínez-Fuentes, 2018).

Preregistration

One key open scholarship practice which has dramatically increased is preregistration. Clear from the title, the purpose here is to publicly state the design, outcomes, and analyses of a research project before you have access to the data (preferably before it exists, although you can preregister analysis of existing data). Preregistration practices have a substantive history in clinical contexts, where randomised control trials of interventions were required to be preregistered

(World Medical Association, 2013) sometimes by law (DeVito et al., 2020). They demand a high standard of evidence to ensure drugs and vaccinations are safe for public consumption, so shouldn't psychological research accept these higher standards too, especially where we attempt to generalise results to improve things for the general public?

Preregistration is often considered valuable for differentiating between the testing of expected effects (prediction/confirmatory analyses) and explanations of why things happened (postdiction/exploratory analyses; Nosek et al., 2018). In context of the research cycle discussed in Chapter 1, preregistration can be seen to have many potential functions (Rubin, 2020). For example, by stipulating that all intended outcomes are captured and reported, this prevents cherry-picking of findings. Let's imagine we conducted a training intervention, and this had a positive impact upon knowledge outcomes but not those of attitudes or behaviour. Without preregistration, we have lots of analytical flexibility, and if results don't tell us what we want, we can manipulate the data, change the analysis, or even selectively report findings to increase the perceived importance. I can champion – *this intervention is fantastic – people learn important things.* This might encourage speculation about its value for other outcomes, including the attitudes and behaviours that we assessed but didn't report. Naughty.

If this work was preregistered, I would have to declare – *this intervention is good for increasing understanding, but does not impact attitudes or behaviour.* A more balanced conclusion but definitely less "sexy" and less appealing for managers to implement, and publishers to print. Therefore, preregistration can minimise publication bias, ensuring more of the research that is conducted is transparently reported: if not through formal publications, then through preregistration records. Through this, it is hoped that syntheses of findings will better represent the evidence available and consider null (statistically "non-significant") results or inconsistent findings as valuable as those which are positive and novel. When we only publish "statistically significant" findings, we are biasing the literature such that we use resources poorly. Multiple teams will waste time evaluating the same research idea because no-one was able to publish null results. Poor-quality work won't get effectively debunked. Plus, don't get me started on novelty as the evaluation criteria we should all be working towards – no-one has tested the sexiness of frogs with different novelty hats and there is a reason why – novelty doesn't mean important or robust.

You might read this and assume that the research community are plagued by terrible people who purposely manipulate every research project for their own personal benefit, presumably meaning replication rates will always be low and evidence will always be untrustworthy. Overtly naughty researchers are not the majority and there are no clear camps between good and evil – it's a continuum and many research practices are suboptimal. There are of course

Figure 7.1 The winner of our novel research programme

some researchers who purposefully operate in this way – there are always individuals who will play the game in whatever way they can to "win" and so, of course, there are a number of high-profile examples of individuals who have manipulated results in reckless and unpredictable ways. There are two other factors to consider, however. Firstly, what do the structures reward? Academics and researchers are normally evaluated by the number of publications and prestige of journal, but journals are more likely to publish "significant" or "novel" results than those which report null findings or replications. This means there is an implicit incentive structure to encourage results of a certain kind when results are literally the *only* thing that researchers shouldn't control. Individuals working in HR are also more likely to be rewarded, promoted, etc. for facilitating work that is evaluated as having an impact compared to projects which report none (or mixed findings). Secondly, education and training can implicitly encourage some questionable practices around study design and data analysis. I completed my degrees only a few years ago and I had very little exposure to the open scholarship practices and norms that are the basis of this book. Questionable practices are often done unintentionally through good intentions but faulty reasoning due to poor learning environments, or are unknowingly committed due to naivety or incompetence (Sijtsma, 2016). Let's not always jump to assuming people are bad – research is tricky and sometimes we can make poor decisions or not know that there are better choices available.

So, how does preregistration help exactly? Let's say we did the very basic aspects of preregistration, the bare minimum to classify as a preregistration. We go to an online website with simple preregistration templates (e.g. AsPredicted. org) and complete a few simple questions. We are interested in whether our health and safety briefing impacts number of injuries reported by staff. We state that we expect number of injuries to be smaller in the 12 months post-briefing compared to the 12 months pre-briefing. Number of injuries will be measured by the number of cases reported through the injury-report portal each month. Our analysis will be fairly simple, we will use a dependent t-test to see whether the average number of reported injuries in the 12 months post-briefing is significantly higher than that of the 12 months pre-briefing, matched across months to account for seasonal variation. Believe it or not, those previous four sentences are enough to constitute preregistration. It doesn't have to be massively complicated.

Now, let's return to the research cycle we discussed in Chapter 1. What has changed now we have preregistered? Well, first, it seems quite difficult to change our minds. We preregistered our hypothesis – our expectation of what was going to happen – that injuries would be lower post-briefing. That's a great outcome. No longer can we pretend we were interested in some other effects, nor can we take back our expectation that we'd hoped for less injuries. It holds us accountable to our original direction and prevents Hypothesising After Results are Known (HARKing). For example, we can no longer turn around and say how great it was that it increased reporting of injuries – we are now better at spotting them and processing them – great! A plausible outcome from a briefing. But that's not what we were expecting so we can no longer pretend.

Furthermore, we can no longer play with the data to massage it into a different story. Having preregistered our expectations surrounding injury data, we can no longer swap this in for near-miss reporting, or for self-reported confidence in reporting injuries. A common practice within clinical practices is switching, misreporting, or failing to report outcomes (Goldacre et al., 2019). Oh no, our drug wasn't good for curing X disease … but it did seem to be useful for managing symptom Y, which was unexpected.

With the current publication and researcher training systems, where manipulation (intentional or otherwise) is taught and rewarded, we should hardly be surprised that preregistration is a valuable step forward. By telling others (often in a public space where the record cannot be altered) the design and analysis approach of your study, you can avoid unnecessary manipulation to game the system, and that will hopefully lead to a body of evidence which is more representative of the research being conducted. With a more comprehensive understanding of the evidence available, hopefully we can make more informed decisions as to how to act.

Preregistration in HR

Given the issues with transparency in applied research highlighted throughout this book, then perhaps preregistration could be of benefit to apply within HR?

I have spent a lot of time mulling over how would preregistrations could work within organisations (Evans et al., 2021). On the face of it, it could be pretty simple and wouldn't add much that wouldn't already be expected from the initiative development process itself. Every HR department could have a website page dedicated to placing preregistration plans and outcomes. I imagine it needs only a few rules to implement consistently:

- Every initiative HR intend to evaluate in any systematic way gets openly reported on the website with timestamped documents.
- The preregistration must include the minimum details needed to evidence transparency at the point of reporting. This includes basic details on the initiative itself, the expected outcomes, the expected sample, and the details on their involvement (e.g. is it compulsory training?), the way in which they will be deal with data (also known as the data management strategy), the way in which they evaluate the initiative (analysis strategy), success criteria, expected date of completion, and an opportunity to add any other comments.
- Every initiative could be updated as and when plans change with a timestamped revision or comment.
- Every initiative should have a final report detailing all actions and evaluations undertaken, explicitly noting any deviations from the preregistration, posted alongside the preregistration no more than three months following the end of the initiative.
- Every external contractor (e.g. advising academics) conducting or supporting such work is required to engage with the preregistration process and follow such guidelines.

That sounds fair right? If you want to go even further, there could be a central database like that for clinical trials (AllTrials) where any organisation can contribute. The benefit of this collation would be that the outcomes reported can be more accessible to feeding back into our collective understanding (e.g. whether diversity training initiatives tend to lead to expected outcomes), meta-data could facilitate interesting meta-research (e.g. are more diversity/ inclusivity initiatives implemented during or immediately following Black History Month than in any other time of the year?), allow opportunities for external evaluation or review, and support facilities to match external academics and practitioners with roles within the projects.

This starts to sound like quite a substantive job to manage but there are benefits to all stakeholders within the process. Primarily, it needs to benefit the company to have any hope for consistent adoption. I think there are quite a few benefits. Firstly, in publishing preregistrations, the organisation has a full, detailed and permanent record of all major initiatives attempted and evaluated. We might imagine that this resource bank in of itself may be of benefit to track progress and developments in organisational priorities. It could also represent a record capable of supporting staff training and development, looking at successes and learnt lessons. These days it seems so much organisational knowledge is only held within the minds of people, with new candidates expected to adopt this slowly through a process of osmosis. Having a transparent account of what initiatives have been conducted, how, and to what impact, could be an extremely fertile ground for facilitating training and assimilation, particularly within HR.

Preregistration can also be a powerful signal to all employees, indicating the importance they place on running such initiatives and carefully evaluating their impact. It transparently demonstrates the organisation's focus (do they care about inclusivity, environmental outcomes, staff welfare, etc.) and helps establish whether more than a token gesture has been directed towards these issues. With employee engagement and awareness of initiatives through the preregistration, it might facilitate more dialogue on the strategic direction and focus of the organisation and encourage greater involvement with such initiatives. For example, if I were concerned about the mental health of a colleague, I could take a look to see what interventions were recently conducted on this issue, and if unsatisfied I could raise the issue with my manager to see whether there could be increased support for staff mental health.

Preregistration, if completed successfully, can also reflect a public signal of organisational trustworthiness, which can help support recruitment and integration of the most promising prospective job candidates and collaborators. Prospective stakeholders can look at what has been preregistered, evaluate the conclusions drawn based upon their own judgement, and chose to engage with the organisations which best meet their values and objectives. For example, a job candidate will get a clearer sense of what goes on in the organisation (through information normally behind closed doors) which might make for a more nuanced selection experience whereby both the organisation and candidate can discuss specific organisational initiatives of interest. Furthermore, the information available can facilitate person–job fit, leading to a financial benefit by attracting applicants who are more likely to be more committed and satisfied in their role, perform at a higher level, and be less likely to want to leave (Kristof-Brown et al., 2005; Verquer et al., 2003).

Preregistration will also facilitate a public comparison of preregistered priorities with those which are disseminated in other forms, e.g. social media claims. Should they be interested in the ethical stance and transparency of the business, customers and other stakeholders will be able to see when and how organisations tackle such priorities. As ethical leadership and ethical business become a greater focus, and issues surrounding climate change make greater and greater impacts upon day-to-day business, the public accounts of action can be a useful strategy for transparently communicating the organisation's commitment to these global issues. Businesses can be held responsible for timely and rigorous evaluation of initiatives and can be held accountable publicly.

Ultimately, preregistration facilitates transparency and ensures outcomes are more representative of the actual work conducted. As such, preregistration seems likely to help prevent businesses making poor decisions through manipulated or distorted outcomes. Again, it's worth noting that this is not normally due to people being purposefully naughty, but often well-meaning naivety, especially when it comes to evaluating their own initiatives (see Chapter 2). No-one can blow smoke up bottoms pretending they have success after success, and this will hopefully lead to a more meaningful discussion on how to evaluate members of HR based upon the quality of work completed, not just the outcomes (subjectively presented). The benefit here is that any attempt to mislead through exaggerated claims can be checked and considered in detail – this minimises the extent to which results can be distorted to draw unreasonable conclusions and thus can inform suboptimal business decision-making.

Other stakeholders can also benefit (Evans et al., 2022). For example, any academics or contractors involved in the activity could be transparently acknowledged and a public record of their work can be available for all to see. Preregistered academic work is often more visible, and therefore seems likely to receive more attention, social media presence, citations, etc. Preregistration represents a powerful act of transparency to support more impactful and acknowledged work. We might expect similar engagement and awareness outcomes in the context of the organisation and industry. This would make such preregistered work more desirable, particularly as the transparency in reporting could encourage greater acknowledgement of applied work by academic tenure/promotion committees, appreciating the importance of real-world impact by placing greater value upon this evidence. A further development in academia is for some journals to offer "badges" to highlight papers that have been preregistered. It's a reward for engaging in what is considered to be a beneficial practice for minimising researcher degrees of freedom, and hopefully improve research transparency and representativeness (Kidwell et al., 2016). So, preregistration in HR could be of benefit to all those working upon the initiatives, particularly academics, and hopefully can encourage growth in academic–industry collaborations.

There is also a wider societal benefit for preregistration. Through the research and meta-research that this data could contribute to, we can help learn some wider lessons about what works and what doesn't, how processes can be improved, and how the bigger societal issues can be tackled. For example, knowing what types of training or initiative seem to capture the widest levels of engagement might facilitate more nuanced public information campaigns. Preregistration could also contribute to a wider culture change which helps to show that business can and do make mistakes, success should not be seen as an inevitability or even expectation, and it is a combination of successes and failures that can take us where we get to – a fair summary of us as humans. Perhaps we won't have to all big-up things in quite the same way, going to extremes to make modest claims, ridiculing minor mistakes to distract from wider issues, by becoming more accepting of disappointing results and placing more focus upon the detail and processes undertaken rather than a dichotomous success/failure outcome label.

Based upon the discussions presented, the preregistration of applied research looks like a valuable opportunity to improve the accuracy and transparency of initiatives. Preregistration can discourage, minimise, or prevent many of the concerns associated with the mainstream yet problematic practices discussed and looks to represent a low-cost intervention which can benefit all stakeholders (Evans et al., 2022). So, we can appreciate why an organisation's HR group might undertake preregistration – for themselves, for their colleagues, for the organisation as a whole, and for society more broadly. There are certainly some financial benefits to justify such effort, particularly if the work required is a modest addition to that which is already done (but not publicly or transparently reported or evaluated). I hope I have convinced you that this idealistic plan could be quite beneficial, so I now want to cover off some initial concerns that might be raised here.

Firstly, one of the main critiques of preregistration is that it is inflexible. What if something changes in the meantime? What if you learn a more appropriate analysis to conduct? What if you have to slightly change the initiative in some way or change how you recruit volunteers to ensure engagement levels are high? This is a predictable and justified concern surrounding preregistration, particularly in occupational contexts where uncertainty and change seem like the only constant. The joy here is that preregistration should be considered a plan, not an all-constraining prison (DeHaven, 2017). It's not designed to punish you if things change, but to provide a transparent account of what you were planning at the time of design. At any stage of the research process, you can make changes, just so long as you transparently report them and adjust conclusions to account for them. Whilst they have not been major, I am confident that there are no preregistrations I have been involved with that have been completely followed to the letter. I have always need to make deviations. They have always been justified by resources or circumstance or such, but nevertheless changes have always taken place.

Secondly, organisations encourage and reward early results. This seems like it's contrary to the careful development of the initiatives and their evaluation. I might imagine that a manager, expecting a system to be up-and-running, and instead presented with a carefully thought-out plan, might be a little disappointed. I personally would be thrilled. Your preregistration demonstrates conscientious planning and should make many future decisions much easier (so we can say the initiative met the expected targets for outcome one but not outcome two, rather than making more general claims about receiving mixed results or cherry-picking the best outcomes – can I classify these as equally successful?). Similarly, practical challenges can influence the need, study design, or data by the time it has all been carefully logged and implemented. It's worth noting that the type of preregistration we are suggesting here isn't asking for any more details than that which should be fully considered before being properly implemented anyway. For example, if I hadn't had a good think about how I might evaluate whether the initiative is successful, I probably shouldn't be running the initiative. Also, we should acknowledge that we can make changes to the preregistration as and when we need to, meaning that any changes made shouldn't be problematic as long as they have been transparently logged. It's a very modest amount of paperwork to reap quite a substantive reward.

There can also be some more practical concerns. For example, I might expect that my initiative is only useful for a few people in an organisation employing thousands – do I need to preregister this? Won't the sample size be too small to make any meaningful contributions to our understanding? Let's unpick these two arguments. Firstly, preregistration will confer the benefits of enabling a more transparent reporting of outcomes regardless of niche focus or sample size. Within academic research, we often find larger effects with smaller samples (often in error; Simmons et al., 2011), so it's definitely worth treating such initiatives with the same level of attention. Secondly, sample size is only one factor to consider when evaluating a study. As I noted in Chapter 4, some work on diversity training has been conducted with as few as seven participants. This work got past peer review and was based on a phenomenon (diversity training) that most of the working population experience. To me, that isn't good. Sample size is particularly important in context of the extent to which it represents the population it's attempting to generalise conclusions about. Let's say 15% of your workforce identify as LGBTQ+ and your intervention captures engagement from half of this group – I'd say that was probably useful evidence even if the actual numbers of individuals involved were low. Furthermore, there are a number of statistical processes that can help synthesise multiple small samples (e.g. Meta-analysis). Finally, an initiative designed for a small group of people is likely to be quite focussed and tailored, so perhaps could be more relevant, achieve greater engagement, and signpost clear investment into this group. For the employee, employer, and broader scientific perspective, preregistration seems to be of benefit regardless of the size or focus of the work tested.

Preregistration in Academia

In principle, preregistration can improve the transparency and dissemination of your work and ensure the final outcome is representative of the work conducted, and it should be fairly easy to do, even if you work with organisations (Evans et al., 2021). But is the type of preregistration discussed here enough or should we be aiming higher for academic research? It's the same with all sorts of issues that as soon as you make something a target, that ceases to be a good measure (Goodhart's Law). Change the rules and the game changes. The same can unfortunately be said for preregistration. It's quite easy to write a vague preregistration, being purposefully ambiguous to afford yourself more decision-making later down the road. Take the perceived credibility of preregistration without any restrictions on your actions. This is sometimes called "openwashing": when you communicate endorsement or adherence to such practices but don't do them properly. For example, an Excel file that accompanies a manuscript labelled "data.csv" but is simple one line of text which says the data is available on request. Cheeky! Similarly, one can always act differently to the plan by arguing why such an approach would be justified. The robustness of such a justification can be – but is not always – problematic. Sometimes we must act outside of the plan to produce the best quality evidence, but it's hard to infer intent behind the change.

Unfortunately, questionable value shouldn't even be a surprise. Clinical Trials have a much longer history of preregistration than social sciences, and the writing is on the wall. There's a brilliant paper by Cuijpers and Cristea (2016) which is a scathing review of the field, presenting guidelines for how to create evidence that therapies will be effective even when they are not. Mocking (rightfully) the field for its poor practices. For example, increasing expectations of participants that it will be successful, using multiple outcome assessments and only publishing those with significant results, using a small sample size and calling it a pilot, and not publishing non-significant results. Makes it sound easy doesn't it!

The brilliant Dr Ben Goldacre leads AllTrials, a unit looking at how trials are registered and conducted. He has contributed to provide strong evidence to effectively highlight the problems with quality and accessibility of preregistration in clinical trials (e.g. DeVito et al., 2020). As such, it probably means that being "preregistered" doesn't actually mean much. I mean, you saw how simple it was right? Would you happy to take drugs evaluated through that sort of framework? You say "no", but let's be honest – you might have... I would encourage you to read Dr Ben Goldacre's (2010) *Bad Science* if you want to dig deeper from a more clinical/medical perspective. Not especially reassuring though.

The other question to ask is whether it all matters? I mean if no-one checks it, if there's no meaningful processing of the information, if people can game it in a way which might make no public information better than something then does this achieve much? Whack a badge on it, you've tried, well done.

So let me introduce you to the new future of research. It's called Registered Reports and it's been masterminded by Professor Chris Chambers of Cardiff University. The principle here is like preregistration on jetpacks. Not only do you create an in-depth and detailed preregistration plan, preferably including all bells and whistles, including mock data and analysis code scripts, but this whole body of work gets peer-reviewed before you even collect data. It sounds incredibly intimidating, but I have been involved in a number of these, including a massive international collaboration on social perception (Jones et al. 2021) and my own slightly more modest research on humour (see Chapter 2; Evans et al., 2020) and in my view it's the most meaningful development in scientific publication this decade. It always seemed odd to me that scientists would invest *masses* of public or university funding completing various bodies of research, and the first time they are likely to get any meaningful critical feedback is when they submit a manuscript they could have massaged in any way they liked to give them the best chance of being accepted for publication, before placing it into a peer-review process without the data, and without any need to prove authenticity of data or process. Unfortunately, the peer-review process is no guarantee of quality. The literature suggests peer review has small but meaningful impacts upon quality (Carneiro et al., 2020; Klein et al., 2019), but its ability to establish consensuses on the extent to which work should be published or not is highly questionable (Kravitz et al., 2010; Pier et al., 2018). It's easier to gain agreement in outcome for the following controversial question: how should you hang toilet roll, a or b (see Figure 7.2)?

The correct answer, like this debate, should be over. Registered Reports are the future of confirmatory research and I for one, can't wait. Registered Reports are a two-part process. The authors write a proposal, prepare all materials, and often create mock data and analysis scripts too. All of this then undergoes peer review and is given Stage 1 In Principle Acceptance (IPA) following changes to feedback. This IPA is a promise to the authors that if they conduct the study they planned, the journal will publish the results regardless of the size, direction, or nature of the findings. The authors are then clear to collect the data using the approved plan, write up the results and discussion, and then these two

Figure 7.2 Is it *under* or *over?*

final sections go through peer review again to check that the plan was followed, any deviations were justified, and the conclusions drawn are appropriate to the design of the study. Even if the quality of peer review is poor (not my experience!), you have a transparent account of what was planned and implemented, and the extent to which they match. It's a step forward.

When we're thinking about the evidence used to inform our HR practices, this method would provide a much more convincing basis for action. Firstly, it represents a highly detailed and evaluated preregistration, so confers further opportunities for minimising publication bias and p-hacking. With the level of detail expected from Registered Report submissions, there is much less researcher degrees of freedom to influence analysis decisions, and the final publication is all but guaranteed if conducted appropriately, therefore all Registered Reports should accurately reflect all aspects of the research conducted. If RRs were consistently adopted and in ten years' time we did a review of all the RR literature on diversity training, we could be confident that we would be missing less unpublished work due to the findings (also known as the file-drawer effect).

Registered Reports are a powerful opportunity to minimise some of the other problematic practices within the research cycle too. Registered Reports need to include a clear recruitment plan, including a rationale and justification for the proposed sample size, and often the plans and rules informing when data collection starts and stops. This often means issues surrounding small sample size, and thus power, are foreseen and mitigated. Furthermore, whilst RRs don't ensure data quality, a data management plan is normally produced, which stipulates how data will be checked for authenticity and quality (e.g. removing participants who complete a questionnaire in an unusually quick or slow time) and allows for transparency in the process adopted.

Finally, RRs help minimise post-hoc rationalising of results. For example, in our earlier example we hypothesised that a health and safety briefing might increase the number of accidents reported. If the results suggested they actually decreased, then we might be tempted to have presented that as our expectation all along. This is called HARKing – Hypothesising After Results are Known. With RRs, hypotheses are peer-reviewed and publicly logged – no chance of trying to play that game. As a result, null findings are far more likely in RRs than normal publications (Allen & Mehler, 2019). Equally, if we do want to entertain possible reasons why the results might be contrary to expectations then that's absolutely fine. We can write these up for the discussion section of our paper, and everyone will know that these are more tentative interpretations of data that would require further testing to be confident of.

Registered Reports are still not a panacea, a cure-all, to all of academia's problems. There is no guarantee that the quality of the final work will change or improve based upon this process. I know my experience of the process would encourage that conclusion, but it is not inevitable. However, investing time into planning research, considering the minutiae, and having critical feedback examining every decision along the way is surely a valuable investment in progressing the eventual quality of the body of the evidence available to inform decision-making. It is an opportunity to question assumptions and practices, and means that the content available for us to examine is more transparent and hopefully much more reflective of the actual work being conducted. I am hopeful that one day preregistration, and certainly more nuanced versions demanding greater detail and critical engagement, will be used more to inform evidence-based practice in HR. In particular, I hope that HR will become ambassadors for preregistration and integrate it into their methods of working, reaping the benefits for improving the quality of decision-making.

My Experience of Preregistration and Registered Reports

Since being catapulted into the world of open scholarship through Twitter, I have learnt a lot more about what quality means in science. It's been a pretty painful learning experience. I started off a wide-eyed student, hopeful at the prospect of changing the world through objective *science*. I am now sitting here today writing the literary equivalent of a scowl, highlighting how science has been a misleading veneer of objectivity over a shambolic but well-meaning attempt to produce some actionable and thus useful pieces of information. Preregistration work has contributed much to my change in stance.

To return to the mouldy bread, a biologist wouldn't just add a rubber duck to the bag on a whim. They might postulate the anti-mould properties of a certain material, so justify it that way. They might argue for the role of different quantities of air in the bag. They might add salt or lemon juice to the bag to test the impact on mould growth. They wouldn't do this at random though. They wouldn't just keep throwing in different things without a justification. Unfortunately, without preregistration, this is exactly what many researchers are doing. They throw in another variable in their questionnaire to see how it interacts with the other things being measured, and then provide some post-hoc rationale if there is an interpretation of results that makes the impact look possible. If it doesn't, then they can dig around with the data to see if it's possible by making minor changes to the analysis approach, and if all else fails they just don't try to publish it. In occupational contexts, I think this most commonly manifested as adding additional outcome measures in, just in-case the intervention or training tangentially impacts them... I just don't think this is sustainable or helpful. If we don't have a transparent overview of everything that has been done, we don't know what has and is likely to work and what has and is likely to fail.

Based upon my experiences outlined in Chapter 2, I have tried to embed preregistration into my project planning, and I now publish using Registered Reports wherever possible. I also encourage my students to do this, but amongst their other priorities I infrequently make it mandatory. As I reflect upon my first research project on humour (Evans & Steptoe-Warren, 2018) I feel the analytical freedom I had wasn't a positive thing. It made out as if there was only one way to analyse the data, and only one correct answer to report. That's not at all true. I couldn't help but feel that the published examples of similar analyses on similar data produced different conclusions partially because of this flexibility. I felt incredibly privileged to be in the position where I could attempt to constructively challenge my own research and introduce greater caution and criticality to the literature. In my subsequent Registered Report replication, looking at the value and consistency of the original findings (Evans et al. 2020), I was expecting to see contradictions and had fully thought through the different options.

I have only one regret about my Registered Report – that I did not provide mock data and analysis scripts as part of my Stage 1 Submission. I, of course, detailed much of my analysis plan in the report, but I did not make explicit how my plans for analysis would translate into code. It was quite a learning curve attempting to produce this during the period of data collection, particularly as I was learning to use R (coding-based software for statistics and visualisation) as an alternative to SPSS (proprietary point-and-click software) which I used for the original research. This was a mistake in judgement, and I am grateful to some amazing collaborators for bringing me up to speed on such practices.

I have learnt from such experiences through these experiences and the quality of my work has certainly increased. In my latest work, a project I am doing as part of the SCORE replications (see www.cos.io/score), I created all the materials and mock data, I created an analysis script, and I even created the questionnaire online before I had started data collection. I am now at the point of analysis, and I simply download the data, replace "MockData.csv" with "Data.csv" in my code, and I have the results of my research completed in seconds. Literally seconds. Not even long enough to make a cup of tea. What makes this piece of work so strong is the transparency and detail of preregistration. I might have made mistakes – I am always open to that – but at least I have made every decision consciously, planned in detail, and reported in a way that can't be edited or falsified. You might not agree with what I have done, but you can see it in all its detailed glory. And because all the resources are openly accessible, you can even go back and change analysis decisions to see what impacts upon the results. I look forward to the science practices of the future where data can be re-used much more and where we can learn more from taking a meta- approach by looking at how and why we accumulate knowledge in the way we do.

Preregistration isn't going to solve all our problems. It might help with transparency but not change quality. But it can help us get to a place where we can begin to make better decisions by holding a more detailed and representative understanding of the literature available. It'll help better preserve the right of others to reach independent conclusions about our work and data (Rouder, 2017) and this is what gets me up in the morning. That and/or my two-year-old and/or five-year old.

Conclusion

There are two clear ways in which preregistration should be part of HR's future. Firstly, organisations should invest greater attention into preregistered work which may inform their decision-making. For example, if doing diversity training, I would take a look through meta-analyses to establish general consensuses, but pay particular interest in Registered Reports/preregistered works like that by Chang et al. (2019), which had a good sample size (over 3,000!) and was a realistic intervention (online training). I don't automatically put greater faith in their conclusions, but I can look in detail about what they did, how it was evaluated, and consider the extent to which the effects observed might be possible for our organisation. Secondly, HR can begin to publicly preregister its own work. Whilst this may be of benefit to the scientific community, the organisation itself is likely to be the main benefactor – it improves the quality of decisions made by facilitating more accurate evaluations, it'll collate loads of resources to train HR staff, and will be able to improve reputation by publicly discussing their priorities through their actions. The first organisation brave enough to take up this challenge can contact me, and I will happily offer consultancy for free. For me, embedding preregistration into HR is a vital opportunity to take a few positive steps forward on a path to recover from some of the issues highlighted throughout this book surrounding the quality of evidence informing practice.

Starting Preregistering

For the reasons we have discussed, and I talk more about why elsewhere (Evans et al., 2021), preregistration within HR is incredibly rare. It's all very well and good encouraging preregistration, but the better/more detailed the preregistration is, the more we have to potentially gain. The more we preregister, the better we get at it too; it's certainly a learning curve. We therefore need to invest in good resources and education to facilitate preregistration. In an effort to bridge the gap, I want to highlight a few resources and examples of high-quality preregistration to help you get started.

Resources of Interest

Discussion on application of preregistration in applied contexts: Evans, T. R., Branney, P., Clements, A., & Hatton, E. (2021). Improving evidence-based practice through preregistration of applied research: Barriers and recommendations. *Accountability in Research*, 1–21. http://dx.doi.org/10.1080/08989621.2021.1969233

An accessible and updated list of preregistration templates: https://osf.io/zab38/wiki/home/?view

Comprehensive preregistration template: http://dx.doi.org/10.23668/psycharchives.4584

Simple public preregistration: aspredicted.org

Examples of preregistration: https://osf.io/e6auq/wiki/Example%20Preregistrations/

Registered Reports

Registered Report template: https://osf.io/93znh/

List of Registered Reports: www.zotero.org/groups/479248/osf/collections/KEJP68G9/items/RP5KTAGD/collection

My first Registered Report as lead (Evans et al., 2020): https://osf.io/uqg8c/ (Stage 1) -> https://osf.io/385sz/ (Stage 2)

Large-scale collaborative Registered Report (Jones et al., 2021): https://doi.
org/10.6084/m9.figshare.7611443.v1 (Stage 1) -> https://psyarxiv.com/
n26dy/ (Stage 2)

Further Introductory Reading on Open Scholarship Practices

Allen, C., & Mehler, D. M. (2019). Open science challenges, benefits and tips in early career
and beyond. *PLoS Biology, 17*(5), e3000246.
Crüwell, S., van Doorn, J., Etz, A., Makel, M. C., Moshontz, H., Niebaum, J. C., ... & Schulte-
Mecklenbeck, M. (2019). Seven easy steps to open science. *Zeitschrift für Psychologie, 227*,
237–248.
Kathawalla, U. K., Silverstein, P., & Syed, M. (2021). Easing into open science: A guide for
graduate students and their advisors. *Collabra: Psychology, 7*(1).
Klein, O., Hardwicke, T. E., Aust, F., Breuer, J., Danielsson, H., Mohr, A. H., ... & Vazire, S.
(2018). A practical guide for transparency in psychological science. *Collabra: Psychology, 4*(1).
Munafò, M. R., Nosek, B. A., Bishop, D. V., Button, K. S., Chambers, C. D., Du Sert, N. P., ...
& Ioannidis, J. P. (2017). A manifesto for reproducible science. *Nature Human Behaviour,
1*(1), 1–9.
Parsons, S., Azevedo, F., Elsherif, M.M., Guay, S., Shahim, O.N., Govaart, G.H., ... & Aczel,
B. (2022). A community-sourced glossary of open scholarship terms. *Nature Human
Behaviour, 6*(3), 312–318.
Pownall, M. (2020). Pre-registration in the undergraduate dissertation: A critical discussion.
Psychology Teaching Review, 26(1), 71–76.

References

Anvari, F., & Lakens, D. (2018). The replicability crisis and public trust in psychological
science. *Comprehensive Results in Social Psychology, 3*(3), 266–286.
Bergmann, C. (2018). How to integrate open science into language acquisition research.
Student workshop at the 43rd Boston University Conference on Language Development
(BUCLD), Boston, USA. Accessible: https://docs.google.com/presentation/d/1bdICPzP
OFs7V5aOZA2OdQgSAvgoB6WQweI21kVpk9Gg/edit#slide=id.p
Carneiro, C. F., Queiroz, V. G., Moulin, T. C., Carvalho, C. A., Haas, C. B., Rayêe, D., ...
& Amaral, O. B. (2020). Comparing quality of reporting between preprints and peer-
reviewed articles in the biomedical literature. *Research Integrity and Peer Review, 5*(1), 1–19.
Chang, E. H., Milkman, K. L., Gromet, D. M., Rebele, R. W., Massey, C., Duckworth, A. L.,
& Grant, A. M. (2019). The mixed effects of online diversity training. *Proceedings of the
National Academy of Sciences*, 201816076.
Cuijpers, P., & Cristea, I. A. (2016). How to prove that your therapy is effective, even when it
is not: A guideline. *Epidemiology and Psychiatric Sciences, 25*(5), 428–435.
DeHaven, A. (2017). Preregistration: A plan, not a prison. Accessible: https://cos.io/blog/
preregistration-plan-not-prison/

DeVito, N. J., Bacon, S., & Goldacre, B. (2020). Compliance with legal requirement to report clinical trial results on ClinicalTrials.gov: A cohort study. *The Lancet*, 395(10221), 361–369.

Eggleston, C., Lee, M., & Talhelm, T. (2015). Replication of study "The Face of Success" by Rule & Ambady (2008, Psychological Science). Accessible: osf.io/4peq6.

Evans, T. R., Branney, P., Clements, A., & Hatton, E. (2021). Improving evidence-based practice through preregistration of applied research: Barriers and recommendations. *Accountability in Research*, 1–21.

Evans, T. R., Johannes, N., Winska, J., Glinksa-Newes, A., van Stekelenburg, A., Nilsonne, G., ... & Masson, I. (2020). Exploring the consistency and value of humour style profiles. *Comprehensive Results in Social Psychology*, 4(1), 1–24.

Evans, T. R., Pownall, M., Collins, E., Henderson, E. L., Pickering, J. S., O'Mahony, A., ... Dumbalska, T. (2022). A Network of Change: United Action on Research Integrity. *BMC Research Notes*. www.osf.io/ebr3w.

Evans, T. R., & Steptoe-Warren, G. (2018). Humor style clusters: Exploring managerial humor. *International Journal of Business Communication*, 55(4), 443–454.

Goldacre, B. (2010). *Bad science: Quacks, hacks, and big pharma flacks*. McClelland & Stewart.

Goldacre, B., Drysdale, H., Dale, A., Milosevic, I., Slade, E., Hartley, P., ... & Mahtani, K. R. (2019). COMPare: A prospective cohort study correcting and monitoring 58 misreported trials in real time. *Trials*, 20(1), 118.

Hüffmeier, J., Mazei, J., & Schultze, T. (2016). Reconceptualizing replication as a sequence of different studies: A replication typology. *Journal of Experimental Social Psychology*, 66, 81–92.

Jones, B. C., DeBruine, L. M., Flake, J. K., Liuzza, M. T., Antfolk, J., Arinze, N. C., ... & Sirota, M. (2021). To which world regions does the valence–dominance model of social perception apply? *Nature Human Behaviour*, 5(1), 159–169.

Kidwell, M. C., Lazarević, L. B., Baranski, E., Hardwicke, T. E., Piechowski, S., Falkenberg, L. S., ... & Nosek, B. A. (2016). Badges to acknowledge open practices: A simple, low-cost, effective method for increasing transparency. *PLoS Biology*, 14(5), e1002456.

Klein, M., Broadwell, P., Farb, S. E., & Grappone, T. (2019). Comparing published scientific journal articles to their pre-print versions. *International Journal on Digital Libraries*, 20(4), 335–350.

Kravitz, R. L., Franks, P., Feldman, M. D., Gerrity, M., Byrne, C., & Tierney, W. M. (2010). Editorial peer reviewers' recommendations at a general medical journal: Are they reliable and do editors care? *PLoS One*, 5(4), e10072.

Kristof-Brown, A. L., Zimmerman, R. D., & Johnson, E. C. (2005). Consequences of individuals' fit at work: a meta-analysis of person–job, person–organization, person–group, and person–supervisor fit. *Personnel Psychology*, 58(2), 281–342.

Munafò, M. R., Nosek, B. A., Bishop, D. V., Button, K. S., Chambers, C. D., Du Sert, N. P., ... & Ioannidis, J. P. (2017). A manifesto for reproducible science. *Nature Human Behaviour*, 1(1), 1–9.

Nosek, B. A., Ebersole, C. R., DeHaven, A. C., & Mellor, D. T. (2018). The preregistration revolution. *Proceedings of the National Academy of Sciences*, 115(11), 2600–2606.

Open Science Collaboration. (2015). Estimating the reproducibility of psychological science. *Science*, 349(6251).

Parsons, S., Azevedo, F., Elsherif, M.M., Guay, S., Shahim, O.N., Govaart, G.H., ... & Aczel, B. (2022). A community-sourced glossary of open scholarship terms. *Nature Human Behaviour*, 6(3), 312–318.

Pier, E. L., Brauer, M., Filut, A., Kaatz, A., Raclaw, J., Nathan, M. J., ... & Carnes, M. (2018). Low agreement among reviewers evaluating the same NIH grant applications. *Proceedings of the National Academy of Sciences, 115*(12), 2952–2957.

Pontika, N., Knoth, P., Cancellieri, M., & Pearce, S. (2015, October). Fostering open science to research using a taxonomy and an eLearning portal. In Proceedings of the 15th international conference on knowledge technologies and data-driven business (pp. 1–8). Graz, Austria.

Rouder, J. (2017). Tweet. Accessible: https://twitter.com/jeffrouder/status/9381 47822431502337?

Rubin, M. (2020). Does preregistration improve the credibility of research findings? The Quantitative Methods for *Psychology, 16*(4), 376–390.

Rule, N. O., & Ambady, N. (2008). The face of success: Inferences from chief executive officers' appearance predict company profits. *Psychological Science, 19*(2), 109–111.

Sijtsma, K. (2016). Playing with data – or how to discourage questionable research practices and stimulate researchers to do things right. *Psychometrika, 81*(1), 1–15.

Simmons, J. P., Nelson, L. D., & Simonsohn, U. (2011). False-positive psychology: Undisclosed flexibility in data collection and analysis allows presenting anything as significant. *Psychological Science, 22*(11), 1359–1366.

Tennant, J., Agarwal, R., Baždarić, K., Brassard, D., Crick, T., Dunleavy, D. J., ... & Tzovaras, B. G. (2020). A tale of two 'opens': Intersections between Free and Open Source Software and Open Scholarship. *SocArXiv*. Accessible: https://doi.org/10.31235/osf.io/2kxq8

Verquer, M. L., Beehr, T. A., & Wagner, S. H. (2003). A meta-analysis of relations between person–organization fit and work attitudes. *Journal of Vocational Behavior, 63*(3), 473–489.

Vicente-Sáez, R., & Martínez-Fuentes, C. (2018). Open Science now: A systematic literature review for an integrated definition. *Journal of Business Research, 88*, 428–436.

Wingen, T., Berkessel, J. B., & Englich, B. (2020). No replication, no trust? How low replicability influences trust in psychology. *Social Psychological and Personality Science, 11*(4), 454–463.

World Medical Association. (2013). WMA declaration of Helsinki – Ethical principles for medical research involving human subjects. Accessible: www.wma.net/policies-post/wma-declaration-of-helsinki-ethical-principles-for-medical-research-involving-human-subjects/

Sharing and Collaboration

8

I did my undergraduate degree in psychology only a few years ago really. When I started it really surprised me that scientists working in social science fields wrote up studies in a way I was familiar with from chemistry or biology experiments. A nice little neat paper focussing on what I expected to happen and why, the materials and procedure adopted, a report of what happened accompanied with a conclusion of the interpretations drawn. During my A-levels, I don't think I ever came into contact with a journal article in psychology, so at the start of my undergraduate degree the idea of an academic "journal" as the optimal strategy for dissemination slightly disturbed me. I think at the time I simply considered it a suboptimal method of communication.

The idea of what felt "wrong" didn't click for a few years. Following my undergraduate degree, I nearly immediately began teaching on the same course for the subsequent cohort, and soon afterwards started to study for my doctorate (PhD). It was an interesting experience negotiating a highly unusual deviation from the UG -> MSc -> PhD -> Academic Post trajectory and I am eternally grateful to have had the most inspiring and supportive supervision from Dr Gail Steptoe-Warren. During my PhD, I began to redefine my interests. As I noted earlier (Chapter 3), my PhD changed from the application of emotional intelligence to the study of theory and evidence quality in emotional intelligence. I was beginning to question some of the conventions of the academic research workflow. One of the greatest intrigues was the following statement:

Data is available upon reasonable request.

DOI: 10.4324/9781003035794-8

This sentence can be found in a large number of academic works. It's often right at the end, before the references, or in the methods section. It raises some testing questions: why won't you share your data? (what have you got to hide?!). On what conditions would you allow or deny me a copy of the data file? (Is this just posturing? Do you have any intention to share this? Why do you have concerns about how others' might use your data?). Once you think about it, it makes total sense that if you invest lots of time, money, and resources in collecting data that could help study a number of different hypotheses in a number of different ways, that you would want to make it as accessible as possible right? Unfortunately not. I spent my undergraduate research methods classes practising analyses using datasets that were purposefully collected for the purposes of teaching and often weren't "real" data simply because the norm wasn't to share.

There's loads of reasons to not share data, and many of them are selfish. Wanting to publish multiple derivate works from the same data set (also known as salami slicing) to secure a larger number of publications which can all cite each other thereby boosting citation numbers. Stopping your data from being examined by others who might "scoop" your research ideas. Stopping others finding issues with your work which would otherwise be mostly undetectable without the data and therefore undermining your reputation. Saving your time from carefully curating resources so you can move onto the next project.

This six-word sentence about data, short and sweet, perfectly exemplifies my concerns about so much of academic research. It encourages researchers to prioritise the number of publications and citations rather than the quality of the work and its impact, perpetuating the publish-or-perish aphorism. It reinforces power dynamics that the researchers are the "experts", and that science is an individual game rather than a team effort designed to serve the wider society within which we live. It focusses upon control and gatekeeping rather than accessibility and inclusivity. It's about hiding mistakes rather than being human and showing that we all make errors and bad decisions and shouldn't feel shame about any perceived failures. It tells us that science has far to go before we can expect dramatic changes in norms. In my role as Associate Editor for the journal *Current Psychology*, nearly all submissions feature this six-word abomination, and I send each of them back with a request to place data in an accessible depository. It's disheartening, but in my role as co-Editor-in-Chief for the *Journal of Open Psychology Data*, I also have the pleasure of working with lots of researchers keen on sharing data and changing the prehistoric status quo in science (Evans, 2022).

Without labouring the point too much, open data is really important. Firstly, it can be used to help independently verify analyses. We can check that what is reported is what we find – this is often called a computational reproducibility analysis and often relies on researchers sharing their analysis code too.

Second, often as a result of such analyses, or indeed just closer examination of data, we can identify errors or corruption and help correct the scientific record. Simonsohn (2013) has provided two clear examples where raw data been instrumental to confirm fraud by identifying purposeful manipulations and discounting innocent explanations or indeed authors' explanations for the discrepancies. Whilst there are examples of errors and fraud identified using open data, there are much greater concerns about the errors not being identified due to restricted data access. Reluctance to share data has been associated with smaller effect sizes and lower quality reporting (Wicherts et al., 2011).

Third, we can use this data to check the conclusions under different analytical decisions. For example, we might exclude a certain subgroup within the analysis to see if the effect remains within certain parameters. Research methods are seen as unchanging and there is certainly the perception that academics teaching them can continue to roll out the same slides and materials every year because nothing changes. This is far from true, and thus open data can also be helpful not just for checking different analysis decisions but also considering different analysis approaches as they continue to be improved or replaced with superior strategies.

Fourth, the data can be used for secondary analyses – they can be used to assess different hypotheses, theories, and approaches. Indeed, the *Journal for Open Psychology Data* is predicated on the value of such work.

Fifth, open data is of benefit for data synthesis. For example, in Chapter 4 we discussed the meta-analysis on diversity training. The original meta-analysis was based upon interpretations of the data made through whatever detail was reported in the papers. Sometimes details are inconsistent, poorly presented, inaccurately presented, or, indeed, otherwise generally obfuscate clarity. If the data was open, a more consistent analysis approach could be taken across data sets which would allow a more robust outcome and would foster more confidence in the conclusions drawn.

Sixth, shared data is an important resource which can be used to reduce barriers to access in communities where communication, discrimination, or resources limit involvement. Other such benefits include reuse of data in different or non-academic ways, e.g. for teaching, exploring policy decisions, etc., making the work more accessible and discoverable, and facilitating greater understanding of research already conducted. As a result of all such factors, sharing your data helps scientific progression.

So how inaccessible really is data at the moment? Some researchers have attempted to find the hidden data. Wicherts et al. (2006) asked authors for 249 datasets apparently "available upon reasonable request" and only secured 64, even after proving ethical approval, reassurance that they wouldn't be shared, and CVs to evidence their competence. Is that not reasonable? Vanpaemel et al.

(2015) had a similar goal and asked for 394 datasets. They received 22% after an initial request and a further 16% after follow-up, with similar figures reported in other scientific fields, e.g. phylogenetic data (Magee et al., 2014). An increase over the decade between such studies, but still a relatively low percentage of sharing. Of course, not all data is suitable for sharing. For example, data can identify participants or can contain commercially sensitive information. These are important and justified concerns and hold an important role in highlighting the ethical barriers to sharing sensitive data reported within such discussions (Gewin, 2016). As can be expected, such discussions are particularly prominent in psychiatric and clinical fields where the implications of identifying any given participant can be particularly negative (Walsh et al., 2018). Sharing data isn't necessarily so absolute, however. There are a number of strategies whereby an individual can share without disclosing all information publicly and immediately. If immediate risk is a concern, data can be embargoed. If there are certain parts of the dataset that might easily identify participants (often demographic details like age and sex) these can be removed or edited and the remaining partial data can be shared. You can also make synthetic data which has the same properties to the original data except that no individual person is identifiable. There are also a wide range of gatekeeping services available to allow access to those with legitimate reasons but exclude those whose motivations may be questionable. There are many shades of grey between fully open and fully closed.

One key driver of an increased rate of sharing is likely to be policy changes. For example, in a sample of 500 papers from high-impact journals, only 47 included data (Alsheikh-Ali et al., 2011). In a subset of 149 of these papers in journals without data availability policies, none had provided open data. Policies have great potential to drive long-term changes towards greater frequency and quality of data sharing (Hardwicke et al., 2018) but a review (Banks et al., 2016) reported that only 13% of management journals had such policies. Furthermore, you can make people state where the data is, but that doesn't necessarily mean the data will be accessible and reusable. Inclusion of data availability statements relatively infrequently leads to actual availability of the data (20%; Federer et al., 2018) so the exact policies do seem important.

The time needed to curate resources is a significant barrier to sharing effectively (Houtkoop et al., 2018). Sharing an Excel file online doesn't take much work – popping it on the Open Science Framework website (osf.io) would take less than one minute. Sharing an Excel file that can be meaningfully interpreted by someone mostly naïve to the research takes serious time. For example, data should be accompanied by a codebook which explains what each element of the data is and how it was collected – see my basic example here: osf.io/e2hbn. To be useful, data ideally needs to be FAIR – Findable, Accessible, Interoperable, and Reusable (Wilkinson et al., 2016), such that all data and meta-data (data about the data) can be found and used easily by humans and computers alike. Compliance to such principles requires significant investment to maximise the value of the data, some say around 5% of research budgets (Science Europe, 2016), but there is evidence that support is growing for such practices (Mons et al., 2017).

Research practices are changing but issues are likely to remain problematic and thus it's easy to conclude that "research data cannot be reliably preserved by individual researchers" (Vines et al., 2014). This issue only becomes more problematic with time passing when we acknowledge that resources can be easily lost and individuals infrequently have consistent contact methods, so the odds of obtaining an old data set reduce dramatically with every year that passes (Vines et al., 2014). The lack of data sharing is problematic in that it is used to justify continued reluctance to sharing – a self-perpetuating defence against progressive change (Houtkoop et al., 2018). It also perpetuates the need for this individualistic and subjective gatekeeping approach and highlights a fundamental inadequacy of training and education to support effective sharing (Houtkoop et al., 2018). I am confident that dramatic changes to practices will take hold eventually. For example, born-open data, where data is archived (and often shared) immediately or with a short processing delay, with no human action required, has begun to be more widely adopted (Rouder, 2016).

Much of the debate thus far has focussed upon data, but there are many other outputs from research which fail to be shared, but for similar reasons could support faster progress in science. Some of the most useful but rarely shared materials are the analysis codes used to report the statistical findings. Within such code, the assumptions made about the model, data, and interpretations are laid clear. Part of this issue taps into wider issues within academia surrounding the widespread education and use of proprietary software to analyse data, using a point-and-click format which is not reproducible and requires minimal understanding of the statistical processes being adopted. So I don't go into a full rant about how every department I have ever worked in has perpetuated such problematic practices, I will move on, but you can read more about this sort of thing elsewhere (e.g. Obels et al., 2020).

In addition to analysis code, research materials are also important to share. Materials used to collect data (the exact questions asked during interview, the stimuli used for experimental works, or the specific items of any questionnaires adopted) are rarely shared. Even more ridiculous is that papers published in academic journals presenting a new scale or method, or translation/adaptation of such resources, frequently fail to provide such details. Can you imagine such occult practices in any other field claiming to facilitate societal progression? It may seem obvious to share materials, but there has been a culture of individuality within science to such an extent that someone can write a paper evaluating how ten good questions capture a specific psychological construct, but they do not face any pressure to share those ten questions with the academic community. Such resources are not just useful for direct replication projects, they also provide valuable meta-data to better understanding current research and facilitate more rigorous measurement practices (Flake & Fried, 2020).

Do practitioners do more to share their work? This is more of an unknown. One key barrier to more transparent practices is the competitive nature of organisations. Academics, and indeed academic institutions, have a number of ugly metrics with which they compete with each other. For organisations, the competition is more direct and its consequences are more serious – profit or loss, life or death. Of course, competition is a fundamental aspect of life and certainly not inherently negative. However, competition is a central barrier to sharing in this context. Knowledge is power and sharing information with competitors is hardly an obvious course of action. One mustn't conflate the expectations of a body of individuals with the actions of an individual however – there are many reasons why an individual working in an organisation would benefit from increasing the rigour and transparency of the work they complete.

Sharing materials, data, and other such content is a mere conscientious extension of a portfolio. It's an opportunity to systematically log project work, evidence skills, and learning, and provide an account of work that can be shared with others. To ensure this is public and to provide a comprehensive and detailed account is additional work but it's likely to represent a strong signal of rigour and allow potential recruiters, selection panels, and collaborators to engage with the work in a detailed way and evaluate the work based on exactly what was completed, not just a sentence in another CV. There are some clear personal reputational gains for promoting transparency and rigour in applied work, with consequences for prestige and subsequent recognition. Even if we were to adopt a purely introspective perspective, it can be super useful to provide yourself a clear and open account of work, particularly when training others, answering questions, reminding yourself of specific details, and building upon any previous work. From my experience, Future Tom is always grateful to Past Tom in that regard.

Sharing is of great benefit to both academics and practitioners when reviewing what work has been completed and to what outcomes. I'm confident that academics would hope to see all resources comprehensively shared, including data, to build a detailed view of the grey literature available (Evans et al., 2021). This can be help negotiate discrepancies in findings from the more theoretical literature (see Grey Literature Bias; Chapter 6) but it can also help identify communities of practice and establish a clearer understanding of expected outcomes and preferable strategies. However, for practitioners, we might expect the main materials adopted are likely to be some of the most useful dimensions to share. Materials that can be easily re-applied to different contexts, whether that be intervention content or even evaluation strategies, can represent desirable and highly valued resources to the community.

Institutional resistance is likely to be the primary barrier to sharing. Creating materials that require resources and may provide the organisation a competitive advantage, using additional resources to curate such materials, and then openly sharing them with potential competitors is obviously going to create resistance. The nature of a competitive market is such that this should be expected and not considered unreasonable. The goal here is to make the value of sharing much greater than any potential risks and to slowly change norms. It may help to reflect upon a common open scholarship mantra to help negotiate planning here: as open as is possible, as closed as is necessary.

The second key barrier to this level of sharing is that work is infrequently attributable to individuals but to teams of individuals, often with different professional backgrounds and goals. We all have different stakes in the projects in which we contribute. In my current post, I take a leading role in a few projects within which I take primary responsibility for all areas. For many of my other projects, I have less substantive and more passive responsibilities for. I can appreciate reluctance for others to share projects with our own passive involvement should they be used to publicly represent our capabilities, particularly in situations where you have less choice in which projects you get asked to contribute to (academics are suckers for taking on "side-projects", myself included). Furthermore, sharing may be more valuable and desirable in some fields and subfields than others. Sharing in these collaborative spaces is best collaboratively negotiated and represents as much of a logistical/planning negotiation as it is an interpersonal one. Making a clear contribution statement for the project (Sam was responsible for project leadership, Sujal was responsible for evaluation design, etc.) might help acknowledge contributions of different kinds and extent (see Brand et al. (2015) discussing the CRediT taxonomy for an academic but quite accessible example) and anonymising those who wish to be unnamed seems likely to negate most potential conflicts.

I have two solutions to potentially mitigate both issues. Firstly, we can negotiate with all the stakeholders involved as to what exactly can be shared and when (Evans et al., 2021). For example, you could have a team meeting to decide what could be the best way of sharing the lessons learnt with the wider practitioner community. Similar to the discussion from Chapter 7 on preregistration, discussing sharing openly with management and then agreeing on what could be shared and how, and the potential for personal and organisational benefit, is particularly valuable prior to the project commencing. Any actions towards sharing potentially commercially sensitive materials should always be approved by organisational representatives with the necessary authority to do so. Here ends my legal responsibility.

The second recommendation is to be strategic about what is shared and where. Sharing some intervention content, intervention evaluation materials, decision-making processes, and outcomes, with practitioners in a professional environment may be a far more permissible and desirable outcome for the organisation in building reputation and may require less dramatic organisational gatekeeping. Sharing data is highly desirable but we should be realistic in context of current sharing norms, and work towards such goals by recognising that there are many other aspects of the process which can be of value to share.

Practitioners currently have several widely accepted avenues available to disseminate their learning externally. Everything from community networks, social media, professional conferences, and engagement with continuing professional development events. Whilst many of these routes are now incredibly popular, the quality of such dissemination strategies is variable, typically placing little-to-no emphasis on the level of sharing and detail that might be necessary to drive valuable additions to the body of evidence. Increasing the level of detail and transparency in these paths is a worthwhile strategy to help establish new benchmarks of quality and transparency.

In a conference targeted at practitioners and academics just a few years ago, I attended a session where the quality of evidence for their approach was "testimonials". That was the serious evidence they wanted to portray. Short clips of individuals endorsing the work we'd spent the last few minutes "learning" about, no doubt prepared for the marketing team to pump out to gullible minds excited about buzzwords. It would have been OK if everyone who heard the word testimonials immediately walked out, and the test publishers never returned, ashamed of their brazen cowardice in the ability to create better quality evidence for their product. That didn't happen and I have clearly still not forgiven them for the 20 minutes of my life that were stolen for such psychometric debauchery. In a similar conference, which was slightly more practitioner-focussed, the conference focus du jour consisted of prospective claims about what the future of HR might look like. They were mystical charlatans dressed in business suits. This was also one of the weirdest conferences I have attended in that after all the presentations and discussions they shepherded us into a communal changing room together (one each for men and women, obviously, but you can guess which was busiest), where everyone automatically got dressed up into black tie for the evening awards as if it were part of the celebrations to expose your nipples to strangers suggesting HR policies to you. Very odd. I didn't win an award and I certainly didn't go back to another conference hosted by that association.

Are We Learning?

The British Psychological Society (BPS) is the Professional Body of Psychologists in the UK. It is a well-respected and active voice for psychology students, academics, and practitioners. There are a number of Occupational Psychologists and individuals with a passion for applying psychology to the workplace, academics and practitioners alike, housed in the Division of Occupational Psychology (DOP). The DOP have an annual conference to unite all these parties, from test publishers running training sessions to students presenting their MSc or even BSc dissertation research projects. Research presented at the conference regularly attracts media attention, so I thought it might be a bit of fun to have a look at the extent to which the positive and problematic practices highlighted throughout this book have been present in the conference, holding this as a potential tentative representation of the wider body of work being conducted in the field. The conference submissions are peer-reviewed, so in principle the chances of seeing problematic practices should have been minimised, and vice versa for best practices. Furthermore, in 2018, Dr Brian Nosek, executive director of the Centre for Open Science, was a keynote speaker for the broader BPS Annual Conference, and, in 2020, he was a keynote speaker for the DOP conference, so replications and other such open scholarship practices should be prominent. It therefore seems like a prime space to question our recent learning from the replication/credibility crisis and look at the central priorities moving forward.

Let's have a look at the BPS Division of Occupational Psychology Conference extended abstracts for 2020 (BPS DOP, 2020). In an attempt to emulate the methods adopted by Charles et al. (2019) who explored the state of understanding in the psychology of religion, I coded all 160 abstracts for a range of positive and negative facets and practices, ranging from preregistration to sample size. One might think I have better things to do with my life, but obviously not. The abstracts included were of variable length, but each were systematically read and any evidence of the relevant criteria was logged. I think you can probably guess what happened…

So, there's some good news and some bad news.

- One study was preregistered. Congratulations go to Hannah Collis, a PhD student, and Prof Mark Cropley of the University of Surrey. This lovely pair were also the only ones to explicitly report a replication study.
- With respect to informed sample size estimates, I identified two examples of use of power analyses. Work led by Jenny Koehring, an MSc student at the University of Wolverhampton, and Joel Slater, a BSc student from Birkbeck, University of London, both contained a power analysis using the

G*Power software. This is good, although best practices were not reported. One had a sample size less than half of that suggested by the power analysis, and the second conducted the analysis after data collection (which makes it nearly completely redundant). Furthermore, both used a rule-of-thumb to state expected size of effect.

- Dr Dietmann of HM Courts and Tribunal Services was the only one to report using open-access software for analysis (R), however findings were reported only as statistically significant, with no comment or details of the size of effects reported from the analyses.
- I ran the PDF of abstracts through StatCheck (Rife et al., 2016). StatCheck is a programme that extracts central statistics, re-runs analyses, and then checks for inconsistencies between the results calculated and those reported. Of the 57 statistics checked, four were statistically inconsistent. These are not necessarily wrong or indicative of wrong-doing, but might suggest that a little closer attention is needed.
- References to openness, open scholarship or open practices were only noted for one presentation – the keynote from Dr Brian Nosek. At least they were in his presentation!
- There was no evidence for open data or code, and only a single link to the Open Science Framework (OSF) throughout the whole document. Sample sizes for quantitative research was as low as seven, with a handful of studies representing over 1,000 participants.
- A number of references to evidence-based practices were noted, including an evidence-based case study (?), and were more common in presentations delivered by test-publisher or commercial representatives than academics or students. This raises the question what calling actions "evidence-based practice" might be attempting to do…

A similar investigation of European (EAWOP) and international (SIOP) conferences drew highly similar conclusions. So, have those working within this sphere been quick to adopt open scholarship practices? No. But are there signs of growth? Also no. Well, maybe a little bit. Open scholarship practices have an extremely low uptake. Tenney et al. (2020) did a review of the literature published in academic journals around organisational behaviour and found pretty similar results. Open scholarship practices like replication, preregistration, and open data have been growingly adopted very recently, but are still relatively rare, even in academic publications at highly respected journals, and this is likely to be hampering our ability to make meaningful developments in understanding and practice.

It's easy to see the extreme worst of this situation. There is a dissemination system that is structurally biased to reward quick outputs and there is little systematic encouragement for adoption of open scholarship practices. This runs through the research lifecycle – from the design (no preregistration as part of ethics applications) to dissemination (conferences and journals). So, we have a workflow whereby quality is not being sufficiently prioritised, and it's a cyclical process – individuals at all stages of their career are being shown that, hey, this is the right way to do it if you want to make it in this field. This perpetuates the status quo, which we have established is problematic, and leads to another issue of representation.

Unfortunately, the systems we operate within reward individuals who secure early success with disproportionate levels of recognition, resources, credit, rewards, and thus subsequent success; something known as the Matthew Effect (Merton, 1968). This accumulative advantage is well described as "the rich get richer, and the poor get poorer", and whilst commonly related to economic outcomes, can also be seen in many outcomes including attention, investment, social media following, reputation, etc. We tend to accelerate the careers of those willing to "play the game". In research, it's those who salami-slice or don't waste time sharing resources. In practice, it's those who piggy-back onto projects with minimal contributions and tend to make noise over preliminary, and thus less robust, findings. We all know these sorts of people and yet we prioritise the voice of these increasingly "prolific" individuals in favour of those who are less well known – even when the quality of work is similar or better. For example, independent of research proposal quality, projects from recipients of previous research funding are rated more highly than those who have not yet secured previous funding, and those who were previously successful tend to have higher levels of self-belief, support, and resources to submit more subsequent applications (Bol et al., 2018). We should question which work and voices we should be championing much more – our time, investment, and respect should be invested in appropriately. By not changing anything in how we provide recognition of rigour and transparency, we are perpetuating the status quo when we know that current practices could be considerably improved.

Before getting carried away based upon a few conferences, I should acknowledge that the information I analysed were abstracts. They were not a full representation of the work conducted, so they are likely to represent lower estimates of best practices. For example, we might expect (and hope) that many of these works might be using power analyses, open-access software, include plans to make data openly available, etc. but the authors simply prioritised different content on their submissions. This ultimately then suggests changes in signposted priorities from conference organisers might be of benefit. For example, this particular conference asks, as part of their abstract submission process, what resources will be shared. People normally talk about slide handouts or pdfs of relevant products etc. but they could be steered to note what will happen to the data, materials, etc. Indeed, some conferences have begun to curate OSF pages to help encourage this transparency. This might help slowly change expectations and practices, and direct reviewers to more heavily weight the transparency and robustness of the work conducted in their evaluations. I now primarily attend conferences to run training sessions on open practices (e.g. preregistration) or to lead/support collaborative projects – it's far more impactful and rewarding.

There is, of course, some hope too. Open scholarship practices are seemingly most championed and actioned by early career researchers, and I am hopeful that this means the next generation of academics and practitioners will be focussed on addressing meaningful questions through robust and transparent methods and analyses. As the old brigade slowly march out the building, novelty ties and nostalgia in-hand, the new troop are excited to change research norms and structures. A key part of such transition should be development of more sophisticated opportunities to share and collaborate.

One such opportunity comes in the form of active practitioner conferences. The conference norm is to focus upon securing highly prestigious keynote speakers and provide an inane and broad conference theme (history and progress in …) allowing innumerable short presentations on a variety of any niche fields. I have to beg for money from my employer to attend such events. When I finally have a very brief slot to present my work, the exact timing of my opportunity is more dictated by the conscientiousness of the previous speaker than the time on the clock. My expectations for meaningful feedback and interesting questions are rapidly lost to the man in the middle row who, in his infinite experience, has more of a statement than a question.

We should instead be providing a much clearer focus based upon priorities within our communities – equality, diversity, and inclusivity; green initiatives; corruption; staff mental health, etc. Having established a single and clear priority for the conference, we should solicit a mixture of sessions based upon projects tackling such work, and practical sessions designed to *do* something. The Society for the Improvement of Psychological Science (SIPS) conference includes "hackathons" where individuals collaborate to create open resources together, e.g. how-to guides, resource banks, and similar. Imagine going to a conference and returning to your organisation with practice project examples, ideas of how to drive change in that area, and a collection of resources to help implement them. My recommendations for such conferences, and indeed any conference:

- Make an explicit statement of support for open practices during the call for submissions. This helps establish norms and expectations, encouraging those who complete such work to submit.

- Conflict of Interest statements should be declared at the point of submission and should be repeated at the start of every session. These should be a consideration when evaluating which submissions to accept and reject.
- A code of conduct should be explicit throughout all conference documentation. See the SIPS code of conduct as a good example: http://improvingpsych.org/sipsinaction/code/
- Submissions should be evaluated on evidence quality and transparency. If data has yet to be collected at the point of submission, it should be made clear what type of evidence would be presented.
- Encourage and facilitate sharing of materials and resources. This can be as easy as placing a checklist of recommended resources to share (e.g. presentation materials, data, study materials, etc.) alongside a dedicated platform to host them (e.g. an OSF page).
- Caps should be applied to limit the number of sessions any one individual or commercial party can present. Submissions during previous years should also be considered to maintain a diversity of voices (e.g. you can be acknowledged as a contributor on a maximum of two submissions, or one submission if you presented in any session last year).
- If submissions cannot be anonymised for evaluation, then organisers should consider implementing additional strategies to maximise transparency, e.g. by having publicly named reviewers.
- Conferences should collect and evaluate diversity data of delegates and presenters and make public statements about any meaningful discrepancies between such groups.
- Training sessions and hackathons are far more valuable than lots of brief presentations and should be prioritised as such. I would recommend a combination of opportunities for in-depth evaluations of recent projects, training sessions on specific techniques, tools or approaches, and practical sessions focussed on creating practical materials to share and apply.
- Make things as inclusive as possible. These can be structural changes, such as running the conference online or through local hubs, or by embedding practices, e.g. minimising barriers to access and contribute to projects by using formats which can be easily shared and edited, such as online documents that can be edited in real-time synchronously.

Another opportunity to share and collaborate, and an idea I have discussed elsewhere (Evans et al., 2021), is the possibility of a hybrid academic-practitioner journal, whereby applied work that is transparently reported can be published in a journal led by individuals who represent both communities. There are very few pathways to disseminate this sort of applied work in formal ways where it can be acknowledged by the relevant practice community whilst also providing the level of detail necessary to feed into broader scientific understanding. This community of academics interested in supporting practice, and practitioners invested in feeding back into scientific understanding, would represent a powerful force for changing norms and developing important resources of wide benefit. I would imagine that all submissions would be reviewed by an academic and practitioner reviewer, to ensure relevance to their respective communities, and evaluated based upon both transparency and rigour. This is not an ideal solution because new recognition and incentive initiatives are required outside the problematic academic publication structure, but this journal has potential to narrow the academic–practitioner gap until the point at which new structures can facilitate longer-term culture change.

Future Collaboration

Opportunities to share are valuable for speeding up incremental progress and represent a key part of collaboration, something prevented by so many structures that both practitioners and academics typically operate within. My early research portfolio was a solitary endeavour and after processing/wasting the excitement of being able to study whatever I liked (e.g. whether chillax represents something different from chilled or relaxed; Evans & Steptoe-Warren, 2015), I realised that only alongside others would I be able to make the type of differences I hopelessly dream about making. From that point, I became active in collaborating. One of the first groups I contributed to was the Psychological Science Accelerator (Moshontz et al., 2018), the CERN of psychology – a forum for international collaboration. It's all about crowd-sourcing expertise and resources with decentralised authority to tackle big psychological projects. The first published work identified the cultural specificity of influential models of social perception (Jones et al., 2021) through data collected from 11 world regions, 41 countries and 11,570 participants. The scale of work being conducted was previously unimaginable and I now proudly sit on the metascience subcommittee. This sort of collaborative approach to working now represents nearly all of my research focus, whether that be supporting undergraduate students to conduct a collaborative replication project for their dissertation (CREP; Wagge et al., 2019), conducting applied research with practitioners within the Fire Service (Evans & Steptoe-Warren, 2019), or contributing towards the development of research synthesis tools for the scientific community (e.g. NIRO; Topor et al., 2020).

Whilst collaborations between academics are becoming more frequent and well-structured, the academic–practitioner gap remains an ongoing barrier to effective academic–industry work. This is not solely an issue of having two independent groups though. There are many roles an individual can hold and in the wardrobe of many academics, in addition to regrets and shoulder-pads, there are both applied and basic research hats. There are also many individuals working in HR who have education in many areas of academic study that provide a basis for their work, whether it be from psychometrics, evaluation, and analysis, or theory behind practices. It's a divide not of people but in communication and application of different practices across different contexts and communities. Greater openness, and improvements in rigour (e.g. preregistration; Evans et al., 2021), from both basic and applied research provides an exciting opportunity to negotiate this divide whilst also providing opportunities for tackling wider social issues.

One of the greatest strengths of such collaborations is the opportunity to draw upon expertise from many different fields and perspectives. As we begin to recognise that it's probably best that one individual doesn't do everything (see Chapter 2) and indeed that you can't be an expert in every aspect of the research cycle, we should begin to accept that good research and HR work is likely to require a team effort. Whilst this provides some exciting opportunities for training to encourage specialisation, hopefully causing more rapid and consistent adoption of developments in practices to occur, this is also likely to raise other concerns for working within industry. For example, single individuals or pre-existing teams (e.g. consultancy organisations) might become more preferable to organisations due to lower resource cost and the promise of a more coherent and fluid response. Without suitable experience in each dimension of the work, this might lead to lower quality work than a team-driven project, although there are obviously variations in quality of individuals and teams and much of this will be down to careful vetting of such collaborations. We might therefore begin to see a conflict, as discussed in Chapter 2, where a cost-benefit analysis will be necessary to determine to what extent the additional value offered by a diverse team can be justified over the costs of a single individual or pre-existing team. We might see that the divide between individuals prepared to generalise and specialise widen, however what I hope this will lead to is greater fluidity between groups with diverse membership, such that individuals with different skills and specialisms, academic or practitioner, can flexibly contribute to different projects, making the most of their expertise by contributing to areas where they can have the greatest impact. I sincerely hope this will help shake off the complacency and negate the use of old-boy networks to secure contracts and instead promote a culture of collaboration and teamwork where we value and reward contributions not memberships.

Sharing, disseminating, and collaborating in a commercially sensitive space is often complex and represents a likely obstacle course of negotiations. Changing the way we see the role of academics and practitioners and changing our practices to prioritise both rigour and transparency are valuable steps forward. Making minor changes to what we share and how might feel insignificant, but such changes will have incremental value as we continue to revise our norms towards increasing the likelihood that what we do in HR will make a difference.

References

Alsheikh-Ali, A. A., Qureshi, W., Al-Mallah, M. H., & Ioannidis, J. P. (2011). Public availability of published research data in high-impact journals. *PLoS One*, 6(9), e24357.

Banks, G. C., O'Boyle Jr, E. H., Pollack, J. M., White, C. D., Batchelor, J. H., Whelpley, C. E., ... & Adkins, C. L. (2016). Questions about questionable research practices in the field of management: A guest commentary. *Journal of Management*, 42(1), 5–20

Bol, T., de Vaan, M., & van de Rijt, A. (2018). The Matthew effect in science funding. *Proceedings of the National Academy of Sciences*, 115(19), 4887–4890.

Brand, A., Allen, L., Altman, M., Hlava, M., & Scott, J. (2015). Beyond authorship: Attribution, contribution, collaboration, and credit. *Learned Publishing*, 28(2), 151–155.

BPS DOP. (2020). DOP Annual Conference Abstracts. Accessible: www.bps.org.uk/sites/www.bps.org.uk/files/Events%20-%20Files/DOP2020%20Abstracts_0.pdf

Charles, S. J., Bartlett, J. E., Messick, K. J., Coleman III, T. J., & Uzdavines, A. (2019). Researcher degrees of freedom in the psychology of religion. *International Journal for the Psychology of Religion*, 29(4), 230–245.

Evans, T. R., & Steptoe-Warren, G. (2015). Why do word blends with near-synonymous composites exist and persist? The case of guesstimate, chillax, ginormous and confuzzled. *Psychology of Language and Communication*, 19(1), 19–28.

Evans, T. R. (2022). Developments in Open Data Norms. *Journal of Open Psychology Data*, 10(1): 3. Accessible: http://doi.org/10.5334/jopd.60.

Evans, T. R., & Steptoe-Warren, G. (Eds.). (2019). *Applying occupational psychology to the Fire Service: Emotion, risk and decision-making*. Palgrave Macmillan.

Evans, T. R., Branney, P., Clements, A., & Hatton, E. (2021). Improving evidence-based practice through preregistration of applied research: Barriers and recommendations. *Accountability in Research*, 1–21. Accessible: http://dx.doi.org/10.1080/08989621.2021.1969233.

Federer, L. M., Belter, C. W., Joubert, D. J., Livinski, A., Lu, Y. L., Snyders, L. N., & Thompson, H. (2018). Data sharing in PLOS ONE: An analysis of data availability statements. *PLoS One*, 13(5), e0194768.

Flake, J. K., & Fried, E. I. (2020). Measurement schmeasurement: Questionable measurement practices and how to avoid them. *Advances in Methods and Practices in Psychological Science*, 3(4), 456–465.

Gewin, V. (2016). Data sharing: An open mind on open data. *Nature*, 529(7584), 117–119.

Hardwicke, T. E., Mathur, M. B., MacDonald, K., Nilsonne, G., Banks, G. C., Kidwell, M. C., ... & Frank, M. C. (2018). Data availability, reusability, and analytic reproducibility: Evaluating the impact of a mandatory open data policy at the journal Cognition. *Royal Society Open Science*, 5(8), 180448.

Houtkoop, B. L., Chambers, C., Macleod, M., Bishop, D. V., Nichols, T. E., & Wagenmakers, E. J. (2018). Data sharing in psychology: A survey on barriers and preconditions. *Advances in Methods and Practices in Psychological Science*, 1(1), 70–85.

Jones, B. C., DeBruine, L. M., Flake, J. K., Liuzza, M. T., Antfolk, J., Arinze, N. C., ... & Sirota, M. (2021). To which world regions does the valence–dominance model of social perception apply? *Nature Human Behaviour, 5*(1), 159–169.

Magee, A. F., May, M. R., & Moore, B. R. (2014). The dawn of open access to phylogenetic data. *PLoS One, 9*(10), e110268.

Merton, R. K. (1968). The Matthew effect in science: The reward and communication systems of science are considered. *Science, 159*(3810), 56–63.

Mons, B., Neylon, C., Velterop, J., Dumontier, M., da Silva Santos, L. O. B., & Wilkinson, M. D. (2017). Cloudy, increasingly FAIR: Revisiting the FAIR Data guiding principles for the European Open Science Cloud. *Information Services & Use, 37*(1), 49–56.

Moshontz, H., Campbell, L., Ebersole, C. R., IJzerman, H., Urry, H. L., Forscher, P. S., ... & Chartier, C. R. (2018). The Psychological Science Accelerator: Advancing psychology through a distributed collaborative network. *Advances in Methods and Practices in Psychological Science, 1*(4), 501–515.

Obels, P., Lakens, D., Coles, N. A., Gottfried, J., & Green, S. A. (2020). Analysis of open data and computational reproducibility in registered reports in psychology. *Advances in Methods and Practices in Psychological Science, 3*(2), 229–237.

Rife, S. C., Nuijten, M. B., & Epskamp, S. (2016). StatCheck: Extract statistics from articles and recompute p-values [web application]. Retrieved from: http://statcheck.io.

Rouder, J. N. (2016). The what, why, and how of born-open data. *Behavior Research Methods, 48*(3), 1062–1069.

Science Europe. (2016). Briefing paper on funding research data management and related infrastructures. Accessible: https://doi.org/10.5281/zenodo.5060104

Simonsohn, U. (2013). Just post it: The lesson from two cases of fabricated data detected by statistics alone. *Psychological Science, 24*(10), 1875–1888.

Tenney, E. R., Costa, E., Allard, A., & Vazire, S. (2020, October 20). Open science and reform practices in organizational behavior research over time (2011 to 2019). Accessible: https://doi.org/10.31234/osf.io/vr7f9

Topor, M., Pickering, J., Mendes, A. B., Bishop, D., Büttner, F. C., Henderson, E. L., ... & Westwood, S. (2020). *An integrative framework for planning and conducting Non-Interventional, Reproducible, and Open Systematic Reviews (NIRO-SR)*. Under review.

Vanpaemel, W., Vermorgen, M., Deriemaecker, L., & Storms, G. (2015). Are we wasting a good crisis? The availability of psychological research data after the storm. *Collabra, 1*(1), 3.

Vines, T. H., Albert, A. Y., Andrew, R. L., Débarre, F., Bock, D. G., Franklin, M. T., ... & Rennison, D. J. (2014). The availability of research data declines rapidly with article age. *Current Biology, 24*(1), 94–97.

Wagge, J. R., Brandt, M. J., Lazarević, L. B., Legate, N., Christopherson, C., Wiggins, B., & Grahe, J. E. (2019). Publishing research with undergraduate students via replication work: The collaborative replications and education project. *Frontiers in Psychology, 10*, 247.

Walsh, C. G., Xia, W., Li, M., Denny, J. C., Harris, P. A., & Malin, B. A. (2018). Enabling open-science initiatives in clinical psychology and psychiatry without sacrificing patients' privacy: Current practices and future challenges. *Advances in Methods and Practices in Psychological Science, 1*(1), 104–114.

Wicherts, J. M., Bakker, M., & Molenaar, D. (2011). Willingness to share research data is related to the strength of the evidence and the quality of reporting of statistical results. *PLoS One, 6*(11), e26828.

Wicherts, J. M., Borsboom, D., Kats, J., & Molenaar, D. (2006). The poor availability of psychological research data for reanalysis. *American Psychologist, 61*(7), 726.

Wilkinson, M. D., Dumontier, M., Aalbersberg, I. J., Appleton, G., Axton, M., Baak, A., ... & Mons, B. (2016). The FAIR Guiding Principles for scientific data management and stewardship. *Scientific Data, 3*(1), 1–9.

The Future of Evidence in HR

9

Revisiting the research cycle we discussed in Chapter 1, it's now easy to see where and how issues arise, and how their consequences can have meaningful implications for both understanding and practice. The complacency evidenced in our example diary entries feel somewhat less concerning now, compared to the wider issues facing science and HR. Up to this point we have ruled out emotional intelligence-based selection, encouraged more consideration for involving external parties to support analyses in HR, provided doubt on diversity training, workplace stress interventions, and organisational change initiatives, and generally discouraged such practices until the body of evidence available to inform the specific practices are convincing. These fields certainly reflect a diverse combination of very specific and very broad areas of practice, however, the common themes between them influence every current practice – the importance of transparency and rigour for evidence to inform strategy.

It would not be unreasonable for you to therefore entertain the idea that I have cherry-picked the worst. That I have been the greatest hypocrite and I have been HARKing on about subjects that I know are problematic. Unfortunately, the problems of transparency and rigour run through most research completed to date and have implications for all fields that I can think of. I have presented the fields in which I have the greatest experience, using the evidence from my own applied practices to ensure the conclusions I disseminate are detailed and robust, but there are so many more which have poor-quality evidence, and they often even have critical reviews pointing out such problematic state of affairs.

As my research has slowly orientated to such critical work, I often get asked about the evidence behind various theories, practices, and ideas outside of my

DOI: 10.4324/9781003035794-9

immediate field of experience. They are often complex questions to answer and require careful evaluation of various sources of evidence to negotiate. I hesitate to provide anything more than tentative opinions initially, and only do so following a good look at a wide range of sources. Having said that, you would be surprised to hear how often sources like Wikipedia provide overviews of relevant concerns raised in the literature. Critique is often out there if you can tolerate hearing it.

One of my former colleagues is training to be a registered occupational psychologist and she is obsessed about mindset theory. This isn't really my area, but given the extraordinary claims made, I was interested in understanding more.

For those who haven't yet heard of this wonderous marvel, mindset theory is a way of looking at people based on a simple continuum as to what they think about their qualities. On one end, individuals believe their psychological qualities are fixed, and thus their success is based on innate ability, and on the other end are those with the believe their qualities are malleable, and thus success is dependent upon hard work, commitment, and effort (Dweck, 2006). Many individuals working within the field of HR have got very excited about the possibility for interventions to encourage more growth mindsets and thus the possibility to improve a plethora of outcomes. For example, Han and Stieha (2020, p. 309) suggest mindsets could be useful for: "a) individual-level outcomes (e.g., work engagement, creativity, task performance, job satisfaction), (b) dyadic-level outcomes (e.g., supervisor-employee relationship and conflict resolution), and (c) organizational-level outcomes (e.g., organizational citizenship behaviours and organizational growth mindset)". It would be powerful if indeed that was possible.

We should first evaluate this idea with an outcome from the context in which it was originally proposed – education. A meta-analysis looking at data from 273 studies and over 365,000 children reported the relationship between mindset and academic achievement to be "very weak" (Sisk et al., 2018). Even then, subsequent analyses suggested this was likely to be an over-estimate due to issues like publication bias. This is a common red flag – in my experience, if central claims about outcomes can't be robustly evidenced then it is either more complex than it has been presented (it has boundary conditions, i.e. the effect can only be observed under certain conditions, e.g. when the outcome is measured in a certain way, or only appears effective for a specific population group), or the original claims were likely to be a result of questionable researcher practices. Replications and meta-analyses are typically quite useful sources of evidence for providing some initial indication of this. In a systematic literature review on school-based growth mindset interventions, it was concluded that "there was insufficient rigour in the conceptualisation and description of interventions, or evidence from outcome evaluations, to be able to describe growth mindset as an evidence-based practice in primary schools" (Savvides & Bond, 2021). Not an especially reassuring conclusion.

When we move on to evaluate specific claims made by mindset theory, this too presents problems. For example, we might expect that individuals who have a greater growth mindset might be more likely to persist, knowing that they have the capacity to improve, refine their practices, and achieve subsequent success. This is just one of six key premises of the mindset model that Burgoyne et al., (2020) aimed to evaluate using a preregistered study. Their conclusion was that no support was found for most of these central premises. All effects reported were very weak, and the strongest relationship they found ran counter to the direction expected from the theory. A modest sample, but pretty clear evidence to suggest that perhaps the basic theoretical principles behind fixed and growth mindsets might be problematic.

Whilst these are only a handful of papers, they begin to paint a picture of yet another field which appears logically plausible and of considerable interest to researchers from a number of fields, whilst also being based upon questionable evidence and theory. To indulge in one final example, let's consider Mental Health First Aid (MHFA) – a massively popular initiative across the globe and particularly within UK organisations, with over 4 million individuals trained. One of the latest evidence reviews conducted by the Health and Safety Executive in 2018 concluded "it is not possible to state whether MHFA training is effective in a workplace setting" and "There is no evidence that the introduction of MHFA training in workplaces has resulted in sustained actions in those trained, or that it has improved the wider management of mental ill-health". This leaves me with a cynical interpretation that organisations want the feeling that they are publicly committing to workplace wellbeing without making any meaningful structural change. A healthy level of suspicion should be applied when looking at any evidence, and action to apply new practices should always be paused until a convincing evidence base is created to substantiate early claims. I found similar results when tackling emotional intelligence for the first time during my PhD (see Chapter 3; Dasborough et al., 2021; Hughes & Evans, 2018) and I am sure that many other fields of research and practice will fall within this bracket. Perhaps, if I write a follow-up to this book, I should solicit topics from the community to critically evaluate, rather than from my own experience, so we can more convincingly evidence how widespread these issues really are.

Some may now say that HR is in a crisis of evidence. I appreciate this sort of statement for recognising the extent of issues and helping encourage meaningful and rapid change, but I don't think that "crisis" truly reflects the nature of our experience. Businesses are continuing to use the practices they always have, innovating HR policies are nearly always slight deviations from existing practices, and leaders still commonly rely upon individuals who convey the greatest confidence in the latest buzzwords as those who should inform their strategy. This doesn't really shout crisis. Crisis conjures pictures of mindless panic, a lack of clear direction as to what is exactly needed, and a lack of control to know how to respond. I don't think we're there. Instead, we have individuals who are predominantly naïve to the state of evidence and the range of potential implications of their actions, and we have a set of clear recommendations for practices which may increase the likelihood that future decision-making will be effective. That leaves us in an awkward position for attempting to renegotiate norms and challenge the status quo.

This discussion raise many questions – what do we do next? The practices we use daily in HR are not based on quality evidence, and many academics and practitioners have little-to-no awareness of this problematic state with the subsequent immediate motivation for change. It can sometimes feel like we're just miniscule parts of a much larger system and that our power to change things is close to non-existent. We mustn't forget, HR has the greatest scope for driving long-term changes within an organisation – they establish the culture and practices of the organisation. Actions in this space really do matter.

My central advice for individuals in this scenario is to consider embedding small incremental changes to your practices. Try to avoid an idealised view of what we should now be doing, as well as attempts to re-imagine completely new approaches – this tends to receive strong opposition and be too overwhelming to accomplish in practice. Instead, start implementing small changes based upon the areas which might drive the greatest impact whilst holding the path of least resistance. This might include external dissemination of some changes to practice as an attempt to encourage transparency, or encouraging a review of the quality of evidence collected to evaluate a given training intervention before automatically running a further iteration. Responses to such actions are normally quite manageable and sometimes changes in processes won't even be noticed until they have already been established. If the changes are in areas which are particularly important (e.g. with an environmental impact or implications for equality, diversity, inclusivity, or justice) then they are especially worth persisting with.

For those in positions of responsibility or power, whether that be formally or informally, the priority should be in reducing barriers to individuals making such small but incremental changes, and frequently facilitating a wider discussion on evidence quality and transparency wherever may be relevant. Cultural change happens slowly, and figures of leadership and authority have a central role in facilitating. Some questions which might help support such discussions follow.

For evaluating interventions:

- What do we want this to change? Why do we want this?
- Can we measure that outcome accurately?
- What evidence do we already have on this? Can we trust this? Is this good evidence?
- Perhaps we could have a closer look at the wider evidence on the likelihood this will work?

For sharing:

- Who do we want to share this with?
- Who would benefit from hearing or having a copy of this?
- Are there any serious concerns about this being shared externally?

Questioning evidence:

- What's the evidence to suggest this will work?
- On what basis are we confident this will happen?
- Is this data/evidence we can trust?
- Is this data/evidence strong enough to base our actions on?
- Why might this evidence/data be problematic?

If you are responsible for budgets, then you have even more scope to make meaningful changes. One practice that represents an ongoing barrier of transparency, and often rigour, is the use of proprietary software, services, and materials. There are a wide number of popular psychometric tools, for example, and much of the evidence to determine whether they are beneficial in practice are subject to gatekeeping from that very same company. It's incredibly difficult to evaluate their value when the use and dissemination of evidence is so tightly controlled. This is publication bias – businesses can control the narrative, providing evidence only in favour of their approach. So many of the terrible "team profiling" questionnaires ("I'm a 'brave thinker', a 'red', a 'lion', oh wait, maybe that is true because I am a Gryffindor…") are clearly questionable even from a brief examination of their marketing materials, yet are nevertheless popularly adopted. My experience in Chapter 8 surrounding the dissemination of testimonials as evidence comes immediately to mind. Using a popular or well-established measure is no guarantee of quality. My suggestion here would be to instead adopt the services of a practitioner or academic who can either provide recommendations for non-proprietary materials, or can work on developing, refining, or adapting open tools to be of greater relevance to the organisation's industry and context. This one change deprives "closed" proprietors from receiving the vital financial contributions they require to sustain gatekeeping, and removes a central external barrier capable of supressing subsequent transparency.

The follow-up question to this, is to consider on what basis academics or practitioners should be recruited and offered the opportunity to contribute. If transparency and rigour is a priority, then this should be the evaluation criteria. Don't take any academic or practitioner on their (buzz)word – take them on the quality of evidence they produce. Examining their commitment to sharing data and resources, their ability to embrace complexity, and their use of rigorous research designs is a good place to start.

It seems like it's only a matter of time until the renewed prioritisation of quality and transparency infiltrate applied research practices (Evans et al., 2021) and subsequent practitioner norms more widely. According to social and behavioural sciences evidence readiness levels (IJzerman et al., 2020) so much of the work we already do in HR is right at the highest levels – either large-scale testing of solutions in the relevant population (level 8), or applying robust methods with feedback evaluation to contribute to the wider base of evidence (level 9). Academics frequently make erroneous claims about how their work might impact real-world practices without a relevant sample to justify such a claim, but those in HR are actually driving the changes in the population of interest. Progress is therefore expected in two central areas. First, the quality of evaluation work is going to need substantive improvements. Most organisations place little emphasis or value on high-quality, in-depth evaluation (Briner & Walshe, 2013) and are content with collating cross-sectional or case-study evidence (Chapter 5). Content of interventions or other such practices are infrequently the central problem. The central factor is that without high-quality evaluation, practices don't improve and don't get questioned. How many training events do I have to attend where minor but meaningful changes could dramatically change engagement or subsequent behaviour change, if only the project was evaluated effectively. Second, levels of transparency, as highlighted throughout (e.g. Chapter 8), are currently problematic. The academic–practitioner gap remains and a large part of resolving this will be when we share and collaborate across the boundaries much more. Sharing resources, learning, approaches, and experience to help design high-quality evaluations will be a substantive step forward for both communities and provides an opportunity to support more application-ready, open, and impactful projects. We all benefit from such collaboration – academics have higher quality, and more relevant, evidence to refine our understanding, and practitioners get quality evidence from which they can make decisions and improve organisational outcomes.

Finally, a message to anyone in research or teaching roles. Things are changing. After running a very fun and accessible training session on R (free software for analysis) for my colleagues two years ago, I was recently contacted by one asking for guidance on how best to get started with R. Their institution has started to use it for teaching undergraduate students and staff were expected to up-skill ready for when these students worked on their dissertations and required supervision. A major change in the way research methods is taught in such a short period would have previously been considered futile. This to some may be considered slow, two years is a long time after all, but up to this point statistics has predominantly been taught either using statistical equations by hand or using proprietary software. Upon graduation, the latter is as useful as securing a pilot's licence when you can't afford a plane and your employer gives out bus passes. Similarly, models of publication via journal articles have not changed much since their original inception, whereby we now have preprint servers, Registered Reports, and even fragmentation of research into separate component publications (i.e. the Octopus model; www.youtube.com/watch?v= ZL2dUA7PPeE). Dramatic changes have been made to research and teaching practices over the last decade, and they are beginning to establish new norms that prioritise quality and transparency, building upon previous themes around "real-world impact" and accessibility. Those which choose not to embrace such opportunities to learn and to update their workflow will have a long and hard battle upwards when they realise the goalposts have moved with regards to how they will be assessed. It can be extremely hard to change but it's most certainly rewarding. I learnt about open scholarship practices through my excessive Twitter use and it was through this that I have got a renewed awareness for my love of learning and the value of challenging norms and standards. For those scared about dipping your toe in the water of open scholarship, fear not, you are already there. I have been discussing the principles and practices of open scholarship throughout this book, despite often not labelling them as such. If you have any motivation to change your practices after reading these pages, I have done my job, and you are good to get started. Welcome to the open scholarship buffet, I recommend the vol-au-vents.

Whilst adoption of many open research practices is increasing, there are a few consequences to consider. One potential negative is the possibility that, at some point, the academic community will prioritise transparency to such an extent that the work of those who work in areas where sharing is not routinely possible (such as those in organisations, and applied researchers more broadly) will be neglected or under-valued. Their work may be similarly high quality and likely high impact, but the lack of transparency may lead to assumptions that the work will be poor and it thus becomes excluded from contributing to the body of evidence to inform practice. Key defences against such segregation include the adoption of open practices wherever relevant (e.g. sharing the materials used to evaluate the work but not the data itself; remember, it is a buffet of options) and collaboration between communities such that the practical limitations and value of work from each direction can be appreciated.

Having changed norms on sharing and openness, we will better accept that transparent poor-quality research has extremely minimal value. We'll then have to start taking more seriously about what we're doing and why. It seems so likely that, once everything is more accessible and open, we're going to find more systemic and fundamental concerns around our foci and quality. The focus of science reformists have already moved beyond the replication crisis and have started tackling deeper issues surrounding theory and measurement practices (e.g. Eronen & Bringmann, 2021; Lilienfeld & Strother, 2020). This may just be my quarter-life crisis speaking but I believe we're going to agree that most theories are too simplistic for the real world. That mainstream measurement practices question the validity of most conclusions we draw. That most effects are too small, and have too many boundary conditions, to be meaningful drivers of real-world change. We will agree that more meaningful structural and foci change are required to best mobilise our collective experience and knowledge. I hope this means that we ask bigger questions of ourselves and, counter to my concern above about segregation, we begin to contribute much more to the daily practices of those within our societies, and prioritise tackling the much wider issues that we face together (like climate change and democracy). I hope we begin to question whether the vast majority of research means anything, or has just become transparent inconsequential garbage, and we choose to re-focus our efforts on building bodies of evidence together through high-quality designs (e.g. longitudinal, multi-source, etc.) that appreciate the inherent complexity of the context, and that we conduct and report them comprehensively, transparently, and with a view to how they can be applied.

In the age of fake-news, deep-fakes, and disinformation, we all need to become more aware and critical of what we see and read. It is my hope that education at all levels will place a much greater emphasis on developing critical skills and strategies to determine the authenticity and quality of evidence. Many courses, including those of HR, will tell you that *X* is important and the best way to do *X* is to follow a specific approach or strategy. They will train you to execute the strategy well. This is fine if this strategy is indeed optimal, however, we need to acknowledge that evidence bases are constantly evolving, and new practice trends emerge regularly. Rather than teaching only the value of specific practices, prioritising the development of critical skills that support individuals to regularly and effectively evaluate the base of evidence on any given practice would represent a much more worthwhile education. There are plenty of online resources available to help encourage such critical thinking skills too, and

I am currently designing (and intend to openly share) a whole module about evidence and evidence-based practice in Occupational Psychology, but I wanted to share a few specific examples and principles here which might be of particular value to the HR context.

Be incredibly wary of things that sound too good to be true. This is often seen in claims that a given tool or intervention will address all outcomes and resolve all your problems. Remember the plethora of claims made about growth mindsets earlier? It's incredibly easy to over-promise but often hard to work out the exact impact an intervention can have. Unless you embed long-term change, a single intervention of any kind is likely to have small and relatively short-term outcomes (see Chapter 5 for some examples). I follow the Sagan standard that extraordinary claims require extraordinary evidence to be convincing. The workplace is messy and we need to look at the bigger picture to work out how changes in one domain might impact upon others. Confident or assertive claims should be treated with immediate caution.

Delivery is important, but it's the content that really matters. Infographics and similar visual tools are great for communicating things, but always prioritise a closer look at the evidence behind them. The devil is in the detail. Flashy infographics and slick presentations can help project credibility, accessibility, and authority, but they often require simplistic messages to work successfully. Look for links or references to the underlying data and do the digging. In particular, look for any meaningful discrepancies between the messages that are possible from the data and those which are disseminated through the graphics. There's even an episode (95) of the podcast EverythingHertz, discussing open scholarship themes, on why badly presented conference presentations can sometimes confer credibility, and why highly polished presentations are often sceptically received and trusted (everythinghertz.com/95). You can't go wrong if you go back to the data upon which the claims are made and provide your own critical judgement on what messages you would take from it.

For consideration of statistical claims specifically, there are very few reasons why I would encourage you to look at, or provide weight to, "statistical significance" or p-values. Indeed, the difference between significant and non-significant is itself often not meaningful (Gelman & Stern, 2006). Instead focus on the size of effect. There are a variety of rules of thumb you can use to interpret these, which are mostly flawed yet occasionally helpful to establish expectations, and the average size of relationship reported in the HR/Organisational Behaviour literature is $r = .227$: relatively small (Paterson et al., 2016). Focus on the scale of impact you want to have, and help the effect size guide your expectations of its likely value.

When you're uncomfortable commenting on the detailed statistics, you can still provide a meaningful critique by examining the central decisions made. For example, we discussed different levels of evaluation (Kirkpatrick, 1959) in Chapter 2, as to whether you capture immediate responses (typically very poor evidence), learning (better, but no guarantee of outcomes), behavioural change (the ultimate evaluation of the direct efficacy of the intervention) or results (e.g. Return on Investment; good to evaluate organisational impact in context but often extremely difficult to do so robustly). Careful consideration of the sample also provides a great insight into the work completed. This can include relevance (e.g. a sample of HR generalists compared to undergraduate students), size, and method of recruitment (e.g. did they self-select, and, if so, might that introduce Selection Bias whereby the sample isn't representative of the population). Finally, in Chapter 5 we also discussed the evidence hierarchy, acknowledging that the most common case-study or cross-sectional data collection is highly problematic, and the highest quality open research conducted is again rare but valuable. These guidelines are quite broad and there are innumerable other factors you could consider. The rules of thumb outlined should be used as an initial tentative guide, but nevertheless a useful grounding which, when considered alongside each other, provide a useful basis to a meaningful critical stance.

Whilst the state of academia is often worrying and can be difficult to negotiate, I remain in place because I am committed to making a difference. I used to think I would make a big difference through my emotional intelligence research – I could save millions of pounds wasted on interventions in schools and selection processes in organisations and apply this to better prepare individuals to negotiate the different types of emotional and social demands in these environments. It was well-meaning but naïve. I'm still driven to make a difference, but I no longer expect to do so through a revelation in my content-specific research. Instead, I want to do so by changing the culture and practices of research as a whole – to change our way of thinking to move beyond thinking of things in "I" terms and embed practices which better acknowledge that research, science, and life, is a team game and that we need to share and do things better, together.

I hope that this text has convinced you that sharing is important. In my opinion, one of the greatest contributions to academic studies in the last decade or so has not been a single breakthrough in theory or evidence. It was not content or subject specific. It was Sci-Hub, a website capable of hosting academic journal articles without any barriers to access, created by Alexandra Elbakyan from Kazakhstan in 2011. Access to academic publications has traditionally stayed behind a paywall by academic publishers, with steep costs to access an article of even a page long. This is often well-exemplified by the meme of a real, two-page paper entitled "The growing inaccessibility of science" which was behind a paywall, costing $8.99 to access. I just checked and the paper (Hayes, 1992) is now openly available but the wider issues remain with various universities and

Profit	Company	Industry
10%	BMW	automobiles
21% (not profit)	PLoS.org	non-profit scholarly publishing
23%	Rio Tinto	mining
25%	Google	search
29%	Apple	premium computing
35%	Springer	scholarly publishing
37%	Elsevier	scholarly publishing

Figure 9.1 Organisations with *large* profits (Holcombe, 2015)

institutions shelling out millions for journal subscriptions. Academic publishers are known to be one of the most profitable industries, relying on academics to submit their own work, peer review others' work for free, and then charge (sometimes individuals, mostly organisations) to access the work.

These financial barriers have direct implications for the speed of progression in science. In response to the high financial barriers to reading scientific articles, Alexandra made a tangible difference to accessibility of scientific understanding. You can now type in the name of a paper or its DOI, and it will pop up with a full copy of the paper ready to digest. No need to log in multiple times to authenticate your identity or provide a university affiliation. It's convenient, free, and most importantly, it makes research accessible to the communities which needed it most. Furthermore, some research suggests that articles downloaded from the website are cited 1.72 times more than those not available, and that the number of Sci-Hub downloads are capable of predicting numbers of future citations of the work (Correa et al., 2021). Regardless of whether these exact figures are robust, they make a valid point in highlighting that science must be accessible to be useful.

Sci-Hub is criticised for sourcing the articles using academic credentials either leaked or sold on the black market and is now considered illegal in many countries, predominantly for violating copyright. Furthermore, Sci-Hub is not really a long-term solution because the work is still not widely available. The impact of Sci-Hub has nevertheless been dramatic, providing access to papers where access was otherwise obstructed, and changing the culture of academic research to encourage sharing and prioritise accessibility.

I maintain my commitment to make a difference as an ever-changing range of international events and crises continue to highlight the need for greater accountability, criticality, and transparency in all areas of research. We, as a community of humans, need to change. We need to take action against corruption, consumption, inequality, and climate change, we need to promote greater peace, education, and life on sea and land (United Nations, 2015). One of the best ways to accelerate action on these issues is to make research transparent and continue to drive improvements in research standards for rigour. We are all growingly aware of ongoing issues surrounding corruption in governments, and the need for immediate and substantive individual, organisational, and societal responses to the climate crisis. It is my hope that by driving changes to the culture of research, we may indirectly, eventually, contribute to tackling such problems. Norms are always being renegotiated and changed, and HR is in a solid position to contribute to this wider culture change in sharing, with the capability of influencing many day-to-day practices of individuals in the workforce and championing wider societal change.

References

Briner, R. B., & Walshe, N. D. (2013) The causes and consequences of a scientific literature we cannot trust: An evidence-based practice perspective. *Industrial and Organizational Psychology*, *6*, 269–312.

Burgoyne, A. P., Hambrick, D. Z., & Macnamara, B. N. (2020). How firm are the foundations of mind-set theory? The claims appear stronger than the evidence. *Psychological Science*, *31*(3), 258–267.

Correa, J. C., Laverde-Rojas, H., Tejada, J., & Marmolejo-Ramos, F. (2021). The Sci-Hub effect on papers' citations. *Scientometrics*, 1–28.

Dasborough, M. T., Ashkanasy, N. M., Humphrey, R. H., Harms, P. D., Credé, M., & Wood, D. (2021). Does leadership still not need emotional intelligence? Continuing "The Great EI Debate". *The Leadership Quarterly*, 101539.

Dweck, C. S. (2006). *Mindset: The new psychology of success*. New York: Random House.

Eronen, M. I., & Bringmann, L. F. (2021). The theory crisis in psychology: How to move forward. *Perspectives on Psychological Science*, *16*(4). Accessible: https://doi.org/10.1177/1745691620970586.

Evans, T. R., Branney, P., Clements, A., & Hatton, E. (2021). Improving evidence-based practice through preregistration of applied research: Barriers and recommendations. *Accountability in Research*, 1–21. Accessible: https://doi.org/10.1080/08989621.2021.1969233.

Gelman, A., & Stern, H. (2006). The difference between "significant" and "not significant" is not itself statistically significant. *The American Statistician*, *60*(4), 328–331.

Han, S. J., & Stieha, V. (2020). Growth mindset for human resource development: A scoping review of the literature with recommended interventions. *Human Resource Development Review, 19*(3), 309–331.

Hayes, D. P. (1992). The growing inaccessibility of science. *Nature, 356*(6372), 739–740.

Health and Safety Executive. (2018). RR1135: Summary of the evidence on the effectiveness of Mental Health First Aid (MHFA) training in the workplace. Accessible: www.hse.gov.uk/research/rrpdf/rr1135.pdf

Holcombe, A. (2015). Scholarly publisher profit update. Accessible: https://alexholcombe.wordpress.com/2015/05/21/scholarly-publisher-profit-update/

Hughes, D. J., & Evans, T. R. (2018). Putting 'emotional intelligences' in their place: Introducing the integrated model of affect-related individual differences. *Frontiers in Psychology, 9*, 2155.

IJzerman, H., Lewis, N. A., Przybylski, A. K., Weinstein, N., DeBruine, L., Ritchie, S. J., ... & Anvari, F. (2020). Use caution when applying behavioural science to policy. *Nature Human Behaviour, 4*(11), 1092–1094.

Kirkpatrick, D. L. (1959). Techniques for evaluating training programs. *Journal of ASTD, 11*, 1–13.

Lilienfeld, S. O., & Strother, A. N. (2020). Psychological measurement and the replication crisis: Four sacred cows. *Canadian Psychology, 61*(4), 281–288

Paterson, T. A., Harms, P. D., Steel, P., & Credé, M. (2016). An assessment of the magnitude of effect sizes: Evidence from 30 years of meta-analysis in management. *Journal of Leadership & Organizational Studies, 23*(1), 66–81.

Savvides, H., & Bond, C. (2021). How does growth mindset inform interventions in primary schools? A systematic literature review. *Educational Psychology in Practice, 37*(2), 134–149.

Sisk, V. F., Burgoyne, A. P., Sun, J., Butler, J. L., & Macnamara, B. N. (2018). To what extent and under which circumstances are growth mind-sets important to academic achievement? Two meta-analyses. *Psychological Science, 29*(4), 549–571.

United Nations. (2015). *Transforming our world: The 2030 Agenda for Sustainable Development.* New York: United Nations.

Index

For Product Safety Concerns and Information please contact our EU
representative GPSR@taylorandfrancis.com
Taylor & Francis Verlag GmbH, Kaufingerstraße 24, 80331 München, Germany